TIME

The Year in Review

1977

Founders: BRITON HADDEN 1898-1929
HENRY R. LUCE 1898-1967

Editor-in-Chief: Hedley Donovan
Chairman of the Board: Andrew Heiskell
President: James R. Shepley
Group Vice President, Magazines: Arthur W. Keylor
Vice Chairman: Roy E. Larsen
Corporate Editors: Ralph Graves, Henry Anatole Grunwald

YEAR-IN-REVIEW STAFF

MANAGING EDITOR: Ray Cave

EXECUTIVE EDITOR: Edward L. Jamieson

ASSISTANT MANAGING EDITORS: Murray J. Gart, Jason McManus

SENIOR EDITOR: Otto Friedrich

Chief of Research: Leah Shanks Gordon; Assistant Chief: Dorothy Haystead

ART DIRECTOR: Walter Bernard

WRITERS: Robert Ajemian, James D. Atwater, David Beckwith, George J. Church, Gerald Clarke, Spencer Davidson, Michael Demarest, John S. De-Mott, William R. Doerner, Martha M. Duffy, John T. Elson, Timothy Foote, Frederic Golden, Paul Gray, Robert L. Goldstein, Robert Hughes, Timothy M. James, Marguerite Johnson, T.E. Kalem, Stefan Kanfer, Ronald P. Kriss, John Leo, Edward Magnuson, Frank B. Merrick, Mayo Mohs, Lance Morrow, Donald M. Morrison, Richard N. Ostling, B.J. Phillips, Burton Pines, George Russell, Richard Schickel, Hugh Sidey, William E. Smith, Peter Stoler, Annalyn Swan, Edward Tivnan, Frank Trippett, Edwin Warner, Roger Wolmuth.

SENIOR RESEARCHER: Brigid Forster

REPORTER-RESEARCHERS: Jennifer Allen, Maureen D. Benziger, Oscar Chiang, Rosamond Draper, Tam Martinides Gray, Georgia Harbison, Allan Hill, Anne Hopkins, Carol Johmann, Adrianne Jucius, Nancy Levering, Laurie Upson Mamo, Gaye McIntosh, Sara C. Medina, Elizabeth Meyer, Gail Perlick, Sue Raffety, Jay Rosenstein, Elizabeth Rudulph, Betty Satterwhite, Raissa Silverman, Bonita Siverd, John Tirman, F. Sydnor Vanderschmidt, Susanne S. Washburn, Genevieve A. Wilson-Smith, Linda Young, Lucille de Zalduondo.

CORRESPONDENTS: Murray J. Gart (Chief),
Richard L. Duncan (Deputy).
Washington: Hugh Sidey, R. Edward Jackson, Bonnie Angelo, William Blaylock, Stanley W. Cloud, Simmons Fentress, Hays Gorey, Jerry Hannifin, Neil MacNeil, Bruce W. Nelan, Christopher Ogden, Don Sider, John F. Stacks, George Taber, Arthur White, Gregory H. Wierzynski. **Chicago:** Benjamin W. Cate, Anne Constable, Patricia Delaney, Barry Hillenbrand, J. Madeleine Nash, Robert Wurmstedt. **Los Angeles:** William Rademaekers, Edward J. Boyer, Joseph J. Kane, Marion Knox, William F. Marmon Jr., John Quirt, James Willwerth. **New York:** Laurence I. Barrett, Gisela Bolte, Mary Cronin, Roland Flamini, Marcia Gauger, Robert Parker, Jeanne Saddler, James Shepherd, Eileen Shields, Evan Thomas, John Tompkins. **Atlanta:** Rudolph S. Rauch III, Neil Shister. **Boston:** Marlin Levin, Jack E. White. **Detroit:** Edwin M. Reingold. **San Francisco:** Joseph N. Boyce, John J. Austin, James Wilde. **Miami:** Richard Woodbury. **United Nations:** Curtis Prendergast.
London: Dean Fischer. **Paris:** Henry Muller, Sandra Burton. **Bonn:** B. William Mader, Barrett Seaman. **Eastern Europe:** David Aikman. **Brussels:** Friedel Ungeheuer. **Madrid:** Karsten Prager, Gavin Scott. **Rome:** Jordan Bonfante, Erik Amfitheatrof. **Athens:** Dean Brelis. **Jerusalem:** Donald Neff, David Halevy. **Cairo:** Wilton Wynn. **Moscow:** Marsh Clark. **Hong Kong:** Richard Bernstein, David DeVoss, Bing W. Wong. **Nairobi:** David Wood, Eric Robins. **Johannesburg:** John M. Scott (Ottawa), Ed Ogle **New Delhi:** Lawrence Malkin. **Tokyo:** William Stewart, S. Chang, Frank Iwama. **Melbourne:** John Dunn. **Canada:** John M. Scott (Ottawa), Ed Ogle (Vancouver). **South America:** Lee Griggs (Buenos Aires). **Mexico City:** Bernard Diederich.
News Desk: Minnie Magazine, Margaret G. Boeth, Al Buist, Susan Lynd, Sara Paige Noble, James Patterson, Lee Powell, Barbara Seddon, Jean R. White, Arturo Yanez. **Administration:** Emily Friedrich, Linda D. Vartoogian.

OPERATIONS MANAGER: Eugene F. Coyle;
Mary Ellen Simon (Deputy).

PRODUCTION: Charles P. Jackson (Makeup Editor); Sue Aitkin

ART DEPARTMENT: Paul Richer, Anthony J. Libardi (Designers), Rose Cassano, Nancy W.W. Coyle. **Maps and Charts:** Paul J. Pugliese, Joseph Arnon. **Researchers:** Nancy Griffin, E. Noel McCoy.

PHOTOGRAPHY: John Durniak (Picture Editor); **Researchers:** Fran Ahders, Jane Colihan.

COPY DESK: Anne R. Davis (Chief), Eleanor Edgar, Susan Hahn (Deputies). Frances Bander, Minda Bikman, Madeline Butler, Joan Cleary, Leo Deuel, Lucia Hamet, Katherine Mihok, Emily Mitchell, Maria Paul, Linda Pocock, Pearl Sverdlin, Shirley Zimmerman.

EDITORIAL SERVICES: Norman Airey (Director), George Karas, Michael E. Keene, Benjamin Lightman, Doris O'Neil, Carolyn R. Pappas.

PUBLISHER: Ralph P. Davidson
Associate Publisher: Reginald K. Brack Jr.
General Manager: Donald L. Spurdle
Promotion Director: Robert D. Sweeney
Circulation Director: S. Christopher Meigher III
Business Manager: John T. Howard

ADVERTISING SALES DIRECTOR: William M. Kelly Jr.

U.S. Advertising Sales Manager: George W. McClellan

Associate U.S. Adv. Sales Directors: Kenneth E. Clarke, John A. Higgons

A Letter from the Publisher

In the wilderness that surrounded Walden Pond more than a century ago, Henry David Thoreau looked with some foreboding on the rise of modern communications. "We are eager to tunnel under the Atlantic and bring the Old World some weeks nearer to the New," he wrote, "but perchance the first news that will leak through into the broad, flapping American ear will be that the Princess Adelaide has the whooping cough." Little did he know. Little could he anticipate the potential of the typewriter and the Linotype machine, much less the computerized electronic phototypesetter and the whirling space satellite, which daily provide millions of words and pictures not only on Princess Adelaide's whooping cough but on gunfire in the mountains of Ethiopia, on an oil spill off Nantucket or a sudden diplomatic breakthrough in Jerusalem.

TIME declared in its original prospectus that it would be "interested not in how much it includes between its covers but in how much it gets off its pages into the minds of its readers." Each week, therefore, TIME's editors labor to compress the hundreds of thousands of words from 86 correspondents around the world into our average of 50 pages of stories per issue. When we decided to introduce new subscribers to TIME by means of this special Year-in-Review issue, we had to compress still further, reducing the 2,600 pages of our regular issues in 1977 into the 96 pages you have before you now.

Looking back from a year-end vantage point gives us a perspective quite different from what we see in the week-by-week scramble. Some stories that seem big at the time almost disappear from memory in a few months—the Hanafi Muslim siege of Washington, for example, or the escape of James Earl Ray. Other stories suddenly thunder out of nowhere—like Egyptian President Sadat's "sacred mission" to Jerusalem. There are other differences, too. As we look back on a year that has gone, obituaries tend to loom large. The world is undeniably changed through the loss of a Vladimir Nabokov or a Charles Chaplin. On the other hand, we can only guess, as men guess the locations of unseen stars, what newly born powers of 1977 have not yet emerged into the sunlight, what geniuses or tyrants-to-be are lying in their cribs.

To impose an order of sorts on the ceaseless tidal waves of news, Senior Editor Otto Friedrich and a staff of 60 have culled through a year's news files in search of what would last, what retained that mysterious combination of novelty and importance that makes a news story stay news. All the stories were written afresh for this project, but wherever a photograph in a past issue of TIME seemed to capture the key moment forever, we simply used it once again. We hope the result is as fascinating to our new subscribers as the making of it has been to us. It is pleasant to think that even Thoreau might have liked it.

Ralph P. Davidson

Index

BACK COVER PHOTOGRAPHS: SADAT—DAVID HUME KENNERLY; REGGIE JACKSON—WALTER IOOSS JR.—SPORTS ILLUSTRATED; ARTOO-DETOO—20TH CENTURY-FOX; CARTER—KIT LUCE

3

TIME/YEAR IN REVIEW 1977

Carter: Promises to Keep

A search for the mystical something that makes successful Presidents

How far away the tranquil fields of Iowa must have seemed to Jimmy Carter not long ago as he heard about the thousands of farmers protesting his leadership. In his home town of Plains, Ga., tractors were lined up by the hundreds, displaying signs of displeasure: "Spring has sprung, fall has fell, Carter went to Washington, farming went to hell." It was in Iowa, the symbolic heart of American agriculture, that Carter had started his quest for the presidency back in 1975, promising the friendly people in the clapboard houses a bigger slice of American prosperity. But once Carter took over as President, farm prices did not rise, they fell. It was not the 39th President's fault. But like so much else in the U.S., it was now his responsibility.

One year of Carter's presidency had wrought other changes in the nation, few so marked as those on the farm but many just as important or more so—some raising questions about Jimmy Carter's ability to lead effectively so nervous and complex a society. At the end of his first year, there were many who questioned whether he had lived up to his promises or to people's expectations. But he believed resolutely that he could.

He made it sound so on the day of his Inaugural. It was a little like a Sunday morning back in Plains. A choir sang *The Battle Hymn of the Republic*. There were prayers. Carter's first words on the Inaugural stand after his oath were a courtly thank-you to Gerald Ford "for all he has done to heal our land." Carter's short address was a subdued message of love and hope, not unlike those lessons he taught in the Baptist Sunday school. There were no eloquent challenges like those of John Kennedy ("We shall bear any burden . . .") nor any of the eager anticipation of power that Richard Nixon had brought to the job. Carter dwelled on humility. "We can neither answer all the questions nor solve all the problems," he told the nation. Then he and his family dramatically walked the mile and a half down Pennsylvania Avenue to the White House. "Where do I live?" he asked White House Chief Usher Rex Scouten. Jimmy Carter had been in the White House only a few times, never overnight.

Almost every one of the plans that Carter brought with him to the Oval Office was soon altered by events or modified to fit political realities. His stance as the new evangelist of human rights was toned down after the Soviets expressed

Fireworks celebrate Carter's inauguration

strong opposition. And while there was progress on SALT II, the emerging agreements for curtailing the arms race were far more modest than what Carter had originally thought possible.

In his obscure political beginnings Carter could talk about almost anything and impress his audiences with his knowledge. His notion that all government concerns should be discussed out in the open grew with each new primary victory. His final campaign for office was waged in part on a pledge to abandon the secretive practices of his predecessors. But even that high-sounding goal had to be refitted to meet the real world in Carter's first twelve months. His casual talk about the Middle East sent shudders through the diplomatic system attuned to the delicate shades of language and meaning. When he called for a Palestinian homeland while answering citizens' questions in the small town of Clinton, Mass., Israelis were startled, for "homeland" was a diplomatic code word implying an independent state on the West Bank of the Jordan River. Slowly Carter retreated, but not before a game defense. Reaffirming his ideas for America's global leadership in a May address at the University of Notre Dame, the President argued: "We are confident of the good sense of our own people, and so we let them share the process of making foreign policy decisions." But no matter how appealing the principle, the practice proved too distressing —if not to Americans, then to leaders of other nations. Carter took his diplomacy backstage.

On the domestic front, Carter's plans for conserving energy had to be severely compromised, reargued and delayed. A hurry-up program to reform the sprawling and costly welfare system bogged down in the overloaded legislature. Carter set a September deadline for massive tax re-

Chief Justice Warren Burger administers oath of office to the incoming President
"We can neither answer all the questions nor solve all the problems."

Nation

form to cure what the President had described as "a disgrace," but the uncertainty of the economy and the mounting concern of the business community caused Carter to pause.

When he became President, Carter insisted that a centerpiece of his Administration would be government reorganization. But even though Congress gave him authority to proceed, there was evidence at the end of 1977 that Jimmy Carter would have to rearrange his hopes. His time and energy were totally absorbed in the tasks of peace and preserving American prosperity.

As winter set in, the President still found himself at odds with a wide range of special interests in U.S. society. Blacks clamored for an intensive program of big-city aid. Early on, Urban League Exec-

tainty. The President has bitten off half a dozen big projects, and all of them generate a tremendous amount of uncertainty." Added Wisconsin's Democratic Congressman Henry Reuss, chairman of the House Banking Committee: "Carter will never win businessmen's confidence by saying that he wants to be loved. What businessmen respect, rightly, is mastery."

In his more philosophic moments, Carter confessed that the Congress was more knowledgeable and independent than he had expected, the Executive apparatus more unwieldy and stubborn than he had imagined, the problems more intractable and complex than he had perceived. It was part of his continuing charm that such candor still was possible in the face of obvious disappointment.

hints that there was a public relations scenario of sorts. In that memo Caddell had outlined a series of actions—almost all of which were carried out by Carter—to build the presidential image, to widen his narrow election margin to a solid base of public approval.

"Too many good people have been defeated because they tried to substitute substance for style," wrote Caddell. "They forgot to give the public the kind of visible signals that it needs to understand what is happening." He wrote out a script for town meetings, fireside chats and visits to the major governmental departments. Caddell suggested that now was the time for the President deliberately to blur political party lines, to create "a fundamentally new ideology." When the Caddell memo appeared in print, the

STANLEY TRETICK

Carter gets up as early as 5:30 a.m. to start a typical day of reading, talking, listening, thinking in the White House Oval Office

"I have learned a lot," he says, and that gives promise of a leader stripped of illusion, with a canny understanding of the world.

utive Director Vernon Jordan said: "We expected Mr. Carter to be working as hard to meet the needs of minorities and the poor as he did to get our votes, but so far we have been disappointed." Women complained that not enough of them had been named to high White House positions. Said Karen DeCrow, former president of the National Organization for Women: "Women's rights are simply not a high priority of this Administration." The AFL-CIO's George Meany, never a Carter enthusiast, declared that Carter's record on labor legislation was "a lot of talking but very little action."

While liberals charged that the cautious Carter had deserted them, businessmen also showed a marked lack of confidence in his leadership. James M. Howell, chief economist for the First National Bank of Boston, spoke for many when he said: "Businessmen thrive on cer-

"I have learned a lot," Carter told a number of interviewers. Sustaining him were the Carter will and determination. At the core of everything was the hope that Carter's first year had been a remarkable period of on-the-job training, and out of the rough-and-tumble would emerge a leader stripped of illusion and with a canny feel for the world. That, at least, was the promise.

Almost from the first hour of his presidency there was an argument whether Jimmy Carter was more style than substance. As it turned out, there was in those first months a deliberate emphasis on style over substance, and the students of such fine detail would contend that in the high art of presidential leadership the two cannot be separated. A secret memo that Carter's pollster, Pat Caddell, had drawn up before Carter took office was leaked to the press in the spring, confirming the

White House was engulfed in embarrassed silence. But the correlation between Caddell's suggestions and Carter's style told the story.

The President pulled on his cardigan sweater for his first fireside chat. His casual, down-home style was a success, and cardigan-sweater sales boomed across the nation. He established press conferences every other week, and his easy and informed manner won plaudits from a jaundiced press corps. In this lions' den it had been, wrote the Boston *Globe*'s Washington Bureau Chief Martin Nolan, "Christians 6, Lions 0." On a visit to the Labor Department the new chief took off his coat and appeared in shirtsleeves. "Just because I am President and because you work for the Federal Government or hold an exalted job," he said, "doesn't make you any better than the unemployed American in Dallas, Texas, that you serve." The Labor employees, most of whom had never seen a President near their offices, cheered lustily. Of course, the incident was duly recorded by television cameras and the press.

Concerned about the late-night work that is such a White House tradition, the new President wrote a memo to his staff: "I want you to spend an adequate amount of time with your husbands/wives and children." Carter humor surfaced about this time, too. "Those of you who are living in sin, I hope you will get married," he told the employees of HUD. "Those of you who have left your spouses, come back home. Those of you who don't know your children's names, get to know them."

One Saturday afternoon, with broadcasting's No. 1 folk hero beside him, Carter opened up the first presidential telephone party line. Walter Cronkite moderated the unique encounter with the

answered questions from the eager townspeople. Later, with his suit bag over his shoulder, he trudged up the front steps and into the Victorian home of Edward Thompson, a jovial father of eight, office manager of a beer-distributing firm. Shedding his coat and tie, Carter talked with the Thompsons for an hour about jobs and family, then went off to bed in the Thompsons' own upstairs room. At 6:30 a.m. the President was up and showering, he penned two notes asking teachers to excuse the tardiness of the Thompson teenagers, and then with a wave and a grin headed back to the presidential world of jets and limousines. Edward Thompson, captivated by his guest, called after Carter, "If you ever come back to Clinton, feel free to stop by." The millions of other Americans who had watched the event minute by minute through television felt the same warm glow. This folksy appeal

transition team had spent $1.7 million to prepare to take over the Government, but once the newcomers were in office it was discovered that many were woefully unprepared. Lots of the huge reports that had been so painstakingly prepared by scholars and former bureaucrats were ignored by the new Cabinet officers and agency heads.

The Carter team had campaigned as outsiders, proud of their lack of involvement with the Washington Establishment. Once in office, however, their task was to subdue the federal monster. They hardly knew how to begin. Nowhere was the inexperience more evident than in the area of congressional relations. Carter brought in Frank Moore, an easygoing Georgian who had helped out with the Georgia legislature. Most state legislatures are heavily tilted toward commercial or regional interests, and they can be

Carter and Wife Rosalynn relax in rocking chairs on White House veranda. For business they get together at working lunch on Wednesdays

"I want you to spend an adequate amount of time with your husbands/wives and children," he told busy staffers.

public. Questions were phoned in, answers were broadcast over the radio. Nine million Americans tried to phone, 42 got their questions on the air. The questions ranged from a query about a 25¢-per-gal. gasoline tax (there would be none) to why Carter's son Chip and his family were living in the White House at taxpayers' expense ("All personal expenses are paid for out of my own pocket"). On several questions Carter disarmed his questioners. "I don't know," he said, but he promised to find the answers—and he did.

In short order Carter was off to Clinton, Mass., for the first of several simulated town meetings, still a part of his meet-the-people program, which also included inviting average Americans to White House dinners. In Clinton's yellow-brick town hall, Carter stood before 850 residents who had won in a raffle the right to be there. For 90 minutes he joked and

was at the heart of Carter's presidential power. In March, 75% of the public approved of how he was handling his job.

This was not mere handshaking. When Carter found he could not do all the reading and thinking he wanted to in a normal day's hours, he arose as early as 5:30 a.m. He devoured memos, picked the brains of visitors. Israel's Moshe Dayan came away impressed with the quick study Carter had obviously done on the history of the Middle East conflict and the proposals made in recent years to resolve it. The President and his family and staff took speed-reading lessons so they could cover more paper in less time. An incurable detail man, Carter spent 20 hours going over the military budget.

Yet not all of this work had real impact or provided real leadership. Carter's

threatened or sometimes coaxed into action. Congress is a different creature, more sensitive to the national interest. The majority of the members now make Congress a career, and some of them show an idealism that exceeds their party loyalty.

At first, Carter's troubles with Congress included only the small things. Phone calls were not returned. Louisiana's Senator Russell Long went to a White House appointment and the receptionist did not recognize him. He waited 30 minutes, then left in disgust. Then more serious differences arose. With little notice, Carter announced he was going to slice into the pork barrel. He cut 19 water-control projects out of the fiscal-1978 budget to the tune of $289 million. Arizona Congressman Morris Udall learned from a reporter that one of his pet projects was to be lopped off. "Zero-based budgeting gone mad," he snorted. While

7

a compromise was ultimately worked out on the water projects, the scar that action left never really healed. "Militant amateurism," scolded Republican Leader John Rhodes. "The Carter people are darned well determined that they are not going to learn."

Upset by White House ineptitude, House Speaker Tip O'Neill privately referred to Hamilton Jordan, Carter's Chief Aide, as "Hannibal Jerkin." Down at the White House, they displayed symptoms of the siege mentality, a Nixon Administration malady, but not without some legislative progress being made. Carter's limited economic-stimulus program was approved by Congress. So was his request for an energy department to consolidate all the energy efforts then randomly scattered

strain consumption and develop alternate sources of energy began. The determined and skillful leadership of Speaker O'Neill prevented major changes in the House, but in the Senate Finance Committee Senator Russell Long presided. While he protested in his soft voice that he favored much of Carter's program, his committee began eviscerating it, clause by clause. Carter was unprepared for such a rough fight. Indeed, his declaration of war on the energy crisis failed even to hold his own attention very long. His exhortations through the summer were mild, his eyes on other horizons. Russell Long is not the son of Huey ("The Kingfish") Long for nothing. Considered by many to be the second most powerful man in Washington now, Long knew when he had the field to himself. The best thing that could be said about the conflict was that Carter

Lance, the banker, sat at his elbow. Balanced budgets and fear of inflation seemed to outweigh the specter of 7% unemployment. Carter was perceived as a "fiscal conservative," little different from his Republican predecessors, Ford and Nixon. Businessmen, on the other hand, were hopeful as individuals, but collectively they were skeptics. The reason, as much as anything, was their uncertainty about Carter's mind, his words. He had promised the oil and gas industry the deregulation of natural gas. But once in office, he wanted to wait. In his campaign, he had endorsed the Humphrey-Hawkins Bill to guarantee jobs, but in power he was hesitant. Yes, he wanted welfare reform, but he also wanted a balanced budget in 1981, and if that meant delay, then so be it. He proclaimed constantly that he was a friend of business, but in the heat of his energy struggle he went on television and attacked the oil industry as greedy obstructionists.Small businessmen were engulfed in rules and regulations from the Occupational Safety and Health Administration, as well as the old-line regulatory agencies, and Carter seemed slow to respond. While inflation at last seemed subdued, the recovery from the previous recession appeared to falter, and unemployment clung stubbornly near the 7% level.

Late in the year, Carter faced a hard decision about reappointing Arthur Burns, the white-haired patriarch of conservative economics. Burns had served Dwight Eisenhower, had been brought back by Richard Nixon as Chairman of the Federal Reserve. In his campaign, Carter had argued for more control over the Fed, an idea that horrified those who felt the separation of the Fed from politics was a foundation of America's flourishing economy. A Burns reappointment might be a telling vote of support for businessmen: thumbs down on Burns would be yet another cause for doubts. As the year ended, Carter sprang another surprise. He dropped Burns, gently and with great praise, and nominated G. William Miller, the chairman of Textron, Inc., a diversified manufacturing firm based in Providence, R.I. It appeared that Carter, through Miller, would retain much of the Burns philosophy but get his own man at the head of the Fed.

Carter's first Cabinet meeting; Vance of State and Brown of Defense flank President

One key adviser urged him to blur party lines and create "a fundamentally new ideology."

through the Government. Jimmy Carter himself seemed to be an apt pupil in congressional relations. He increased his meetings with members of Congress. Hardly a day passed that a group did not troop through Carter's White House for breakfast, lunch or just a chat. Speaker O'Neill was heartened. His frequent dinner companion, Carter turned into the questioner and listener. Why did Congress react in certain ways? he wanted to know. Which members were most powerful? How should he deal with them? "Is Carter a good pupil?" O'Neill was asked. "He's learning," replied O'Neill.

The full nature of the congressional malaise hit Carter first when he sent his energy package up to the Hill, heralding it as his most important first-year initiative. He himself addressed a joint session of Congress, asking the nation to wage "the moral equivalent of war." Almost immediately, the argument about how to re-

finally went to Long to work on the bill that he desperately needed.

In the areas in which Carter held expertise, the results were different. Up before him when he marched into his office was a decision on the B-1 bomber, the $100-million plane being sought by the Air Force. The engineer in Carter emerged. He waded through the complicated data with ease. He listened to the Joint Chiefs of Staff and to Defense Secretary Harold Brown. When he finally decided to shelve the B-1 and base American strategy on the Cruise Missile, the decision stood out as crisp and clean. Carter was playing his hand on American technology, finessing a whole generation of expensive weaponry.

But that kind of decision making was almost impossible in dealing with the U.S. economy. Carter's hopeful allies in the liberal Establishment were alienated when his business instincts took over and Bert

In the world beyond U.S. shores, there was some cheer for the beleaguered President late in the year. His itinerant U.S. Ambassador to the U.N., Andrew Young, who had so riled foreign leaders with his open talk about racism in other nations, had won allies in the African states, then toned down his rhetoric. Carter's own restraint on human rights preaching and his secret communications with the Soviet Union had put the SALT negotiations back on the track. And while there had been a lot of despair in Israel and among American Jews over Carter's insistence that the Palestinian problem be at the center of any Middle East negotiations, this firm Carter stand had brought a degree of reality to the discussions. That same sense of reality prompted him to bring the Soviet Union back into the Middle East picture through a joint declaration of purpose for the Geneva Conference. Even while critics were complaining about the dangers in this move, Anwar Sadat's peace mission to Jerusalem suddenly pushed the whole Middle East situation into a new phase. Carter stayed quiet, content to encourage the new move for peace through secret diplomatic channels.

Carter had said that he did not plan to travel abroad his first year, but he could not resist the temptation of a short European junket. Off he went to London for an economic summit meeting with the major industrial nations. Not much of consequence was settled, but the friendly American President was a hit with British street crowds, and he impressed his fellow leaders with his knowledge and willingness to listen to their concerns.

A plan to journey in November to four continents—nine countries in eleven days—did not fare so well. The scheduled meetings were to be so hasty and the jet hops so long that nothing of consequence could possibly be discussed. Perhaps providence smiled on Carter again. His beleaguered energy plan was coming up in conference committee just at the time he was scheduled to depart, and he wisely postponed the overseas trip, breaking the project into two parts. The first portion—to Poland, Iran, India, Saudi Arabia, Egypt, France and Belgium—was launched in late December. The rest of the itinerary—Brazil, Venezuela and Nigeria—was to be part of a spring journey.

Though doubts persisted about Carter's abilities as a world leader—the Gallup poll showed his popular support dropping from 75% in March to 56% in late November—he obviously was a better-educated man than when he took office. As preacher to the world, his record was spotty. Some had listened, more had turned away. But as a restrained observer and careful manipulator he showed more promise. He seemed to appreciate that Soviet-U.S. relations still lay at the center of his foreign concerns. In 1978 no debate would be more critical than the one over SALT II. The doubters, led by Senator Henry ("Scoop") Jackson, already had given notice of their questions about the new agreements being worked out. But in his first year Carter had been spared any national or international crisis of major proportions. There persisted the hope that Carter had learned and, having learned, would be prepared to cope.

The exact nature of Jimmy Carter still was in question after twelve months on the job. There was always a part of him carefully concealed. He gave more press conferences, talked to more editors, attended more open meetings than perhaps any modern President. Yet in the lonely moments when he went off to decide, there was often great uncertainty about what would emerge.

In his private habits there was remarkably little change except the predictable adjustments required by moving from Plains to the White House. And Camp David, high on the lip of Maryland's Catoctin Mountains, soon became his favorite retreat, a place where he could walk and think or play tennis. He did not participate in Washington social life, though his White House receptions and state dinners had dignity and warmth.

His family was both the joy and bane of many Americans. Brother Billy became the predictable buffoon, clowning all the way to the bank. Miss Lillian retained her spry irreverence, hustling off to India as a special envoy with Grandson Chip, touring Ireland with a group of junketing Iowans on an exchange program. Daughter Amy went about her schooling, the first presidential offspring to attend a Washington public school since the days of Theodore Roosevelt's son Quentin.

Never was Carter's Bible far from his reach. He went to Washington's First Baptist Church, where Harry Truman had worshiped, sometimes led the Sunday school class and even invited the Baptist leaders to the White House to talk about expanding their foreign missionary work. In his office, Carter kept his favorite books by Dylan Thomas and James Agee in a bookcase in his small private study where he did most of his reading and thinking. Classical music was piped into his office. But he could mix culture and corn. On the back lawn when he had his campaign workers from Georgia in for a thank-you reunion, there was fried chicken, and the President in his western shirt hugged and kissed most of the "peanut brigade."

Living in the White House awed the Carters at first. But like others who had preceded them, the family discovered that in some ways their goldfish-bowl existence brought them closer together as a family. "This is home," Rosalynn Carter could say after a few months. Indeed, she became so busy in her official life that she found she needed a special time to talk business with her husband. Not wishing to cut into family hours, the couple scheduled a business lunch once a week. "Every time Jimmy walked in I had a question for him," she explained. "I always tried to look for a good time to do it—but every time it was not a good time. So he said, 'Why don't you do like Fritz [Vice President Mondale] does? He and I have lunch every Monday, and he brings in all the questions he wants to discuss.' " The First Lady got Wednesday lunch—sometimes sandwiched between Prime Ministers and Senators, but rarely squeezed out.

The fervent desire to do what was right was Carter's greatest continuing strength in his first year. No shadow fell on his integrity or his dedication. Yet the mystical something that makes successful Presidents has never been fully defined. Each of the 38 men who have held the job has combined his abilities in special ways to move the nation forward, to respond to crisis—or else he was overwhelmed by events.

In the end, being President is a very personal job. National moods are set by the man who walks each morning to the Oval Office. His whims are translated into fashions, his casual comments become guides for behavior for millions. Truman insisted that the idea the presidency ennobles men was so much bunk. They either had the capacity somewhere down inside them before they got to the office or they did not.

Carter in 1977 proved he was a man of extraordinary intelligence as measured by his ability to learn facts from the papers served up to him. His mastery of the public relations of the office was proved. His vision of a better America stood unmarred. But the journey from dreams to performance is a hard one. Success is a mosaic of talent and work, of instinct and experience. Jimmy Carter still was searching.
— *Hugh Sidey*

Specially marked chair has been provided for Carter's Cabinet-room conferences
His vision stood unmarred, but the journey from dreams to performance is a hard one.

Press Secretary Jody Powell enjoys a close personal tie with Carter   **Special Assistant Hamilton Jordan is clearly the center of power**

Jimmy's Georgia Peaches

What's most noticeable about the new team? The drawl, y'all

As a campaigner, Jimmy Carter regularly promised that he would fill his Government with the very best people available. Like his predecessors, however, Carter soon showed a decided regional preference. John Kennedy had his Irish Mafia, Lyndon Johnson his Texans, Richard Nixon his crew-cut Californians. For Carter, the very best often seemed to mean not necessarily the best for the job but the best from the state of Georgia.

Carter's intimates deny, of course, that he is partial to Georgians. "Jimmy would take someone from Hong Kong if he thought that person could handle the job," says Charles Kirbo, who may well be the President's most trusted confidant. But Kirbo himself is a Georgian, and so are six of Carter's senior White House assistants. So are two of his top Cabinet members (Attorney General Griffin Bell and Andrew Young who, as U.N. Ambassador, has Cabinet rank).

An important part of Carter's team —in terms of trust, ease and intimacy, if not in terms of day-to-day contact—is a group of four Georgians who are older than the President or close to him in age. The first and foremost, Kirbo, 60, is a canny country boy from Bainbridge who has known Carter for 15 years. Kirbo turned down the chance to work in Washington, insisting that his thriving Atlanta law practice "is a better job than anything up there." But he regularly goes up to the cap-

ital to help Carter with tough decisions.

Griffin Bell, 59, of Americus, is another counsellor whose advice the President often seeks. So is Robert Lipshutz, 56, an Atlantan who serves as chief White House counsel. Youngest of the group is Bert Lance, 46, of Gainesville, who resigned under fire in September as budget director, but who has frequently been tapped since then by Carter for advice.

Apart from this council of elders, the main components of Carter's inner circle are his senior White House staffers and a few key Cabinet members. The White House staff shows the most pronounced Southern drawl. Major members:

▶ **Hamilton Jordan,** 33, of Albany, Ga., special assistant to the President and in many ways the *primus inter pares* among the senior aides. Carter calls him "my West Wing Charles Kirbo," and a junior aide comments: "Power groups in the White House? Hamilton is the power group." Jordan has known Carter since 1966 and helped plot the bold strategy that won him the White House. But Jordan seemed more effective plotting maneuvers on the campaign trail than handling administrative details in the West Wing. Usually tieless and shod in clunky work boots, he looks—and in the view of many observers is—out of his depth in the rarefied atmosphere of the White House. Operating out of the office once commanded by Nixon's heavyhanded chief of staff, H.R. Hal-

deman, Jordan resists the notion that he needs a comparable title to help tighten up the staff's often slipshod performance. Says Jordan (with Carter's tacit agreement): "There is not going to be a chief of staff."

▶ **Jody Powell,** 34, of Vienna, Ga., the press secretary. A member of the team since Carter's gubernatorial campaign of 1970, Powell is probably closer to the President than any of the other younger staffers. Like Jordan, he seems unawed by his boss. Once, commenting on the modest accommodations reserved for the aides accompanying the President on a trip, he said irreverently of Carter: "He's tight as a tick." Powell built up a reservoir of good will with the press through his candid, usually good-humored briefings, but he drained some of it away with a single major blunder. During the Lance crisis, he tried to plant a story smearing one of Lance's key critics, Illinois' Republican Senator Charles Percy. To his credit, Powell later apologized and confessed that he had been seriously out of line. He also concedes: "We have not done a good job of placing in context what the Administration is really trying to do."

▶ **Stuart Eizenstat,** 34, of Atlanta, assistant for domestic affairs. An owlish, low-keyed lawyer, Eizenstat was Carter's "issues man" during the presidential campaign and serves in a similar role now. He and his staff weigh the pros and cons of items such as health insurance and welfare reform. Despite Eizenstat's youth and inexperience, he is widely regarded as one of the brightest, most effective staffers.

▶ **Jack Watson,** 39, of Atlanta, Cabinet

Vice President Walter Mondale at work. No one would dream of bossing him around

secretary and assistant for intergovernmental affairs. In a job designed to reach across departmental lines, Watson often serves as a kind of crisis manager and answers alarm bells from Cabinet officers. Complaints persist, however, that the White House is not efficiently coordinating its efforts with those in other parts of the Executive Branch.

▶ **Frank Moore,** 42, of Dahlonega, Ga., congressional liaison. Amiable and slow-talking, Moore was Governor Carter's executive secretary and liaison chief back in Georgia. But he seemed out of his depth at the Capitol, at least initially—courting has-beens and overlooking real comers, failing to keep key Congressmen informed on matters of interest to them, observing only haphazardly the myriad little protocols so dear to U.S. lawmakers. Such complaints are heard less often today.

▶ **Zbigniew Brzezinski,** 49, of Warsaw, Poland, National Security Adviser. When Carter appointed the aggressive, confident Brzezinski, a much-published political scientist from Columbia, Washingtonians wondered whether another Henry Kissinger was in their midst. Such speculation was reinforced by the appointment of Cyrus Vance as Secretary of State, whose mild style recalls that of William Rogers, the Secretary who was so overshadowed by Kissinger. Though Brzezinski can be dogmatic and arrogant, he has been careful not to turn his shop into a rival to the State Department. "A team effort is necessary," he says. "I've made it a practice to tell the Secretary of State all that I do." Not always. Vance was less than delighted when Brzezinski plotted a

five-continent, nine-nation, eleven-day presidential trip that would have given Carter time for little more than a cup of coffee in any one place. The trip was postponed and eventually split into two parts.

Also ensconced in the West Wing but not formally part of Carter's White House staff is an official who ranks among his most important advisers. Vice President Walter Mondale, 50, has been taken more fully into the President's confidence than any of his predecessors. To underscore Mondale's closeness to Carter, he was given a place not far from the President's Oval Office, in addition to the usual suite assigned to Veeps in the old Executive Office Building across from the White House. Says Jordan: "In the past, a President's staff has been able to boss the Vice President around. No one would dream of doing that with Mondale."

The Vice President is one of the Big Four of Carter's foreign policy team, along with Vance, Brzezinski and the President. There is also a kind of backup Big Four: Defense Secretary Harold Brown, Disarmament Negotiator Paul Warnke, CIA Director Stansfield Turner and, most visible of all, U.N. Ambassador Young. A former Congressman from Atlanta, a key figure in the civil rights movement of the 1960s and the most important black on the Carter team, Young, 45, is the first U.N. envoy to be named a permanent member of the National Security Council. He sometimes sits in on sessions of the Big Four as well. "I admit it's a very unlikely team—Brzezinski, Mondale, Vance, Jimmy Carter, me, plus a lot of others," says Young. "The thing that

amazes me over and over again is [that] we've not had a major disagreement on issues of principle."

Young quickly earned a reputation as a kind of unguided missile for a number of unguarded remarks—*e.g.,* accusing the Swedes, the British and a number of past U.S. Presidents of racism—but Carter turned a deaf ear to suggestions that he be sacked. Among other things, Young seemed to be vastly more successful than his predecessors in forging links with the Third World, an area of major importance to Carter.

In economic policy, it sometimes seems that nobody is in charge. Bert Lance's departure left a large gap, and nobody has been able to fill it so far. Carter confers frequently with Charles Schultze, chairman of the Council of Economic Advisers, and Treasury Secretary W. Michael Blumenthal, but he is not really close to either man, and neither is as close to the business community as was Banker Bert.

For Carter's team, and particularly the White House staff, the first days were the worst. Phone calls went unanswered, initiatives were not followed up, Congressmen were not advised of important decisions. Some of that could be blamed on youth and inexperience. Some resulted from a kind of cultural blind spot, a determination on the part of these youthful Georgians to show they were not cowed by the powerful Washington Establishment. Thus when House Speaker Thomas ("Tip") O'Neill complained about the seats assigned to his staff for the Inaugural, Jordan responded with a putdown instead of a pampering. "If you don't like 'em," said Jordan breezily, "send 'em back and we'll give you a refund."

Despite the rocky beginning, the Speaker's relations with the White House have become positively cozy. But even he still has some reservations about the quality of Carter's staff, and there are many in Washington who dismiss much of the inner circle as parochial, amateurish, often inept. As a former member of Gerald Ford's Cabinet put it: "Carter has not made the transition from running for office to the job of leading the nation. All Presidents sooner or later must get rid of people who put them in office in favor of those who know what to do. Carter has refused to do that."

There was increasing talk late in 1977 that instead of changing his team Carter would reorganize it to improve coordination within the President's staff and between the White House and other power centers. Yet when an interviewer asked Jordan whether the President was thinking of hiring outside talent, increasing the size of the White House staff and imposing on it a more hierarchical structure, Jordan replied: "The answers are no, no and no." Unless the team works out some of its serious kinks in the new year, however, pressure may well mount on Carter to make those answers yes, yes and yes. — *Ronald P. Kriss*

Down home in Georgia, Billy, Jimmy and a tenant farmer while away time in a peanut field

New Folks at Home

A tree house and a mutt illustrate a new presidential style

From the moment of his election Americans assumed that Jimmy Carter of Plains, Ga., would bring a fresh style to the White House. Nothing else was imaginable in light of the rigorously folksy ways that Carter, kin and kith had demonstrated all during the campaign. Sure enough, after his Inauguration the new President not only disdained the customary black limousine and walked all the way to the White House, but he also told the Marine Band to stop saluting routine presidential appearances with *Hail to the Chief.*

He cut out the chauffeur service routinely enjoyed by previous White House staffers. Official parties, as the First Lady had threatened, began featuring no beverage more enlivening than wine. Though an ex-sailor himself, Carter ordered the Navy to sell the yacht *Sequoia* (it brought in the sum of $286,000)—a fringe benefit that other Presidents had indulged in without noticeable qualms.

These and other departures, such as Carter's decision not to designate a Chief of Staff, struck many as the end of the so-called imperial presidency. Though it was questionable whether the office could be —or should be—rendered less imperial by mere shifts in style, the changes at least gave the new Carter presidency a distinct tone. It resembled neither Ford's earnest caretaker regime nor Nixon's airless establishment. Nor was there anything to remind Washington observers of L.B.J.'s blustery days or to anticipate an encore to the Kennedy Camelot. On the contrary, Jimmy and Rosalynn Carter made it clear from the outset that they wanted to establish a White House that would be a symbol not of high life but of home life.

In fact, the place quickly became home, or at least home-base, for a sizable swarm of the Carter clan. In addition to the family mutt Grits, Son Jeff Carter and Wife Annette, Son Chip Carter and Wife Caron moved in—soon to be joined by James Earl Carter IV. The down-home complement seemed complete after the Carters obtained the two-months-early release from prison of Murderess Mary Fitzpatrick and fetched her to Washington to serve, as she had when Carter was Georgia's Governor, as nurse to nine-year-old Amy. The comings and goings of Carter's mother, Miss Lillian, filled out a picture of family solidarity. Eventually, Son Chip Carter, his marriage creaking, packed and went back to Plains, but that did not seriously mar the ever-elaborated presentation of the First Family as just plain folks.

Word duly came forth that the Baptist Church–going Carters still joined hands and said a blessing at family mealtime, and that the guest list at state dinners included Amy. The President himself once ushered King Hussein to Amy's bedroom for a visit with the child. Though it was also made clear that the President regularly listened to recorded Verdi and Mozart turned up loud, and though the Carters lent their public presence frequently to performances at the Kennedy Center, such cultural news seemed less central to the emergent image than the fact that the First Couple erected a tree house for Amy in the backyard. With that stroke, they seemed to transform the White House into a quintessential, all-American—if somewhat outsized—home sweet home.

The new mode came as a refreshment to many Americans. True, there were those who found it tempting to make sport of the First Family's public piety, or to mutter about the overload of Georgians in the palace guard. And some citizens felt that Carter sometimes carried informality too far, as when he turned up wearing a beige cardigan on his first televised fireside chat. Yet after an epoch that combined White House pomp and White House scandal, the U.S. generally seemed to welcome the air of domesticity in its symbolic national home on the Potomac.

If there was one place where the new Administration's style did arouse a remarkable amount of disgruntlement, it was in Washington itself. The social movers and seekers, who historically dance to whatever tune the White House plays, had eagerly anticipated introducing the colorful new symbols of power into the endless swirl of cocktail and dinner parties for which Georgetown primarily exists. Said an insider at the Republican National Committee early in the game: "The Carter people are just folks—and folks is in."

Or were they? Mostly, the folks seemed to take pains to remain the outsiders whom they had declared themselves to be en route to Washington. While the President established himself as a model homebody, most of his close associates gradually proved they were just as disdainful of Washington society as of conventional dress while at work. Wisecracking Top Aide Hamilton Jordan, given to coming to the White House dressed as though for a possum hunt, had almost never bothered to go to parties in four years as an assistant to Governor Carter, and he followed the same practice in Washington. Press Secretary Jody Powell almost invariably elected time at home with his family or P.T.A. meetings over the social swim. And even the most-sought bachelor of the Carter coterie, Sam Brown, resisted most invitations on the ground he was too busy with his work as director of ACTION. "Right now," said Brown, "that's more important to me than going to fancy dinners and making the party scene."

Indeed, the Carter folk had a way of avoiding almost any scene deemed smart by fashionable Washington. Even though the popular Sans Souci restaurant is close to the White House, they avoided lunching there "for symbolic reasons," as one of them put it. Translation: the French Sans Souci was first made an In place by Kennedy loyalists back in the Camelot days.

When they did tear themselves away from the White House, work, families and P.T.A.s, the Carter crowd chose to patronize a place not hitherto celebrated —Sarsfield's bar, an L Street saloon distinguished mainly by its tolerance for rowdy drinkfests featuring a lot of chug-a-lugging. Even Hamilton Jordan turned up now and then for a slosh or two with the fraternity of insider-outsiders associated with the President. Why such a place as Sarsfield's? One Carterite, White House Appointments Aide Scott Burnett, explained with revealing candor: "Most of us here at the White House don't like the New York–Washington types who hang out in Georgetown. We prefer to stay by ourselves."

Such stand-oafishness inevitably created an unusual distance between social Washington and the office that remains the foremost symbol of political Washington. For a while it seemed that sociable, high-living Bert and LaBelle Lance, with their love of grand entertaining, might bridge the distance. That hope vanished from Washington with the beleaguered budget director.

Long before the end of the Administration's first year, the local annoyance at its social ways became a public sport. Washington *Star* Columnist Betty Beale sniped at the notion of allowing little Amy in as the dinner partner of visiting dignitaries. Said she: "I couldn't believe my ears when I heard that that kid was sitting at the head table with her parents, reading a mystery story." Sneered another social reporter: "Going to a White House party is about as exciting as going to a P.T.A. meeting."

Finally, according to Feature Writer Sally Quinn of the Washington *Post,* the city stopped talking about the Carter style. The reason, she wrote, was that the Carters "have no style." Maybe so, maybe not. To most Americans the issue was, to say the least, without substance.   — *Frank Trippett*

Clockwise from top: Amy in her new tree house; Amy and father after fishing at St. Simon's; Amy at White House with mongrel friend Grits

From its launch platform on a bomber, the shark-painted Air Force cruise missile can strike within 50 ft. of its target

Nation

Big Gamble on the Cruise Missile

Carter kills the B-1 in a major shift of weapons

After months of hot debate, the final action by Congress went almost unnoticed, yet the bill passed on Nov. 3 gave President Carter authority to start a major realignment of U.S. defenses. At issue: the death of the B-1 bomber and development of two new weapons, the cruise missile and the "neutron bomb."

Since the mid-'60s, the Air Force had been insisting that the nation's safety demanded the development of the B-1. It was a fundamental part of the U.S. defense strategy known as "the triad." According to this concept, the U.S. must be able to rain nuclear warheads on any attacker by three delivery systems: land-based missiles (*e.g.,* the Minuteman III); submarine-launched missiles (the Poseidon); and manned bombers. Of the three, the Air Force argued, the bomber is the only weapon that can "think," can solve problems en route to a target and can be diverted or recalled. Indeed, in an all-out war the Pentagon planned to deliver fully 60% of its megatonnage by aircraft.

That role has long belonged primarily to the B-52, but the Air Force claimed that it was too old (the latest model was built in 1962), too limited in electronics and too slow. It lumbers along at 400

m.p.h. while flying at 200 ft.—barely low enough to duck under enemy radar. The sleek, swing-wing B-1 would overcome the B-52's failings: it could attack at 600 m.p.h. while skimming as low as 70 ft. off the ground; it could be packed with black boxes filled with electronic equipment; and it could carry 57.5 tons of bombs and weapons, almost twice as much as the B-52. But the advantages of the B-1 came at a tremendous price. Each plane would cost $102 million. The bill for building the whole fleet of 244 desired by the Air Force and maintaining it for 20 years would be $100 billion.

Jimmy Carter was skeptical. During his campaign for the presidency he had pronounced the bomber "wasteful of taxpayers' dollars," but he also said he favored continuing work on the aircraft in case it should "become necessary in the future." After taking office, Carter seemed to be warming to the B-1, but at a June press conference he startled both foes and friends of the plane by killing it. The step, said Carter, was "one of the most difficult decisions that I've made since I've been in office." The President had decided that the advantages of the B-1 would

not be worth their cost, that the job could be done cheaper and better by the cruise missile launched from modified B-52s.

The cruise missile is basically a small, unmanned bomber, a descendant of the Nazi V-1 "buzz bomb" that terrorized Britain in World War II. After the war, the U.S. developed drone missiles of its own, including the Air Force's 6,000-mile-range Snark, but in the end discarded the long-range models. They were too big, too slow and too inaccurate.

In the past five years, however, an entirely new generation of cruise missiles has been born, one that Defense Secretary Harold Brown said exceeded expectations. The new missiles, still under development, are powered by a jet engine that is only 30 in. long and a foot in diameter and yet will generate speeds of up to 600 m.p.h. To guide the missiles, engineers worked out a miniaturized computer that is coupled with radar. While flying, the missile studies the passing terrain, compares it to a memorized "map" that bears the correct route, and makes corrections needed to stay on course. The missile will be able to deliver a 200-kiloton warhead within 50 ft. of its target.

The Air Force version of the weapon —the Navy has its own—will have a range of 1,700 miles. Since it is only 19 ft. long and can dart along at 40 ft. above the ground during its final run, the missile would be next to impossible to stop.

What is more, the weapon is relatively cheap—about $1 million each. A refitted B-52 could launch 20 missiles at separate targets while flying hundreds of miles from Soviet borders.

Not everyone, however, is wholly convinced of the cruise's promise. John Taylor, editor of the authoritative *Jane's All the World's Aircraft,* spoke for many military professionals when he declared that the substitution of the cruise for the B-1 was a "disastrous mistake." And congressional supporters of the B-1 are still attempting to keep the bomber alive.

While the debate over the B-1 and the cruise missile was based primarily on military factors, the President's decision to back the so-called neutron bomb quickly became a political, and even moral, issue. Another old idea, the neutron bomb was supported by Carter because of the difficulties NATO would face if the Soviets attacked Western Europe. Not only do the Warsaw pact nations have 27,200 tanks to NATO's 11,000, but the Soviet models are designed to resist the blast and heat of conventional nuclear weapons. More important, NATO might be able to fight off the Soviets by using nuclear weapons, but when the battle was over it would be difficult to tell who had won: war games have shown that the struggle could also kill tens of millions of civilians, mostly Germans, who would be caught in the blast, heat and fallout.

The neutron bomb would solve part of the problem: it kills by releasing far greater amounts of radiation, which can penetrate the thickest armored tanks, but within a smaller range. And because it creates minimal heat and blast, the neutron bomb would take a far lesser toll of civilians and their cities.

These factors led the Pentagon to urge the development of the neutron bomb, but some politicians, both at home and abroad, were appalled at the prospect. The main fear was that the new weapon would be so convenient that an American President would be more likely to authorize its use in time of war—and thus escalate the fighting. Warned Senator Mark Hatfield: "Because of its high precision, [the neutron bomb] invites use." Critics also seized on the fact that the neutron bomb would cause less physical destruction and denounced it as a weapon that kills people but spares buildings.

The Pentagon argued strenuously that equipping NATO forces with the neutron bomb would strengthen the nuclear deterrent, and Carter declared that the weapon "ought to be one of our options." But the Administration said it would not produce the bomb unless the Europeans wanted it, and European leaders, worried about the political implications of such a controversial weapon, said they needed time to reach a decision. ∎

The B-1 could attack at 600 m.p.h. but each would cost some $100 million

Hostages being held captive by seven Hanafi Muslims in B'nai B'rith headquarters. Below, police sharpshooter keeps watch on rooftop

Terror in the Nation's Capital

Muslim gunmen seize three buildings to dramatize grievances

The Hanafi Muslims have never been a particularly notable sect. Their number is minuscule, at most some 100 members nationwide. They originally split away from the Black Muslims in the '60s to follow a less politically radical and more conventionally Muslim creed. Yet for 38 suspense-filled hours last March, a ragtag band of twelve Hanafis proved a point with which the world was becoming increasingly familiar: almost any group willing to run the risk can attract vast public attention to its cause, no matter how inconsequential or irrational, by merely seizing innocent hostages.

The Hanafis did just that in a coordinated attack on three Washington buildings. Seven Hanafis, armed with rifles, shotguns and machetes, burst into the headquarters of B'nai B'rith, the Jewish service organization. Shouting anti-Semitic slogans, they rushed through the building, seizing hostages, slashing some occupants and shooting at others. Two other Hanafis barged into the District Building, just two blocks from the White House, and began firing wildly. They killed a black radio newsman and wounded three other men. Yet another three Hanafis more quietly invaded the Islamic Center on Embassy Row, taking eleven hostages without harming any.

The three buildings were quickly surrounded by local police and FBI agents. Inside, no fewer than 132 hostages, many forced to lie face down on the floor and threatened with imminent death, spent harrowing hours awaiting the highly uncertain outcome. "They never stopped swearing at us," later recalled Besse Zaritsky, 56, a B'nai B'rith editorial employee. "They called us Yahudi [Jew] and bitches. They said they'd chop off our heads."

As television cameras focused on the three besieged buildings, and a police helicopter circled overhead, Washington police and Justice Department officials followed a strategy of waiting out the terrorists and of at least discussing the demands of Khalifa Hamaas Abdul Khaalis, the Hanafi leader. Khaalis, 55, had been discharged from the Army for mental instability in World War II, and then found by a court to be mentally disturbed in 1968, yet he had also been the victim of vicious sectarian rivalry. After he publicly criticized the Black Muslims, seven members of that group broke into his Washington home in 1973 and killed five of his children, plus a grandson and another Hanafi follower. Five of the seven attackers were given life sentences for the murders.

But Khaalis did not consider that sufficient punishment. He now insisted that the killers be handed over to him, presumably for execution. He also demanded interviews with Heavyweight Champion Muhammad Ali, a Black Muslim supporter, and Wallace Muhammad, leader of the sect (Muhammad has actually moderated many of its policies and changed its name to the Bilalians). Khaalis fur-

ther declared that he would not release the hostages until the new film *Mohammad, Messenger of God*, which he considered sacrilegious, had been banned from U.S. theaters. Negotiators quickly agreed to stop current showings of the film but declined to deliver any of the people on Khaalis' list.

The Hanafis threatened to begin beheading hostages, and police took the warnings seriously. Then, as tension mounted amid the glare of vast press coverage, three diplomats from Muslim nations volunteered to try negotiating with the Hanafis. They were Ambassadors Ardeshir Zahedi of Iran, Ashraf Ghorbal of Egypt and Sahabzada Yaqub-Khan of Pakistan. The Pakistani diplomat repeatedly telephoned Khaalis through a long and tense night, reminding the Hanafi leader of appeals for compassion in the Koran. Example: "Help ye one another in righteousness and piety, but judge ye not one another in sin and rancor."

By morning, the citations of scripture had made an impact on the devout Khaalis. At 6 p.m. Ambassador Ghorbal pleaded: "Let us come to you, dear brother, and sit down and talk at a table of peace." Khaalis finally agreed to meet with the diplomats and three police officers. In an emotional two-hour conference, Khaalis burst into tears as he was reminded of his murdered children. But he agreed to surrender all the hostages if he could just return to his home in northwest Washington. Despite some public protests later against letting Khaalis go free without bail, the officials had made a wise bargain. All of the hostages were released; a dozen were cut or beaten, none seriously.

If that was a happy ending for the innocent, there was no such result for the Hanafis. After a 54-day trial last spring, all twelve of the terrorists were convicted of various offenses ranging from murder to conspiracy, and all received stiff prison sentences, which amounted, in effect, to life terms. Khaalis was sentenced to a minimum of 41 years—meaning he will not be eligible for parole until he is 96. ∎

A Man, a Plan, a Canal, Panama!

A hard-won compromise faces strong nationalist opposition

General Omar Torrijos Herrera of Panama

Not since the funeral of John F. Kennedy had so many foreign heads of state come to Washington. Nineteen national leaders of the Western Hemisphere were in town with full glittering retinues. In the flag-draped Hall of the Americas in the Pan American Union Building, on Sept. 7, President Carter and Panama's General Omar Torrijos Herrera signed two documents providing for the U.S. to turn over control of the Panama Canal. Said Carter: "This opens a new chapter in our relations with all of the nations in this hemisphere." Added Torrijos: "You have turned imperial force into moral force." Then the two leaders heartily embraced.

The treaty is skillfully crafted to serve the best interests of both nations. If the U.S. is slowly ceding control over the canal, it also reserves the right to protect, in perpetuity, the neutrality of the waterway. If Panama is allowing a long transition period, it now has a precise date when it will take over the canal that divides its country and wounds its national pride. The U.S. can afford to be magnanimous because the canal is not nearly so important as it used to be; only about 4% of American coast-to-coast trade makes the transit through the canal. The U.S. is also being practical in reaching an agreement with Panama. Without the treaty, nationalist indignation is bound to grow and perhaps culminate in attempted sabotage of the canal.

Few treaties in history were so long in the making. Negotiations began in 1964, after Panamanian students rioted in the Canal Zone, and 24 people were killed. For 13 years, through four national Administrations, the U.S. fitfully pursued the talks. Then, in the fall of '76, on the small island of Contadora off the coast of Panama, the negotiators finally got down to hard bargaining. The U.S. representatives: Veteran Diplomat Ellsworth Bunker, 83, and former Xerox Chairman Sol Linowitz, 64.

The pact they negotiated seemed to be a credible compromise. Panama would acquire control of the Canal Zone but not until the year 2000. In the 22 intervening years, both countries would prepare for the changing of the guard. Panamanians, who now compose 70% of the work force on the canal, would be gradually phased into the management of the waterway. The 14 U.S. military bases and 9,000 troops would be phased out. When the treaty is ratified by the U.S. Senate, more than half of the 648-sq. mi. Canal Zone would be ceded to Panama; the remainder would be turned over in 2000. American Zonians would be able to keep their jobs, but they would lose some of their privileges and perks, and within three years of ratification they would become subject to Panamanian laws.

Until Panama assumes control of the canal, the U.S. would pay 30¢ per ton of shipping and also raise the annual rent it pays from $2.3 million to $10 million; it would provide another $10 million from canal revenues, business permitting. After 2000, Panama is on its own. But the treaty provides for the perpetual guarantee of the canal's neutrality by the U.S. and Panama; both nations are also given the right to move their ships "expeditiously" through the canal in case of some emergency.

Despite the expression of good will on both sides, opponents in the U.S. and Panama denounced the agreement as a

First boat to pass through a preliminary section of the canal was tug *Gatun*, Sept. 26, 1913

Today the waterway is much reduced in value, and vulnerable to nationalist sabotage.

betrayal of the national interest. In Panama, demonstrators protested against another quarter-century of the American preserve, while U.S. conservatives insisted that the canal had been granted to the U.S. "in perpetuity." A Gallup poll showed that Americans opposed the transfer of the canal to Panama by 46% to 39%.

The opposition was strengthened by conflicting interpretations of the treaty. While American officials assured the public that the U.S. retained the right to act in order to protect the canal after 2000, Panamanian negotiators were telling their people that the U.S. could not intervene under any circumstances. In hearings on the treaty, one Senator after another criticized the pact for its ambiguities. Then, in a move suggested by Linowitz, Torrijos came to Washington where he and Carter issued a joint "statement of understanding." After 2000, the lead-

ers declared, both nations would have the right to defend the canal against any threat to its neutrality. They also agreed that the ships of both nations could go "expeditiously" to the "head of the line of vessels" in a crisis.

With those rights spelled out, the U.S. proceeded to rally support for the treaty. Former President Gerald Ford, who had backed negotiations while he was in office, said he was in favor of the treaty. So did former Secretaries of State Dean Rusk and Henry Kissinger. "If the treaties are not approved," warned Kissinger, "it will be a disaster for us all."

Though many Panamanian leftists thought the treaty conceded too much to the U.S., the country approved the pact by a 2-to-1 vote in a plebiscite in October. That left the U.S. Senate as the final hurdle. Most of its members were still not saying how they would vote when the issue comes to a showdown, presumably early in 1978. ∎

"I Let Down the Country"

Nixon's TV "confession" is less than the whole truth

Still amazingly resilient, he looked tanned and far more fit than in his last, exhausted days in the White House. Yet those same discomfiting mannerisms remained. The quick, defensive smile. The look of blank impassivity when the going got rougher. The stammer and twisted syntax when he seemed to know that his answer was inadequate. As the same old Richard Nixon underwent a sharp interrogation by the soft-toned but persistent British interviewer, David Frost, the fallen former President allowed himself only a few fleeting moments of contrition.

"I let down my friends," Nixon conceded in the most emotional moment of an extraordinary series of five 90-minute TV interviews —four in the spring and one in September. "I let down the country. I let down our system of Government and the dreams of all those young people that ought to get into Government ... Yep, I let the American people down, and I have to carry that burden with me for the rest of my life." Later, asked if he felt that he had been punished sufficiently for his transgressions in the Watergate affair, Nixon said quietly: "No one can know how it feels to resign the presidency of the United States."

But that was about as close as Nixon would—or perhaps ever could—come to admitting his wrongdoing. Even as he made his limited confession, he reverted to the Nixonian style, throwing out dark hints of people out to get him and then saying that he, of course, did not necessarily believe this was true, and even if it were, he could understand. "I don't go with the idea that what brought me down was a coup, a conspiracy, etc.," he began. But others had told him that "there is a conspiracy to get you." Agreed Nixon: "There may have been. I don't know what the CIA had to do. Some of their shenanigans have yet to be told." Yes, he did have enemies. "I gave 'em a sword, and they stuck it in and they twisted it with relish. And I guess if I'd been in their position, I'd have done the same thing."

Nixon's more specific defense was to shift much of the blame to his aides, who, he claimed, had devised the bugging and break-ins at Democratic National Headquarters, carried them out and then tried to keep their involvement from being disclosed. He had simply tried to protect them too long. Implying that he should have fired them abruptly, he offered the plaintive defense: "I wasn't a good butcher." Yes, he was guilty of bad judgment throughout the scandal, but his mistakes had been "mistakes of the heart, rather than the head." In the final interview, he offered a quite incredible excuse. His Attorney General, John Mitchell, had let Watergate happen because he had been distracted by the unstable mental condition of his wife, Martha. Claimed Nixon: "If it hadn't been for Martha, there'd have

JOHN BRYSON

Former President Nixon explains to David Frost
"No one can know how it feels ..."

been no Watergate, because John wasn't minding that store."

On the now tedious details of the voluminous Watergate evidence, Nixon seemed not to have mastered the implications of even his own once secret White House tape recordings. Insisting, as always, that he knew nothing about any White House cover-up of the Watergate crimes until his former counsel, John Dean, told him on March 21, 1973, of hush-money payments to the convicted burglars, Nixon was startled when Frost read him portions of his conversation on Feb. 14, 1973, with former Aide Charles Colson. "The President's loss has gotta be cut on the cover-up deal," Nixon had told Colson on that tape. Nixon fell back on the general defense that his whole aim had been to contain political damage, not to conceal any crimes, and therefore he had not been involved in an obstruction of justice. Showman Frost then corrected Lawyer Nixon by telling him that motive is irrelevant under the law if, as in Watergate, the actual result was to obstruct justice.

If Nixon had hoped to begin repairing his reputation in the 28 hours of taping with Frost, he failed. By reasserting the imperial philosophy that "when the President does it, that means that it is not illegal," he merely reminded viewers of how little he had learned from his personal tragedy. The first interview, skillfully publicized by Frost with hints of forthcoming revelations, drew fully half of the viewing audience in New York City and Los Angeles, but in later segments this dwindled to about one-quarter. While the former President generated some sympathy, the reaction of most Americans was that they had heard all they wanted to hear from Richard Nixon. Many were irritated too at the commercialism of the TV spectacular. Nixon made nearly $1 million for his prime-time shows, Producer Frost an estimated $1.5 million.

Despite such criticisms, Nixon is planning still further revelations about his presidency and explanations of what happened to him. He is completing work on his memoirs; the book is scheduled for publication in April.

Some of Nixon's once loyal aides are now showing signs of wanting to produce their own versions of the record. No one expects any revelations from the uncommunicative G. Gordon Liddy, who had initiated the Watergate burglary and who emerged from nearly 4½ years in prison as silent as ever. But under effective prodding from Judge John J. Sirica, the tough Watergate jurist who retired last October from full-time bench duty, H.R. Haldeman, John Ehrlichman and John Mitchell gave the court apologies of varying credibility for what they had done. In return, Sirica reduced their minimum sentences from 2½ years to one year, and all three should be free by next summer. Mitchell is not in the best of health—he had to be given a medical furlough at Christmas because of a hip condition—but he and his two colleagues are plunging into the still lucrative Watergate book market. And Ehrlichman and Haldeman, at least, seem to have lost their devotion to their former boss. Five-and-a-half years after the historic burglary, the Watergate saga is not yet fully told. ∎

Operation White Snow

How a Korean rice broker tried to buy the U.S. Congress

Just a decade ago, Rice Broker Tongsun Park was so broke he had to pawn his mother's jade hairpins to help settle debts of more than $1 million. But he kept on entertaining lavishly at Washington's posh George Town Club. Among his guests there were Gerald Ford, when he was Vice President, and Tip O'Neill, when he was House majority leader.

Another Korean native who liked to entertain was Suzi Park Thomson, 46, an attractive aide to House Speaker Carl Albert. She never earned more than $15,000 a year, but she managed to throw many convivial parties, bringing together Capitol Hill dignitaries, journalists, attractive women and agents of the Korean CIA.

Partygivers Park and Thomson insist that their social activities were perfectly innocent. But according to federal investigators, the soirées were part of a multimillion-dollar attempt by the Park Chung Hee regime in Seoul to buy friends —most of them Democrats in Congress —and head off threatened cutbacks in U.S. aid or the withdrawal of U.S. troops.

When the Korean connection was first publicly disclosed in the fall of 1976, Democratic leaders in Congress belatedly started an investigation with all the gusto of a Westerner taking his first taste of *kimchi*. For months, the probe by the House ethics committee, headed by Georgia Democrat John Flynt Jr., inched along with little noticeable progress. Finally, to defuse growing criticism, Tip O'Neill, who succeeded Albert as House Speaker in January, persuaded former Watergate Special Prosecutor Leon Jaworski to take over the Koreagate case.

Jaworski vowed "to ferret out the facts," but they have been elusive. For one thing, even after being granted immunity from prosecution, Thomson has been a notably unrevealing witness, maintaining that she was only an honest working girl. Said she of her parties: "I cooked and my guests washed dishes." For another, the chief figure in the scheme, Park, stayed out of investigators' reach, slipping away first to London and later to South Korea.

Still, investigators for Jaworski and for a separate Justice Department inquiry have managed to produce tantalizing glimpses of Park's operations. The son of a wealthy businessman, Park studied at Georgetown University (class of 1963), made friends in Washington political circles, tried various small-scale business ventures. In 1965, according to one report, he went to the Korean CIA and offered a deal: if the agency would support his becoming the principal broker in U.S. rice shipments to Korea, he would use his influence to gain congressional support for Seoul. Park won the brokerage. In 1967

Partygiver Suzi Park Thomson

Fugitive Rice Broker Tongsun Park at press conference in Seoul

He had a lot of friends in Congress, and he liked to give them money.

the Korean government put up $3 million so that he could establish the George Town Club and start entertaining.

By 1976 Park had earned $9.2 million from rice-importing fees, part of which he used in his bribery operations. According to former Korean CIA Chief Kim Sang Keun, they were conducted under several code names (among them: "Ice Mountain" and "White Snow") with the approval of President Park, who was known to the conspirators as "the Patriarch." In all, Businessman Park cultivated more than 100 U.S. politicians, mostly House members. They included the leadership of both parties, important commit-

tee chairmen and rank-and-file members of the committees that handle legislation affecting Korea. Park provided his friends with expenses-paid junkets to his homeland, honorary degrees from Korean universities and valuable gifts. And money.

Some of Park's handouts were legitimate campaign contributions; others were simply envelopes stuffed with untraceable $100 bills. Investigators believe that about $190,000 went to former Congressman Otto Passman and at least $100,000 to former Democratic Representative Richard Hanna of California. Other gifts included $10,000 to Edwin Edwards, then a Congressman and now Governor of Louisiana, and another $10,000 to his wife; $5,150 to John Brademas of Indiana, deputy House Democratic leader; $4,000 to John McFall of California.

Despite the large numbers of Congressmen brushed by the scandal, only three people have so far been indicted: Park himself, Hanna and Han Cho Kim, a Korean-born businessman in the Washington area who allegedly handled $600,000 as part of Operation White Snow. The chief obstacle to more indictments is the lack of proof that Park's friends in Congress knew he was a foreign agent or that they changed their votes in return for his gifts. This evidence can probably be pro-

vided only by Park, who now runs a mini-empire of shipping, trading and supermarket interests back in Korea.

Under heavy pressure from Washington, Seoul at year's end agreed to turn Park over to investigators for the Justice Department. Park himself promised, in exchange for the dropping of all charges against him, to testify against anyone indicted for receiving his bribes. Jaworski, whose congressional investigators were not included in the deal, denounced it as "inadequate and unacceptable." He said that Park would be subpoenaed to testify fully before the House ethics committee as soon as he arrived in the U.S. ∎

Carter's First Casualty

Bert Lance's odd banking practices cost him his job

THE NEW YORK TIMES

So close to the President: Lance at work in the Office of Management and Budget

Thomas Bertram Lance, 46, an amiable, bearlike figure (6 ft. 4 in., 235 lbs.), arrived in Washington last January as the $57,500-a-year Director of the Office of Management and Budget. He affected an aw-shucks, country-boy manner, but as one Congressman put it: "You know that kind—when he shakes your hand, you had better count your fingers."

Lance soon established himself as a key economic adviser and the main link between Carter and a wary business community. Said White House Aide Hamilton Jordan: "He's more than a budget officer because he's so close to the President." But the nation's chief budget officer was having trouble balancing his own budget. In January, Lance told the Senate that he had assets of $7,968,354 and "direct liabilities" of $5,343,797, for a net worth of $2,624,557. Those huge debts dated back to 1975 and 1976, when Lance was chairman of the Calhoun First National Bank in northwest Georgia, one of whose founders was his wife's grandfather. He borrowed $3.1 million to buy nearly 200,000 shares of the Atlanta-based National Bank of Georgia. But the stock began dropping, and under the Administration's conflict-of-interest rules, he had to sell his shares by the end of 1977.

By July, an investment that had once been worth $3.3 million was worth only $1.7 million. Jimmy Carter tried to come to Lance's rescue by asking the Senate to release him from the sale. By then, rumors were surfacing almost daily of Lance's irregular practices as president of NBG and

Carter announces aide will go
"Bert Lance is my friend."

of Calhoun. Lance defended those practices as "typical of Southern banking," but eventually three congressional committees and six Government agencies decided they were worth investigating. Among them:

Overdrafts From 1972 to 1975, Lance and his family often overdrew their Calhoun bank accounts by huge sums: Bert by as much as $26,272; LaBelle, his gracious wife, by a high of $110,493; nine Lance relatives by the astounding total of $450,000. Examiners from the office of the Comptroller of the Currency called the situation "abusive" and "appalling" and in 1975 got the Calhoun bank to agree to desist from such practices; that agreement was mysteriously nullified just before Lance's nomination as Budget Director was announced.

Correspondent relations Smaller banks regularly establish "correspondent" relationships by depositing interest-free funds with larger banks in exchange for services such as clearing checks. Federal banking laws prohibit a bank officer from using a correspondent relationship to help get a personal loan. Yet Lance had loans from five banks, and his NBG had correspondent setups with four of them.

Political campaign irregularities When Lance ran unsuccessfully for Governor of Georgia in 1974, his campaign accounts were overdrawn by a total of $228,000. In addition, the Calhoun bank footed campaign bills totaling $78,000 and list-

ed them as "bank expenses." Lance eventually reimbursed the bank. But he also was charged with having used NBG's Beechcraft plane for personal and political purposes without paying the bank. (Carter also took five free flights on the plane; he belatedly reimbursed the bank.)

In mid-August, Comptroller of the Currency John Heimann wound up a five-week investigation. His meticulously worded report neither condemned nor absolved Lance. But it did accuse him of having engaged in "unsafe and unsound banking practices." Unwisely, Carter seized upon the report as a vindication. "My faith in the character and competence of Bert Lance has been reconfirmed," he said. "Bert, I'm proud of you."

Fresh allegations kept appearing, and over the Labor Day weekend, Senate Majority Leader Robert Byrd advised the President to get rid of Lance. So did other key Senators. Lance was determined to have his say at a Senate committee hearing, and his masterful 49-page statement put the Senators on the defensive, but only briefly. Carter phoned Byrd for his reaction. "This matter is not going to go away," Byrd told Carter. Finally, wearily, Lance agreed to resign.

On Sept. 21 Carter went on nationwide television and, with tears in his eyes, said he was accepting Lance's offer to resign. But, still loyal, he added: "Nothing that I have heard or read has shaken my belief in Bert's ability or his integrity." Concluded Carter, visibly shaken: "Bert Lance is my friend."

Lance's duties at OMB were immediately shifted to his deputy, James McIntyre, who had served as Georgia's budget director while Carter was Governor and who was nominated as OMB Director at the end of the year. Even after Lance's departure, the Justice Department, the SEC and the FDIC continued their probes into his affairs. Moreover, Congress was weighing legislation to tighten regulations on overdrafts and insider deals.

All in all, if the Bert Lance affair was less than a full-blown scandal, it nonetheless gave the Administration, barely eight months old, its first major casualty. Perhaps most important, it aroused the suspicion that Jimmy Carter, who insisted so often that Government officials must avoid even the appearance of impropriety, was not above invoking a double standard for the sake of an old friend. As for the Lances, they were not doing badly. The 40-room Atlanta mansion that they bought for $400,000 in 1975 was up for sale, and Bert still owed $250,000 from his gubernatorial campaign. But they were able to hang on to their $100,000 home in Calhoun and their $100,000-plus vacation retreat in Sea Island, Ga. What is more, at year's end Bert seemed to have found a Saudi Arabian buyer who was willing to take 60% of his NBG stock off his hands at $20 a share. That would leave Lance with a tidy profit of $360,000 or so. ∎

The famous skyline of midtown Manhattan plunged into ghostly darkness

The Night of the Locusts

A blackout illuminates a shadowy side of New York

"**Y**ou're going to go right down the pipe," shouted the senior dispatcher for the New York power pool outside Albany. He was trying to warn the men running Con Edison's control center in New York City on the sweltering evening of July 13. Lightning had knocked out four major transmission lines into the city, and the dispatcher's instruments showed catastrophe ahead. For more than half an hour, he repeatedly warned the Con Ed men to ease the pressure on their dangerously overloaded system by acting faster to disconnect some customers. "O.K.," he exclaimed at 9:27 p.m. "I'm going to tell you one more time. All you got to do is push a button. Shed 600 megawatts of power immediately or you're out of business." Nine minutes later, the lights went out all over the city.

"It's Christmas time, it's Christmas time!" The cry echoed through the darkened streets as tens of thousands of blacks and Hispanics poured from their tenements in the ghettos of Bedford-Stuyvesant, Harlem, the South Bronx. But for most New Yorkers of all races, it was, as Mayor Abe Beame said, "a night of terror"— and an ominous change from the 1965 blackout. During both emergencies, most New Yorkers responded with good humor and a willingness to help one another. But this time, roving bands of looters tore steel shutters from storefronts, shattered plate-glass windows and scooped up clothing, TV sets, liquor, drugs, food—anything they could carry.

In The Bronx, looters stole 50 new cars valued at $250,000 from the Ace Pontiac showroom. At an appliance store in Harlem, two boys about ten years old staggered out with a TV set while a woman strolled off with three radios. A number of looters were attacked in turn by other thieves, who wrenched away their booty. Said Frank Ross, a black police officer: "It's like a fever struck them. They were out there with trucks, vans, trailers, everything that could roll."

What the looters did not carry away, they often destroyed. In the South Bronx, burned-out delivery trucks blocked doorways. Twisted steel grilles lay across sidewalks. Several inches of ruined food, squashed hamburger, melted ice cream and broken bottles coated the floor of the new Fedco supermarket. The arsonists were as busy as the looters. The city had 1,037 fires that night, six times the normal number.

For a time, in some neighborhoods, firemen on cherry pickers fought blazes while looters went on about their business below, virtually unmolested. Then after the police moved in reinforcements, doubling the number of officers on duty to 8,000, they began large-scale roundups of suspected looters and gradually regained control of the streets. The final toll: estimated losses of $155 million for more than 2,000 storeowners, including many blacks and Hispanics; 3,772 people in jail on suspicion of looting and arson. There were four deaths—three in fires and one from a shot by a storekeeper.

Next morning, the Spanish-language newspaper *El Diario* headlined the question that was on most New Yorkers'

Looters with spoils in Bedford-Stuyvesant
"It's like a fever struck them."

minds: ¿POR QUÉ? (Why?). The heat and humidity were partly responsible; the 1965 blackout had taken place on a pleasantly cool evening in November. But most urban experts thought that the outbreak reflected twelve years of worsening conditions in the slums of U.S. cities.

As subsequent studies showed, most of the looting suspects (45% were unemployed and 64% had police records) were part of the growing American underclass, a subculture numbering at least 7 million people nationwide. They are predominantly uneducated and unskilled urban blacks and Hispanics, trapped at the bottom of society, where respect for law and authority has increasingly given way to a sense of hopeless anger. Vernon Jordan, of the Urban League, says that this group "in a crisis feels no compulsion to abide by the rules of the game because they find that the normal rules do not apply to them."

But most of the people in New York's ghettos did not loot or set fires, and many of them fully realized that the chief victims in the night of darkness were the poor themselves. Complained a black man in East Harlem: "They run these stores out, and they run out the few jobs in this neighborhood." As the sun rose on Harlem's littered streets, a young woman wearily walked along Third Avenue, looking for any food store that might be open and unlooted. "I'm trying to buy some bread," she said. "I can't find none."

Most storeowners could not afford to close permanently, whatever their fears of staying in the ghettos. Said Gary Apfel, owner of a clothing store in Harlem: "I have to pay off the creditors. I want to close, but I can't afford to close." Added South Bronx Clothier Harry Sperber: "If I close, the building will be empty, and it will be burned down or pulled apart." Thus, within a month, three-fourths of the damaged businesses were reopening, many helped by more than $3.7 million in loans from the Small Business Administration, $1 million in emergency aid from the city, and $2 million from private donations. Con Ed is retraining employees and installing new equipment, which company executives say will help prevent future blackouts. Still, the hidden damages—in terms of lowered morale, increased bitterness and hostility—were incalculable and not so easily repaired. ∎

A Spirit Roaming the Night

New York is terrorized by a killer called Son of Sam

Shortly before 1 a.m. on July 29, 1976, an attractive, brown-haired medical technician named Donna Lauria, 18, left a New York suburban discothèque with a girlfriend. They drove to The Bronx and then chatted for a while in the parked car. Suddenly the shadowy figure of a man loomed up beside the auto. Four shots rang out. Donna was killed instantly—the first victim of a murderer whose random and repeated attacks were to create a wave of fear throughout New York City.

What motivated the murderer, even what he looked like, was a yearlong mystery, but one chilling fact was clear from the start: he was out to kill young, pretty women, particularly women with shoulder-length brown hair. He hunted them down at night in various quiet neighborhoods. He killed four while they were sitting in parked cars with their dates. He killed one on the street. He also killed one young man who was with a female victim and wounded three other males and three females. He always used a .44-cal. revolver.

With every shooting the tension increased. Girls with long brown hair began wearing it up. Young women hurried home from their bus and subway stops, and some—if they had to go out in the evening—wore loose sweaters and caps, hoping they could pass as men.

On June 1 the case took a strange twist. Columnist Jimmy Breslin of the *Daily News* received a ghoulish message,

printed in compulsively neat capital letters, from someone who said he was the murderer. The writer said that he was like "a spirit roaming the night" and warned that he was "hungry" to strike again. The letter was signed "Son of Sam."

Who was Sam? As time went on, a series of peculiar happenings in Yonkers, N.Y., four miles up the Hudson River, led local police to think they knew: Sam Carr, the operator of a small telephone-answering service. Carr said that his dog, a black Labrador retriever named Harvey, had been wounded by a man who lived in a nearby apartment. Carr was getting anonymous hate mail that he guessed came from the same man. The suspect: David Berkowitz, 24, a mail clerk.

Yonkers police did not have enough evidence to arrest Berkowitz themselves, but on Aug. 8 they tipped off New York police—who were swamped with thousands of other leads to check out and did not follow up the tip. On July 31 Son of Sam struck for the last time. He murdered a blonde secretary, Stacy Moskowitz, 20, and partially blinded her escort. A woman later told of seeing a man "who walked strange, like a cat" in the vicinity of the shooting, and remembered seeing a cop ticketing a car that had been parked illegally one block from the murder site. Police found the car, a 1970 Galaxie, registered in the name of David Berkowitz.

Taken into custody, Berkowitz turned out to be a chubby young man with a be-

Sam Carr with his black Labrador
He had lived 6,000 years ago.

mused smile. He talked willingly and volubly about the forces that had impelled him to kill. He got his orders, he said, from "Sam," who had lived 6,000 years ago but had been reincarnated as Sam Carr. Berkowitz said that Sam's messages to kill were transmitted by his dog. Said Berkowitz: "Sam is the devil."

The accused man was born Richard David Falco, but his mother gave him up for adoption at birth, and he was raised in the family of Nathan Berkowitz, owner of a small hardware store in The Bronx. Berkowitz was close to his adoptive mother, but she died of cancer when he was 14. Girls were always a problem for him. Recalls a man who was with him in the Army: "Whenever the subject of women or sex came up, David backed off." Serving in Korea, he reportedly got involved with drugs, including LSD. He was discharged in 1974 and held odd jobs until hired by the post office at $256 a week.

Berkowitz pleaded not guilty and said he would claim insanity as a defense. Two court-appointed psychiatrists declared him too unstable to be tried, but Supreme Court Justice John R. Starkey, 71, ruled that he was capable of standing trial. Starkey released 372 pages of interrogation, in which Berkowitz told the psychiatrists: "I did the shooting. I killed the people. That's all." He described how he had been driven by his demons: "They wanted young blood . . . they were howling. I could hear them howling." Why did he single out young women to be his victims? It all seemed clear to David Berkowitz. "You know," he said, "they're clean. They're washed. Ready to be killed, you know." ■

Son of Sam suspect David Berkowitz being taken into custody
"They wanted young blood. I could hear them howling."

Hooray for HHH

An unquenchable spirit

Old friends and onetime adversaries packed the Senate chamber last Oct. 25 to pay tribute to one of their staunchest comrades. Eleven weeks after he learned that his cancer was inoperable, Senator Hubert Horatio Humphrey, frail but exuberant, returned to the Washington he has known and loved for 28 years. Said Senator Robert Byrd, who only last January beat out the former Vice President for the post of majority leader: "Nothing that life has dealt him has ever dimmed his optimism or quenched his unquenchable spirit."

Humphrey, the Democrats' quintessential New Dealer, preached the politics of hope throughout his 34-year career, and sponsored more major bills than any other legislator of his time. The Civil Rights Act, federal aid to education, the Peace Corps, Medicare—Humphrey had been father to them all. Those years also inflicted painful defeats on the Senator, and four times he failed in his campaigns for the presidency. Another blow came in 1973, when cancer of the bladder was suspected and the Senator underwent painful radiation treatments.

Freed from the ambition for higher office, Humphrey relished his position as his party's elder statesman and Washington's liberal conscience. He set a new goal for himself—to restore harmony in the Senate, to rebuild trust in government. Carter, the newcomer who foreclosed Humphrey's last chance for the White House, soon found Humphrey a valuable ally. In fact the President landed in Minnesota to pick up Humphrey for the tribute in Washington, and in a special inflight ceremony, Carter signed a bill naming the new Health, Education and Welfare headquarters the Hubert H. Humphrey Building. On Dec. 2 more than 2,000 friends and admirers toasted the Senator at a $1,000-a-plate Washington gala, launching a $20 million drive for a Hubert H. Humphrey Institute of Public Affairs at the University of Minnesota.

While working on the Hill, Humphrey continued to undergo chemotherapy. But he suggested that Washington offered an even better remedy: "The therapy of the excitement of being back on my job —there's no substitute for it," he said. ∎

Time to Retire?

No, say many over 65

There was a time when the old were held in reverence, and people retired from their life's work mainly as a result of illness or death. The Age of Reason, with its notions of reordering society scientifically, led to the first mandatory retirement laws. By 1889 when German

Chancellor Otto von Bismarck introduced the world's first social security system, he more or less arbitrarily chose 65 as the time at which German workers could get a state pension. The average life expectancy then was about 37 years. It has increased ever since, to nearly 72, but Bismarck's retirement deadline stuck.

Unfortunately, mandatory retirement often means mandatory poverty. Of the nation's 23 million elderly people nearly 4 million survive on $50 per week or less. Last fall, the increasingly discontented old finally rose in revolt. They were led, appropriately, by Democratic Congressman Claude Pepper of Florida, now 77. Pepper served in the U.S. Senate for 14 years until being forcibly retired by Florida voters in 1950, then started a second career in 1962 by getting himself elected to the House of Representatives. Says he: "Mandatory retirement is an extravagant waste of people."

Gray Panther Leader Maggie Kuhn testifies
The discontented old finally rose in revolt.

Last October, Pepper's bill to extend the age of mandatory retirement from 65 to 70 for private industry and remove it altogether for federal employees passed the House by a stunning 359-to-4 vote. A month later, the Senate also approved it, but with some modifications that required a conference committee.

The old now have growing organizations like Maggie Kuhn's Gray Panthers and the National Council on the Aging to lobby for their needs, but experts are not quite sure what the effects of the new law will be. General Motors, for instance, points out that only 2% of its blue-collar hourly workers bother waiting until age 68, the official GM time for them to retire. The Senate Committee on Human Resources estimates that only about 200,-000 people a year will choose to work beyond 65. But a recent Louis Harris poll found that a full third of Americans now between 65 and 69 would go on working at least part time if they had the chance.

That is about 2.8 million people—or roughly enough to raise the national unemployment rate from 7% to nearly 10% —if every one kept a younger worker from entering the labor force. ∎

Badge of Honor

Is it a patriotic duty to lie?

There was no doubt that the former director of the Central Intelligence Agency had quite deliberately committed a crime. On Feb. 7 and March 6, 1973, while being questioned by the Senate Foreign Relations Committee on his new appointment to be U.S. Ambassador to Iran, ex–CIA Chief Richard Helms was asked whether his agency had secretly financed groups opposed to Chile's late Marxist President Salvador Allende Gossens. Knowing full well that the CIA had done exactly that, Helms said, "No, sir."

After the CIA's covert activities—and Helms' lie—became public in 1975, the Ford Administration left it to its successors to decide the ticklish question of whether to prosecute a 31-year public servant for doing what he conceived to be his patriotic duty. Helms made the issue even more ticklish by hinting that if he had to defend himself in court, he would find it necessary to summon some high officials and disclose some high secrets. After months of plea bargaining, Attorney General Griffin Bell worked out a compromise: Helms, who could have faced up to ten years in prison, would plead *nolo contendere* (no contest; but in fact, an admission of guilt) to two misdemeanors. That brought him a suspended two-year sentence and a fine of $2,000. But in agreeing to that mild punishment, U.S. District Judge Barrington D. Parker gave Helms a harsh scolding: "You now stand before this court in disgrace and shame . . . There are those employed in the intelligence-security community who feel that they have a license to operate freely outside the dictates of the law . . . No one, whatever his position, is above the law."

Senate liberals were quick to denounce the bargain. Said Democratic Senator Frank Church, chairman of a Senate committee that had probed CIA activities in Chile: "I thought there was to be an end to the double standard of justice for the big shots. Apparently Helms was just too hot to handle." On the other hand, Helms was perfectly candid about the dilemma he had faced. Said he: "I had sworn my oath to preserve certain secrets . . . I didn't want to lie . . . I was simply trying to find my way through a very difficult situation." Others were more emphatic in support. His attorney, Edward Bennett Williams, declared that Helms would "wear this conviction like a badge of honor." The ex–CIA chief himself said: "If I had done anything else, it would have been a disgrace." As for the $2,000 fine, Helms' friends had a lunch and raised the money before the coffee was served. ∎

Abortion Battle

Who should pay for the poor?

In 1973, the U.S. Supreme Court established the principle that a woman has the right to an abortion during the first six months of pregnancy. This had the effect of expanding the use of Medicaid funds for those who wanted abortions but could not afford them. By 1976 Medicaid was providing funds for nearly one-third of the estimated 1.1 million abortions performed annually in the U.S.

Then the tide changed. As the result of pressure from "right-to-life" forces, Congress voted in 1976 to eliminate federal Medicaid funds for abortions except when women's lives were in danger. Several states took similar measures, and the Supreme Court ruled last June that states were not obliged to provide Medicaid funds for "nontherapeutic" abortions.

The majority opinion, written by Justice Lewis F. Powell, did not restrict the practice of elective abortions but held that neither the Constitution nor the law requires the states to provide for them. The question of public funding of abortions, it contended, should be resolved by legislators, not by judges. In an angry dissent, Justice Thurgood Marshall charged that the decision would "brutally coerce poor women to bear children."

In November, the National Women's Conference in Houston took a strong stand for public funding of abortion, but many Congressmen opposed such a step (as did President Carter). In December, after a five-month deadlock in Congress, the House and Senate voted to prohibit Medicaid payments except in cases in which 1) a woman's life was in danger, 2) there was a risk of "severe and long-lasting" damage to her health, or 3) the pregnancy was the result of rape or incest.

The right-to-life movement hailed the compromise as a victory and vowed to fight this year for a law that bans Medicaid abortions without exception. ∎

Ray's Escape

Reviving talk of conspiracy

Brushy Mountain state prison in eastern Tennessee seems virtually immune to any attempt at escape. Its brown stone walls are 14 ft. to 18 ft. high, topped by electrified barbed wire. Eight watchtowers overlook the main yard, and the Cumberland Mountains beyond the walls are alive with rattlesnakes and copperheads.

At 7:30 p.m. on June 10, the impossible occurred. A gang of convicts started a brawl, which diverted the guards' attention. Seven other prisoners quietly edged over to the northern corner, uncovered a hidden ladder and began scrambling over the wall. When the guards opened fire, they hit only the last of the fugitives. Already gone was James Earl Ray, 49, serving a life term for the 1968 assassination of Martin Luther King Jr.

The ease with which Ray escaped immediately provoked speculation that he had received outside help—and that his helpers might even have been involved in a conspiracy to kill King (Ray has claimed at different times that he had help and that he acted alone). The Rev. Ralph David Abernathy, who succeeded King as head of the Southern Christian Leadership Conference, hinted that Ray could implicate "a lot of people in very high places in this country." Said Louis Stokes, chairman of the House Select Committee on Assassinations: "My real concern is whether Ray was lured into this escape and, if so, whether for the purpose of killing him to stop him from talking."

Some 150 state and local police—all

Ray at time of recapture
Sandy and Little Red led the way.

under strict orders to capture Ray alive —combed the Tennessee forests. Five helicopters whirred overhead. President Carter sent in 60 FBI agents equipped with elaborate infrared tracking devices. After two days of hunting, the supervisor of the Brushy Mountain prison kennels, Sammy Joe Chapman, finally picked up the trail, and two of his bloodhounds, Sandy and Little Red, started their triumphant hallooing. As the leashed hounds dragged him forward, Chapman could hear Ray crashing through the darkened forest. Then a sudden silence fell. The dogs led Chapman to a mound where Ray had tried desperately to bury himself under some dead leaves. They stood wagging their tails.

"Are you all right?" asked Chapman.

"I'm all right," said Ray.

By the following day, all seven fugitives were back in prison. And for the time being at least, the specter of a conspiracy was put to rest. ∎

Kennedy Probe

House committee finds little

Despite a series of investigations, deep suspicions and public doubts persist about who was really responsible for the killing of John F. Kennedy and Martin Luther King Jr. Late in 1976 a Gallup poll showed that some 70% of the American people believe both assassinations were conspiracies. So when the House of Representatives established the Select Committee on Assassinations last September to make a fresh study of the killings, there was hope that the issue might be resolved.

The committee named as counsel Richard A. Sprague, a tough former assistant district attorney from Philadelphia who had won 70 convictions in 71 murder cases. The investigator said all the right things—"I'm under just as much obligation to disprove as to prove" and "I'm willing to go to wherever the investigations lead me"—but his ambitious plans soon aroused congressional suspicions. While there had been talk in the House about a $1 million annual budget for the committee, Sprague proposed $6.5 million —for just the first year of the committee's mandated two-year life. The huge sum was to go for a staff of 170, the lease and purchase of polygraphs and the installation of a computerized cross-reference system for thousands of documents.

In April, the committee thought it had hit pay dirt when a Dutch journalist, Willem Oltmans, turned up with a new conspiracy story. Oltmans said he had been friendly with a Russian-born oil geologist (and former mental patient) named George de Mohrenschildt, who claimed he was part of an anti-Kennedy plot headed by the late Texas oil tycoon H.L. Hunt. Oltmans asserted that De Mohrenschildt said that not only Lee Harvey Oswald but several anti-Castro Cubans were assigned to shoot the President. What gave spice to this tale was that when a committee investigator asked to interview De Mohrenschildt, the mystery witness killed himself with a shotgun. That left the House probers with another unprovable tale.

By this time, the committee was at war with itself. The chairman, Texas Democrat Henry B. Gonzalez, tried to fire Sprague for being power-hungry and insubordinate, but when the rest of the committee opposed him he resigned. Three weeks later, Sprague resigned, too. That persuaded the full House to approve a continuation of the investigation on a reduced annual budget of $2.8 million.

Under its new chairman, Democrat Louis Stokes of Cleveland, and chief counsel, Cornell Law Professor G. Robert Blakey, the controversy surrounding the committee quieted. With a gag rule now in force, whatever is turned up in the investigation will not be publicly aired until the end of this year. ∎

On the Warpath

Indians claim much of Maine

Who owns the U.S.? The Federal Government, to be sure, is the largest titleholder. Then there are state and local properties, and millions of individuals and private businesses account for the rest of the country. Well, not quite. At the moment, more than half of the 266 federally recognized Indian tribes are seeking court settlements of disputes over land ownership and tribal rights.

Most of the largest land claims have come in the East. The Indians' legal argument centers on the Nonintercourse Act of 1790, which required congressional approval for any local acquisition of Indian land. Since many such deals between the Indians and the European settlers in the original 13 states never got federally sanctioned, the Indians maintain that the 180-year-old law still applies. And so in five states—Massachusetts, Rhode Island, Connecticut, New York and South Carolina—tribes have claimed nearly half a million acres.

The largest single case is in Maine, where the Passamaquoddy and Penobscot tribes claim 5 million to 10 million acres, up to nearly half the state. At first, the state government and local landowners guffawed at the claim, but when the Indians' lawyers compelled the U.S. Justice Department to support the Indians' treaty rights, local bond issues were delayed and real estate business was disrupted. On July 15, President Carter's special representative on Indian land claims, Georgia Judge William B. Gunter, recommended that the tribes be given $25 million and 100,000 acres of state-owned land. While the tribes have indicated that they would not press their claim to residential land, they found the recommendations inadequate and threatened to take the case back to federal court. Maine officials refused to give up any land—private or public—and are preparing their case for court.

While the Eastern cases are basically claims to land ownership, Western tribes have been pushing for legal remedies in disputes over mineral and water rights and states' fishing and hunting regulations. Further, many tribes are demanding either to be immune from state taxes and liquor laws or to be allowed to institute their own. Seven tribes in Oklahoma, for instance, are asserting a claim to a portion of the bed of the Arkansas River, while in Washington various tribes are embroiled in a legal tiff with the state government, commercial fisheries and sports anglers over Indian fishing rights in, as one early treaty put it, their "usual and accustomed places." Throughout the country, the Indians' claims are presenting a difficult problem of how to balance legally justifiable rights with the weight of history. ∎

Golden mask of Tutankhamen

King Tut Strut

Wonderful things on view

After years of negotiation, 55 of the splendid furnishings from the richest royal tomb ever uncovered—the four burial rooms of King Tutankhamen—began a six-city, two-year tour of the U.S. "Wonderful things," British Archaeologist Howard Carter whispered in 1922, when the dim light of his candle first flickered into the dark tomb. The place, he said, was filled with "strange animals, statues, and gold—everywhere the glint of gold."

The Tutankhamen show presents these objects, more or less in the order in which Carter found them, so that visitors get to share something of the discoverer's original excitement. Tutankhamen was about 18 years old when he died in 1325 B.C., perhaps by assassination, but he was sent into the land of the dead with alabaster cups for his wine, bejeweled amulets to ward off evil spirits, unguent jars shaped like lions with lolling tongues, even an ivory-inlaid wooden seat to make him feel regally at home.

The boy king's artisans wrought skillfully in silver, alabaster, obsidian, lapis lazuli, wood, glass and gems, handling each material as easily as if it had been clay. But their most glorious work was done in solid gold. The exhibit's most famous object is the full-size golden mask that once covered Tutankhamen's mummified head. Though every bit as haughty as might be expected of an art aimed at celebrating pharaonic majesty, the mask's burnished, artfully molded surfaces give off a resplendent inner life that all but defies mortality.

The show, currently in New Orleans and scheduled to reach Los Angeles by February 1978, has set off a kind of Tutmania. Hundreds of thousands of people have stood in line, many of them as long as five hours, to be happily awed by the long-dead king's gilded hoard, then snap up postcards, calendars, color slides and replicas of Egyptian jewelry. Especially in Chicago, the Pop Tut Cult spread to include pyramid hair styles, Cleopatra eye makeup, scarab rings and mummy bead necklaces. And the latest disco dance is a provocative shuffle called the King Tut Strut. ∎

Hail, Lousewort!

A rare plant v. the engineers

In a few woody acres along the St. John River in Aroostook County, Maine, grows a slender, 18-inch-high yellow-green-blossomed plant known as the Furbish lousewort. Named after Kate Furbish, a 19th century spinster and tireless field botanist, this lousewort looks a lot like a snapdragon. It toils not, neither does it spin. Yet it has helped block construction of the $690 million Dickey-Lincoln hydroelectric project on the St. John.

Ironically, the Furbish lousewort was thought to be already extinct when naturalists working for the dam project stumbled upon it in 1976 in the area that the dam was expected to flood. Since the Endangered Species Act of 1973 requires that all federally financed constructions refrain from "jeopardizing" any officially endangered species, plans for the dam were threatened until the fate of the lousewort could be legally resolved.

The lonely lousewort was not alone in its ability to frustrate the nation's builders. Consider, for example, the 3-in. perch known as the snail darter, which lives in a 17-mile-long stretch of the Little Tennessee River. The TVA had nearly finished the $116 million Tellico Dam on the Tennessee—to create an industrial-development project with 4,000 new jobs—when the snail darter's obscure presence was discovered. In response to a suit by environmentalists, a federal court order has blocked the dam's completion ever since January. Consider, too, the inch-long primeval pupfish, one species of which lives only in the Devil's Hole in Nevada. Since 1976, the pupfish has been protected by a Supreme Court ruling that blocked use of the water in the Devil's Hole for irrigation, because it would drop the water level—and cut the pupfish off from its only supply of life-giving algae.

Builders and bureaucrats also have their ways of struggling for survival, however. Last August, Congress passed a bill appropriating $9 million for efforts to remove endangered species from the path of federal projects. TVA biologists thereupon netted 117 snail darters, released them upstream from the dam and waited with fingers crossed. In Maine, meanwhile, at a cost of $17,000, the Army Engineers scoured 300 sq. mi. along the St. John River. They announced in August that they had found five other clumps of Furbish lousewort well beyond the site of the proposed dam. ∎

The Moral Equivalent of War

Carter attacks the worsening energy crisis and ends in a donnybrook

Georgian Jimmy Carter is a son of the Sunbelt, but he wasted no time in confronting the long-term challenge of the nation's looming energy shortages. The Big Freeze in the winter of '77 helped, for as Carter took office, much of the U.S. was shivering through its coldest January in 177 years. The cold sent more than a million workers and as many students home from factories and schools, mostly because of a lack of natural gas for heating. Symbolizing his concern about energy, the new President reviewed his Inaugural parade from a stand warmed by solar heat.

More substantive action came quickly. The first bill Carter proposed—and the first one he signed into law—was an act giving him the power to order natural-gas companies in such fuel-rich states as Texas, Louisiana and Oklahoma to share their supplies with other regions where gas was running out. In return, the producers could charge the unregulated higher prices normally permitted only on gas that does not cross state lines.

"We must face the fact that the energy shortage is permanent," Carter warned in his first fireside chat, delivered as he kept comfortably warm in a cardigan sweater. How Carter handles the energy problem, Presidential Aide Hamilton Jordan predicted, would pose "a greater test of his leadership than any other single issue." The President later fully agreed, declaring: "I expect the first year of my presidency to be judged more on energy than on any other domestic issue. None is more important."

The dimension of the problem could be clearly seen in a few key statistics. The U.S., which already consumes one-third of the world's energy, wastes roughly 30% of that supply and yet keeps increasing its demand by 6% per year. In 1973, when President Nixon proclaimed "Operation Independence" to free the U.S. from its reliance on foreign oil, the nation imported 36% of its supply. Since then, far from becoming independent, the U.S. has increased its imports (and its vulnerability to boycotts and price-gouging) to 49%.

Carter tackled the long-range problem head-on, and at first he seemed to enjoy considerable success. He called for creation of a Department of Energy—the first new Cabinet addition since 1966. Congress quickly complied. Dubbed DOE, the new department consolidated the work of three independent agencies (the Federal Power Commission, the Federal Energy Administration and the Energy Research and Development Administration) as well as various energy functions

previously spread through nine of the other eleven Cabinet jurisdictions. The department was launched with a formidable 19,000 employees and a first-year budget of $10.5 billion. To head it, Carter selected his key energy adviser, James Schlesinger, the assertive ex-professor of economics who had previously directed the Atomic Energy Commission, CIA and Defense Department in Republican Administrations. Choosing Schlesinger, Carter said, was "the most important nomination" he would make as President.

Schlesinger addressing oilmen in Houston
He now has a budget of $10 billion.

Even before he became a Cabinet member, Schlesinger's assignment from the deadline-conscious President was to draw up a comprehensive national plan by which existing supplies of oil and natural gas could be stretched to last at least until the end of the century. Long before then, solar energy will be economically competitive for providing heat and electricity. On April 20, Schlesinger and an overworked staff produced a plan aimed at curtailing waste and soaring consumption, encouraging increased oil production, setting out new price policies and unwinding some of the Government's regulatory red tape.

With his popularity then running high in polls, Carter threw his full prestige into the energy fight. He had helped shape the plan, sitting in on some of 21 White House energy conferences with oilmen, builders,

union leaders and economists. Then he personally launched it in April with a triple TV blitz: a solemn prime-time address outlining the scope of the problem; a statistic-studded list of recommendations to a joint session of Congress; a press conference defending his program against the largely uncritical questions of reporters.

To Carter, the energy crisis was imminent, and he described it in apocalyptic terms. If the nation failed to wage what he grandly called "the moral equivalent of war" against the steadily rising U.S. dependence on foreign oil, Carter warned, "the alternative may be a national catastrophe." The country would "constantly live in fear of embargoes" imposed by oil-exporting nations, and "we could endanger our freedom as a sovereign nation to act in world affairs." To wait too long, he said, would create irresistible pressures to "plunder the environment" in an orgy of strip-mining for coal, drilling for offshore oil and building of nuclear power plants.

Later events were to prove Carter correct on two points: 1) that the rising oil imports were a serious obstacle to achieving a favorable trade balance (by year's end oil imports had cost the U.S. $45 billion and contributed to an alarming $28 billion deficit in the balance of trade); 2) that his own popularity would fall at least 10% as many citizens and special interests objected to parts of the energy plan (although the energy bill was far from the sole reason, his poll ratings slipped by 9% from the week following the energy speeches to mid-November).

The Administration's energy plan set three goals to be reached by 1985: 1) cut the annual growth in total U.S. energy demand from its present 6% to 2%; 2) slash the daily consumption of gasoline, now at 7.2 million bbl., by 10%; 3) reduce the average daily imports of oil, which were running at about 8.2 million bbl. in 1977, to 6 million bbl. To reach those goals, the plan included these major proposals:

Crude Oil. A wellhead tax would be levied against existing production of domestic oil to bring the price up to the level of imported oil (the boost would be roughly from $8.25 per bbl. to $13.50). Intended to encourage conservation by raising prices, this tax would eventually be rebated to consumers through income tax credits to avoid depressing the economy. But producers would have an incentive to find new oil because they could charge the world price and the wellhead tax would not apply to such new discoveries.

Natural Gas. The regulated price of "new"

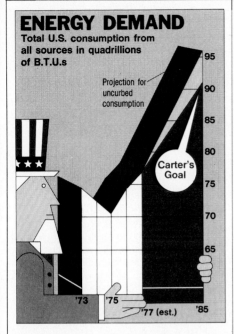

ENERGY DEMAND

Total U.S. consumption from all sources in quadrillions of B.T.U.s

Projection for uncurbed consumption

Carter's Goal

95 90 85 80 75 70 65

'73 '75 '77 (est.) '85

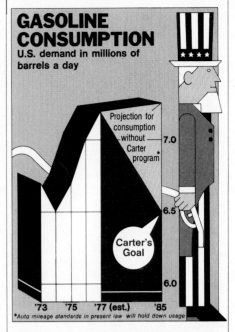

GASOLINE CONSUMPTION

U.S. demand in millions of barrels a day

Projection for consumption without Carter program*

Carter's Goal

7.0 6.5 6.0

'73 '75 '77 (est.) '85

*Auto mileage standards in present law will hold down usage

---

gas sold across state lines would be allowed to rise from $1.45 per 1,000 cu. ft. to $1.75 (each dime increase costs consumers some $2 billion a year). New gas sold within the producing state would command the same price—a drop of more than 25¢ from its current unregulated cost. The aim was to prevent regional hoarding. "Old" gas from existing wells would not get interstate price hikes.

Coal. Mass conversion to coal, without much relaxation in clean air standards, would be encouraged by a 10% tax credit on the machinery needed by factories to make the switch from oil and natural gas —and those which failed to do so would be penalized by a tax rising from 90¢ per bbl. of oil to $3 by 1985. Users of natural gas would be taxed at a similar rate. The tax would go into a fund to aid this conversion to coal.

Gasoline. In each year in which total gasoline consumption exceeded specified national goals, a tax of 5¢ per gal., up to a maximum of 50¢ by 1989, would be levied. A combination of heavy taxes on new

gas-guzzling cars and price rebates on gas-sippers would encourage the purchase of more fuel-efficient automobiles.

The initial response to Carter's call to arms was mixed. While polls showed that most Americans considered the energy situation serious, few viewed it as the potential catastrophe Carter had described. Oil and gas executives, knowing they could be exploited politically as villains, generally applauded Carter for addressing the long-neglected problem but fumed at his emphasis on conservation instead of all-out development. Some also felt that Carter put too much emphasis on tax incentives, too little on the free market. Other critics pointed to some glaring omissions, like the absence of any improvement of mass transport to make up for the curbs on auto traffic.

Probably even to Carter's surprise, his package moved smoothly through the House. The shrewd Speaker, Democrat Tip O'Neill, saw the danger of piece-by-piece legislation that could be sliced up by each of the many groups opposed to one or more of the plan's many parts. Aided by Carter's careful cajoling of key Congressmen, O'Neill created an *ad hoc* committee to coordinate all action on the package—and watched it pass the House virtually intact. The chamber killed only the President's 50¢ gasoline tax (which looked like an Administration bargaining chip anyway) and the rebate on small cars (it kept the tax on big ones).

With that relatively easy victory, Carter relaxed his attention. But he had no such loyal ally in the Senate, where Majority Leader Robert Byrd routinely sent the legislation item by item to the normal committees. There strong chairmen, most notably the Finance Committee's Russell Long, hacked the package into bits. With no one keeping watch on the broad perspective, various lobbies effectively asserted their influence.

Natural-gas producers, not satisfied with Carter's price increases, pushed for total deregulation of prices—and they wanted the higher profits applied to old as well as new gas. After a bitter fight and a liberal-led filibuster, deregulation

passed the Senate. Oil companies asked that the proposed wellhead tax on old oil be dropped—but the increased price maintained—arguing that they needed more incentive to finance exploration. The two houses differed on that, but the Senate approved a generous program of tax credits to promote conservation. Companies that might have to switch to coal contended that environmental safeguards must be lifted. The Senate exempted a broad range of plants from the requirement to burn coal. Car manufacturers fought the guzzler tax—and got it killed.

Carter's package emerged from the Senate in mid-October in a series of shredded remnants. The angry President then went on television and lashed out at the oil companies in one of the most emotional moments of his first year. He accused the oil companies of "potential war profiteering" in the energy fight and seeking "the biggest rip-off in history." His program involved "immense amounts of money," he said, and yet the oil executives "want it all."

An unwieldy 53-member Senate and

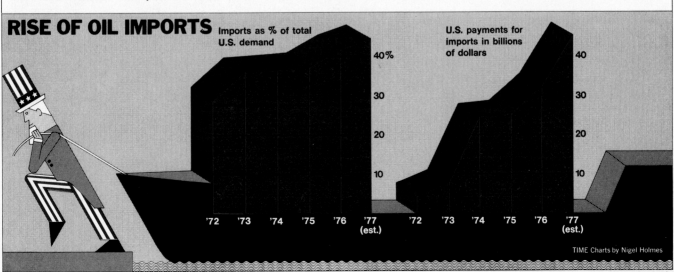

RISE OF OIL IMPORTS

Imports as % of total U.S. demand

40% 30 20 10

'72 '73 '74 '75 '76 '77 (est.)

U.S. payments for imports in billions of dollars

40 30 20 10

'72 '73 '74 '75 '76 '77 (est.)

TIME Charts by Nigel Holmes

House conference committee quickly became locked in weeks of indecisive wrangling over ways to resolve the vast differences between the two chambers. Carter cancelled a scheduled nine-nation trip and remained in Washington to try to save his embattled plan. In another prime-time TV pitch, he took a more conciliatory approach toward opponents of his proposals—but it was so low-key and soft-sell as to have little effect.

As the conferees struggled to reach agreement on the plan's many provisions, some progress was made. They approved a program of loans and grants to encourage homeowners and industry to improve the insulation of buildings, mandatory conversion of certain factories and utilities to the use of coal and a reform of electricity rates designed to reduce usage during peak hours of consumption. But just a few days before Christmas, Senators on the committee overwhelmingly rejected a proposed compromise on natural gas under which prices would remain regulated but would be allowed to rise more sharply than Carter had proposed. New Hampshire Democrat John Durkin denounced it as "the moral equivalent of mugging the consumer on Christmas eve," while other Senators just as angrily protested its failure to lift all controls over gas prices.

With that, the conference committee ended its deliberations for the year without even taking up Carter's key tax on crude oil—and without giving him an energy bill to sign. They agreed only to try again when Congress reconvenes. The President called the committee's inability to find a compromise "regrettable" and warned that until some decisive action is taken by the Congress the nation's energy problems "will simply continue to get worse."   — *Ed Magnuson*

The Search for Fuel

The obstacles keep getting harder

How to find more oil and gas, how to get this fuel out of the earth, how to transport it to the facilities that will refine it and to the people who will use it—these are questions that are taking on life-or-death importance to the energy-hungry U.S. economy.

The year 1977 provided some important answers as American oil and gas prospectors intensified their efforts to find new supplies. Indeed, the search led to a drilling boom—a record of more than 42,000 wells were sunk last year—and even to a shortage of drilling equipment. For the moment, in fact, there is a surplus rather than a scarcity of oil, but the long-range search demonstrated several serious problems as the fuel hunters found themselves forced to work in the depths of turbulent oceans, the deadly cold of the Arctic and the numbing mazes of the law.

Ever since oil was discovered under Alaska's frozen North Slope in 1968, U.S. technicians have been devising plans to pump it out, for the vast field is capable of producing 2 million bbl. of oil and 3.4 billion cu. ft. of natural gas a day for the next 20 years—an increase in U.S. output of 23.7% for oil and 6.2% for gas. But the problem of how to ship the oil represented a major obstacle. For three years a consortium of eight U.S. oil companies has been working to construct an 800-mile-long pipeline from the North Slope's Prudhoe Bay to the all-weather port of Valdez, 120 miles east of Anchorage. In doing so, the oilmen have had to battle not only the Alaskan cold but the opposition of organized environmentalists, who charged in various legal actions that the pipeline would destroy Alaska's fragile tundra, place an insuperable obstacle in the path of caribou migrations, and hold the entire Alaskan ecosystem hostage to the risk of an oil spill.

To overcome these objections, the oilmen built refrigerating units into the pilings supporting the pipes so that the oil-warmed conduits would not melt Alaska's delicate permafrost. They also constructed earthen overpasses in some places and actually raised the pipe itself in others so that migrating caribou could follow their traditional routes.

The long-delayed opening of the $9 billion pipeline last June was auspicious. As a first step, some 6 million cu. ft. of nitrogen was blown through the pipe to purge air from the system and reduce the risk of an oil-vapor explosion. Then a cylindrical plastic plug, known to oilmen as a pig, was inserted into the 48-in.-diameter pipe. Finally, after an all-clear signal from Valdez, workmen opened the valves at Prudhoe and started the oil on its way. Helped along by pumps, the oil pushed the pig through the pipe, clearing out any refuse and tools left behind by the workmen.

The trip, which took five weeks, was a tense one. The pipeline passes over or under 800 streams and rivers, including the mighty Yukon, cuts through muskeg swamps and dense forests, crests passes at 4,800 ft. in the Brooks Range and 3,000

Alaskan pipeline, here cutting through mountains 75 miles north of Valdez, can carry 1.2 million bbl. of oil a day

ALYESKA

Offshore drilling like this spidery operation off Louisiana is beginning to tap vast riches in Gulf of Mexico

ft. in the Alaska Range. It is dotted with eight pumping stations—one of which was disabled shortly after start-up by an explosion caused by an open valve, which permitted the highly volatile crude oil to gush through a turbine.

Despite the length of its journey, the oil arrived only slightly behind schedule, filling storage tanks at Valdez until it could be loaded on tankers for shipment. Where it will be shipped, however, is still being argued about. Californians have opposed the idea of unloading the tankers at a Los Angeles oil terminal because they fear further pollution of the area's already unacceptable air. But in December the impasse neared an end when Standard Oil Co. of Ohio indicated a willingness to spend $20 to $30 million on antipollution equipment at an oil-burning power plant in the area as a trade-off for the pollution created by its tankers.

Sohio hopes to move the Alaskan crude on to refiners in the Gulf states by converting and linking more than 1,000 miles of existing natural gas pipelines. About 250 miles of new pipeline must be built, and the project will take two years and $500 million to complete. Two competing plans for piping Alaskan oil to the Midwest from a tanker terminal in Washington State have also been proposed. One is the Kitimat project, which would run through Canada at a construction cost of $500 million, and the other is the "northern tier" project through the U.S.—a larger pipeline at a larger cost: $1.2 billion. Either could be ready by 1982, but will certainly face strong challenges from environmentalists.

By March, the Alaska pipeline will have reached a capacity of up to 1.2 million bbl. of oil a day, with an eventual total of 2 million bbl. a day—cutting U.S. dependence on foreign oil by 14% and reducing the nation's bill for imported crude by a significant $6 billion in 1978. Another pipeline could move the country even closer to the energy independence it seeks. The U.S. and Canada agreed in September to build a trans-Canadian pipeline that would carry 2.4 billion cu. ft. of natural gas per day from the North Slope to the Lower 48.

Competition for the right to build the gas pipeline began in the late 1960s, when leading Canadian and U.S. firms, among them Pacific Gas & Electric and Texas Eastern Corp., banded together into what seemed like an unbeatable consortium called the Arctic Gas Pipeline Project. This group, which at one time included no fewer than 27 companies, proposed to construct a 48-in. line that would begin at Prudhoe Bay, follow the northern coastline to Canada's Mackenzie Delta gas deposits, and then head south to the U.S. But, encountering strong opposition—first from environmentalists, who feared it would endanger Canadian and Alaskan wildlife, and then from the Canadian government, which backed the environmentalists—the consortium quit.

But a small Salt Lake City firm called Northwest Energy Co. did not. Under its chairman, a peppery Texas oilman named John McMillian, Northwest joined forces with two Canadian firms to form a consortium called Alcan, then came up with a plan that proved acceptable by following the already developed routes of the Alaskan oil pipeline and the Alcan Highway. The new line, which could be ready by 1983 if everything goes according to plan, will run from Prudhoe Bay south to Fairbanks, then swing southeast across Canada's Yukon Territory and

south through British Columbia and Alberta near Calgary. There the line will split; one branch will run south to a terminus near San Francisco, the other will run east to Dwight, Ill., near Chicago. The construction cost alone could reach $14 billion, and the eventual cost of the gas to consumers is expected to be about twice the present regulated rate.

The newest and most difficult fields for U.S. oil hunters lie in the waters off the nation's coasts. Already, off California, Louisiana and Texas, work crews put in long hours on platforms that rise spiderlike from the sea, sinking wells that not only plumb several hundred feet of water but often probe several thousand feet below the sea bottom in search of natural gas and oil.

The plan to extend this vast exploration along the Atlantic continental shelf was abruptly halted last January, when a federal district court in New York voided the leases that the U.S. Department of the Interior had sold to a number of oil companies back in 1976. The court ruled that the department had failed to comply with requirements protecting the coast against oil spills and other environmental dangers. The ruling infuriated oilmen, who had paid $1.1 billion for five-year rights to explore and produce oil and gas and who hoped to start exploring by midsummer. Their anger—and their appeals—proved effective. In September a federal appeals court threw out the lower-court decision, declaring that the lease sales did not violate any environmental law and holding that the district court judge had exceeded his authority. That decision, however, is being appealed to the U.S. Supreme Court by New York's Suffolk County.

The oilmen, who grumbled that they had lost at least $44 million in interest payments on their lease purchases, now predicted that they would be able to begin test drilling in the Atlantic early in 1978. Many also expected that the appeals court decision would encourage oil companies to bid on additional leases scheduled for sale by the spring of 1978.

There are a lot of such agreements to go around. The leases sold so far lie in two tracts 50 to 90 miles at sea almost due east of Atlantic City, N.J., in an area called the Baltimore Canyon. Those remaining to be sold are on Georges Bank, a shallow section of the sea off Nantucket Island, which is also one of the world's richest fishing grounds; the Southeast Georgia Embayment, a region near the Georgia-Florida line; and three areas in the Gulf of Mexico. All are potentially rich not only in oil but in natural gas, which is found in the same types of geological formations. Experts estimate that the Baltimore Canyon may contain reserves amounting to some 1.4 billion bbl. of oil and 9.4 trillion cu. ft. of gas. The two other sections should be at least as productive.

But getting to this fuel will not be easy. Though the continental shelf includes the shallowest sections of the ocean, the oil-bearing strata in the Baltimore Canyon lie anywhere from 8,000 to 13,000 ft. below the ocean bottom. Drilling to these depths will be costly; so will the suits that are sure to be brought by environmentalists opposed to any undersea oil exploration.

Despite these drawbacks, exploration is expected to go forward. The Carter Administration has come out in favor of offshore oil and gas operations that meet environmental standards. Congress has also taken steps to provide for more orderly offshore development. It is considering setting up a $200 million fund to compensate property owners who suffer from oil spills and offshore accidents. But the bill has been stalled in the House Rules Committee by intense oil industry lobbying. Among the reasons oilmen oppose the bill are provisions for test drilling by the Government, a greater role for state governments, and more competitive bidding for leases.

A Harris survey has indicated that a majority of the American public favors offshore operations. The country nonetheless needs to find safer ways to pump and move this oil, for, as events in 1977 showed, drilling can be dangerous and transportation uncertain. One dramatic demonstration occurred last May, when a well on a Phillips Petroleum Co. platform in the North Sea oilfield southwest of Norway let go with a roar and shot a column of mud, oil and highly flammable natural gas nearly 200 feet into the air. The blowout was not a bad one as such accidents go, but it was costly. Before a team of American oilfield troubleshooters, led by the legendary Paul ("Red") Adair, managed to cap the well, more than 20,000 tons of oil had spilled into the sea, threatening the fragile spawning grounds of herring, mackerel and other species that provide rich catches for fishermen in the area. Another dramatic example of the uncertainties of international oil shipping occurred in December, when two huge tankers operated by Gulf Oil collided off the coast of South Africa, killing two crew members and causing an ocean slick that covered 12 sq. mi.

Closer to home, Americans have had a number of demonstrations of the dangers of oil spills. The year had barely begun when the Liberian-flag tanker *Argo Merchant,* which had run aground off Nantucket shortly after Christmas, broke in half, spilling its cargo of 7.6 million gal. of oil into the sea. Shortly afterward, another Liberian ship, the tanker *Sansinena,* exploded in her berth at Los Angeles harbor, killing nine crew members. While she was still smoldering, a third Liberian tanker, the *Olympic Games,* ran aground in the Delaware River below Philadelphia, puncturing her hull and spilling 135,000 gal. of thick crude oil into fertile tidal marshes.

The three accidents, and several minor ones that followed, raised the fear that the U.S. might have to pay for its petroleum imports by the gradual ruin of its waterways. Demands for reform have had mixed results. Though American-flag tankers must meet strict safety standards, most oil companies prefer to carry their cargo in foreign-flag ships. These vessels, registered in nations such as Liberia and Panama, avoid U.S. and European taxes, wage scales and expensive safety regulations for crews and equipment. The U.S. Coast Guard has moved to prevent spills by imposing tough new regulations for foreign vessels entering U.S. waters, but comprehensive worldwide compliance is doubtful.

The dangers of tanker spills are not likely to diminish. The *Argo Merchant,* a relatively old ship, measured 640 ft. in length and had a cargo capacity of 30,000 deadweight tons. Many of the newer ships are twice as big and carry up to 200,000 tons of oil—and thus can cause much more damage if they break up. Despite the *Argo Merchant* and other 1977 disasters, the continuing high volume of oil imports makes new tanker spills all but inevitable. For, as one Coast Guard officer explains, "we need the oil they're carrying." — *Peter Stoler*

The Liberian-flag *Argo Merchant,* aground off Nantucket, spreading a 100-mile-long oil slick
Money-saving foreign registry permits looser safety rules—and so more accidents.

Siege at Seabrook

A nuclear clash in New Hampshire mirrors a national dilemma

When the sun finally chases away the chill of winter, tourists from all over New England flock to the quiet New Hampshire town of Seabrook (pop. 5,300) to enjoy its beaches. But last year's spring invasion was something else. One early May day, 2,000 youthful protesters, toting knapsacks and waving signs demanding NO MORE NUKES, converged on a muddy construction site owned by the Public Service Co. Arriving from several directions—some from a beach where they had been landed, marine style, from boats piloted by local lobstermen—the invaders put up tents and announced their aim: to block the utility's plan to build a twin-reactor, 2,300-megawatt nuclear power plant there.

Thus began the siege of Seabrook, which quickly became a symbol for the battle that has raged nationwide through the mid-1970s between those who say that nuclear power is necessary and those who say it is costly and dangerous. The day after the invasion, New Hampshire's conservative Republican Governor Meldrim Thomson Jr. warned the Seabrook demonstrators to clear out or be arrested: "Whether this is a nuclear plant or an oil refinery or a nursing home, you are trespassing." An hour later, police moved in. Many of the 1,400 demonstrators who were seized refused to post bail, thus forcing the state to house 500 of them at a crowded armory for several days.

That did not end the struggle over Seabrook. Two months later, 3,000 pro-nuclear demonstrators—including many utility-company employees waving banners proclaiming NUCLEAR IS THE POWER OF TODAY—staged a march in favor of a resumption of work on the plant. The Seabrook protesters, a coalition of New England antinuclear groups that call themselves the Clamshell Alliance, say they will be back again this spring.

The Seabrook plant, first proposed in the late 1960s, had been stalled for five years as the utility fought to get the 48 separate local, state and federal permits needed to build it—against stiff opposition almost every step of the way. Among other concessions, the company agreed to build costly facilities to cool the sea water used to absorb the extreme heat generated by the reactors; environmentalists charged that otherwise the heated water would have endangered marine life.

In the 25 years since the first atomic plant was built in the U.S., 65 nuclear stations have gone into operation, and today they supply about 10% of the country's electricity. But the growth of nuclear power, which was once considered a natural replacement for the dwindling supplies of conventional fuels, has slowed sharply: only three new plants were ordered in 1976, compared with 30 in 1974. Because the cost of both building the plants and buying the uranium fuel to run them has been rising, nuclear-generated electric power has not been as cheap as once predicted—although it still costs less than electricity produced by oil or gas. But much more discouraging, from the power companies' viewpoint, has been the difficulty of getting plants approved by the regulatory machinery.

During his campaign, even Jimmy Carter, the former Navy nuclear engineer, said that the atom should be considered only as a "last resort" energy source. As President, Carter has joined in attacking the main target of the nuclear opponents' ire: the so-called fast-breeder reactor. The breeder uses uranium not only to generate power but also to produce new supplies of atomic fuel in the form of plutonium. Although the breeder reactor promises a guaranteed long-term source of fuel, it is reviled by antinuclear groups, because plutonium wastes are highly toxic and hard to dispose of. They also argue that because plutonium is the key ingredient of the nuclear bomb, plutonium production could contribute to the proliferation of atomic weapons.

As a sign of his antiplutonium intentions, Carter vetoed the authorization for construction of the nation's first large-scale fast-breeder reactor on the Clinch River near Oak Ridge, Tenn. (Congress later voted enough funds to keep the project ticking over).

At the same time, however, Carter quietly backed the expansion of standard nuclear power. As part of its overall energy program, the Administration is counting on completion of all of the 75 nuclear plants now planned or under construction. That would increase the percentage of U.S. electricity needs generated by the atom to 20% by 1985; by the year 2000, Administration planners say, another 240 atom plants should be in place, bringing the total to 380 facilities, producing 32% of the nation's electricity.

Carter's nuclear safety reform bill, introduced in September, promised further action to speed the construction of atomic plants. A complex, something-for-everyone proposal, the bill would, among other things, require Government to pay the legal expenses of antinuclear organizations challenging a particular plant, while also barring such groups from raising the same objections to a project with each of the various agencies that must rule on it. The bill would also encourage states to set up nuclear "site banks" that could be prescreened by regulatory authorities and thus ready for immediate construction when an atomic facility is needed. Although the outlook for passage of the bill is uncertain, Carter seems determined that there should be no more Seabrooks. Says he: "Even with the most thorough safeguards, it should not take ten years to license a plant." ∎

Largest U.S. nuclear energy plant is in operation at Rainier, Ore.

Such installations now provide 10% of nation's power, and that will soon double.

MIDDLE EAST

"Sacred Mission" to Israel

President Sadat tries a historic gamble for peace

The welcome at Tel Aviv's Ben Gurion Airport was quite unlike any such scene in the three decades of Israel's existence. The red carpet, and the honor guard and the ceremonial trumpeters were all standard, but the military band was provided, for the first time, with the music for the national anthem of Egypt, *By God of Old, Who Is My Weapon*. Red, white and black Egyptian flags fluttered over the terminal, and signs proclaimed the incredible message: WELCOME TO ISRAEL, PRESIDENT SADAT.

The Boeing 707 marked with the words ARAB REPUBLIC OF EGYPT maneuvered briefly over the airfield and then swept in for a landing at 7:58 p.m. on Saturday, Nov. 19, just after the end of the Jewish Sabbath. Out stepped the waving and smiling figure of Egypt's President Anwar Sadat, arriving on an unprecedented peace mission of his own invention. Four times in 29 years, Egyptians and Israelis had fought to the death, and even in the recent state of armed stalemate there was no official relationship between them—no commerce, no airline traffic, no telephone lines. President Sadat, hard pressed by the desperate poverty of his people and the repeated failures of all peace efforts, was determined to change all that.

He invited himself to Jerusalem for what he called a "sacred mission," and in just 43 hours he changed the whole structure of Middle Eastern conflict. Old rigidities cracked; new doors opened. In the negotiations that continued throughout the rest of the year, it was far from clear exactly what concessions Israel's ailing Prime Minister Menachem Begin might make, or whether the militant Palestinians and their allies could block any compromise (after the announcement of Sadat's visit, Palestinian explosions rocked Egyptian embassies in Damascus, Athens and Beirut). Indeed, it was far from clear whether any official settlement could be worked out at all, but after years of deadlock, a sudden change had occurred. And at last, with President Carter using his good offices to help the talks along, there was a real prospect for peace.

Said Sadat: "The process that we started will enable us to solve all the problems." Said Israel's once bellicose Menachem Begin: "Everything is open to negotiation." And they both agreed on a joint pledge: "No more war."

Quite apart from anything Sadat said

Egypt's Sadat addressing the crowded Knesset in Jerusalem

His message: "We accept to live with you in permanent peace with justice."

in Jerusalem, his trip was itself a remarkable phenomenon. Among the assembled dignitaries who welcomed Sadat was former Premier Golda Meir, the iron grandmother with whom he had once traded insults. "Madame, I have waited a long time to meet you," Sadat said gallantly. Meir later twitted him for having called her "that old lady," and Sadat burst into laughter. Everywhere, Sadat encountered the past in strangely different forms. He stayed at the King David Hotel, which Begin's guerrillas had blown up in 1946. He went to pray at the Al Aqsa mosque in Old Jerusalem, Islam's third holiest shrine. He toured Yad Vashem, the grim Israeli memorial to the Jews who perished in the Holocaust. Wherever he went, Sadat was hailed by jubilant Israelis waving Egyptian flags or wearing T shirts bearing his visage along with Begin's and the inscription: ALL YOU NEED IS LOVE.

The focal point of Sadat's voyage, though, was the Knesset (parliament), for Sadat had told his Arab critics that his basic purpose was to state the Arab position in "their house." He carried out that pledge—and firmly. Of the Arab territories captured by Israel in the 1967 war —the West Bank, the Sinai, Gaza Strip, Golan Heights and East Jerusalem—he declared that they were "equal to the Holy Valley where God Almighty spoke to Mo-

ses." The Arabs would not even bargain about giving up a single inch of their land. Said Sadat: "We insist on complete withdrawal from these territories, including Arab Jerusalem." As for the Palestinians, "the cause and essence of the conflict," Sadat insisted on "the fundamental rights of the Palestinian people ... including their right to establish their own state." Along with these demands, however, Sadat also proclaimed the one fact that Israelis yearned to hear: "We welcome you among us with full security and safety... We accept to live with you in permanent peace with justice."

Begin, in reply, offered no immediate concessions. He cited the ancient Israeli claims to the land and acknowledged that he and Sadat "have a different position ... with regard to borders." But he declared once again that Israelis "seek peace, a full peace, true peace." Sadat's private meetings with Begin, Foreign Minister Moshe Dayan and other Israeli leaders made little immediate progress, though the Jerusalem mood nevertheless remained jovial. "One day, God willing," joked Begin, "I shall visit Cairo and see the pyramids. After all, we had a part in building them." "I'm not sure whether they will get the Nobel Prize," sighed Golda Meir as the visit ended, "but for certain, both should get an Oscar."

U.S. officials were first startled, then pleased by Sadat's personal diplomacy. It was the latest of many necessary shifts in U.S. policy. Once, the U.S. had favored bringing all the combatants to the Geneva Peace Conference of 1973, but after two fruitless days, the conference was recessed to allow then Secretary of State Henry Kissinger to try step-by-step diplomacy. Kissinger retrieved two pieces of the Sinai for Egypt from Israel, widened the buffer zone between the two armies and helped to reassert American influence in the Arab world. But peace remained elusive.

to Rabin's successor, Begin. Carter also met with Syria's President Hafez Assad in Geneva and found him "brilliant."

All year long, however, the Geneva timetable slipped. The President had hoped for a Middle East conference by the end of the year, but new trouble kept flaring. Gradually, though, his conversations narrowed the U.S. view to what Washington considered three "essentials of peace." Carter called for a return of most occupied Arab territory, a commitment to "the legitimate rights of the Palestinian people," and termination of the

Clockwise from upper left: Israeli Prime Minister Begin welcomes Egyptian President Sadat at Tel Aviv's Ben Gurion Airport; the two leaders in cordial exchange at dinner; Sadat bows in prayer at Al Aqsa mosque

Sadat left Israel with an escort of Israeli fighters and a feeling of satisfaction. He has frequently insisted that roadblocks along the way to peace were 70% psychological and 30% substantive. By his historic flight, he rightly felt, he had wiped out much of the 70%. Back in Cairo, where he was welcomed by hundreds of thousands of cheering supporters, Sadat decided to keep up the momentum by summoning a follow-up conference at the Mena House Hotel, in the shadow of the great Pyramid of Cheops.

The Carter Administration decided to start afresh. "Of all regional conflicts in the world," Carter warned at the U.N., "none holds more menace."

To get back on the route to Geneva, Carter, Secretary of State Cyrus Vance and White House National Security Adviser Zbigniew Brzezinski undertook a series of trips and talks. At the White House, the President played affable host to Sadat, Saudi Arabia's Prince Fahd, King Hussein of Jordan and Yitzhak Rabin, then Prime Minister of Israel, and then

state of war followed by "true peace."

This was in many ways a major shift in U.S. policy. The U.S. had always acknowledged that something must be done about the Palestinians, but Carter was the first U.S. President to put so much public emphasis on a Palestinian "homeland" —*i.e.*, a hostile entity on Israel's very frontier. On both sides, Carter's new plans, which he had almost offhandedly announced to the world, drew sharp criticism. The Palestinian Liberation Organization, for one, refused even to recognize Israel, much less to promise "true peace." Begin, in turn, refused to deal with "demented genocidists." He also defied Carter by authorizing 51 Jewish settlements in the occupied West Bank, which would be the heart of any Palestinian homeland. And when Palestinian guerrillas in Lebanon threatened Israeli border settlements, Israeli troops crossed the border to wipe them out. Even as Sadat prepared to visit Israel, Israeli warplanes raided southern Lebanon, killing more than 100 people.

The new U.S. diplomatic position, together with such Israeli incursions, threatened the "special relationship" that has long existed between the two countries. Nor was it helped when Carter turned to

He Needed a Touch of Daring

The great moment for Egypt's Anwar Sadat came when he saw Israeli schoolchildren waving Egyptian flags and chanting a raucous welcome. "Just look at what has changed in 40 hours," he said on the plane back to Cairo. "Anwar Sadat, the man who launched the 1973 war, welcomed as a hero in Israel."

Sadat's year had begun in just the opposite mood. All moves toward peace were bogged down, yet his army was too poorly equipped to make war. Inflation was so bad and wages so low that an affluent minority was spending as much on a lunch at the Sheraton as a civil servant earned in a month.

Things came to a head in mid-January, when mobs protesting price increases surged into the streets of Cairo and Alexandria in the most savage rioting since the last days of King Farouk. In the end, the army moved in to quell the violence (after 79 were dead), but the event shook Sadat badly, and many predicted that his end was only months away.

Sadat reacted by looking to the West and to the oil-rich Arab states for help. Saudi Arabia and the U.S. led the way in putting together a $5.4 billion aid package that enabled Sadat to keep the price of a disc-shaped loaf of bread to 1½¢. But most important of all, Sadat looked to America to help him get the peace that he considers essential for Egypt's economic development. Over and over this year he said: "In the Middle East peace game the United States holds 99% of the cards."

DAVID HUME KENNERLY

Egypt's President Anwar Sadat
"Just look at what has changed."

Being chummy with Americans comes easily for Sadat. Now 59, a onetime journalist and longtime army officer, he is accustomed to dealing with a wide variety of people. He quickly moves onto a first-name basis with visitors like "Dave" Rockefeller and "my friend Henry" Kissinger. He enjoys immensely the company of American newsmen. He is at home in the English language and can enjoy joking with American friends. That made it simple for him, when the time came, to open up some new diplomatic paths with the help of the U.S. TV networks. Sadat's liking for Americans is matched by his loathing for the Soviets. His conservative village background and his deep religious faith contribute to his distrust of Communist ideology. He also was much impressed by the callous way the Soviets made use of his predecessor Gamal Abdel Nasser. A leading Egyptian editor says: "Unlike Nasser—who allowed his emotions to color his policies—Sadat shapes policy on the basis of reason. The only exception is his attitude toward the Russians. He hates them with a passion that is hard to explain."

Throughout 1977 Sadat saw the Soviets as the villains in all his crises. He blamed them and their local "agents" for the January riots. In midsummer he accused the Russians of building up leftist regimes in Africa. He replied by sending his air force to bomb a series of Soviet-built military airfields inside Libya. In the autumn he announced cancellation of further payments on his huge debt to the Soviet Union. In December he closed Soviet consulates and information offices in Alexandria, Port Said and Aswan.

With his bridges to the Soviet Union now in ashes, Sadat's dependence on the U.S. was almost total. But as the months rolled on, it became apparent that this reliance on America posed serious dangers. Though Jimmy Carter had uttered encouraging phrases about a Palestinian homeland and substantial Israeli withdrawal from occupied territories, Sadat's military commanders warned him that if Carter used American economic power to put heavy pressure on Israel, the newly elected and fiercely nationalist Menachem Begin might use his military superiority to launch a pre-emptive war against Egypt. And so the Egyptian President decided to risk his career with the most daring stroke of his life. He went straight to the enemy camp.   *— Wilton Wynn, Cairo*

In Cairo, the crowds give Sadat a hero

the Soviet Union. The two powers had been co-chairmen of the original Geneva Conference four years ago, but Kissinger froze Moscow out of the peacemaking process with his step-by-step and shuttle diplomacy. On Oct. 1 the U.S. brought the Soviets back in again by means of a 700-word joint declaration calling for peace on the basis of Carter's three points.

The Israelis protested bitterly. In New York for a session of the U.N. General Assembly, Carter and Vance sat up late one night with Moshe Dayan to draft a joint working paper that would overcome the objections. In a session that Dayan later called "brutal," Israel agreed to accept the Palestinians as part of a "unified Arab delegation" at Geneva. Who the Palestinians would be and how much participation they would be allowed were left purposely vague. Amid such maneuvers, the Geneva timetable slipped over into the new year.

Small wonder that Sadat was frustrated enough to seize on a possibility so startling that no one had even thought of it. In the course of a televised speech to the Egyptian People's Assembly on Nov. 9, Sadat said that he was ready to take a calculated gamble: "The Israelis are going to be stunned when I say this, but I am prepared to meet them at their own home. I am ready to go to the Knesset."

In many places, Sadat's statement was largely dismissed as mere rhetoric, but Begin offered a quick response: "We stretch out our hand to you." Then, in a unique bit of electronic diplomacy, U.S. TV Broadcaster Walter Cronkite interviewed both leaders by satellite and elicited a commitment from which neither could gracefully withdraw. What had seemed rhetoric was suddenly the biggest diplomatic drama of the year. In four days, Sadat's advancemen descended on Jerusalem.

Egypt is by far the most populous of the Arab states, but Sadat took considerable risks in acting so completely on his own. Not only did the Palestinians re-

MINGAM—GAMMA, LIAISON

elcome home from his "sacred mission"

He Has a Touch of the Messianic

Eretz Israel. That is the Hebrew name for the ancient land of the Jews—and the dream that has inspired the life of Menachem Begin. As a schoolboy in Poland he used to long for the creation of a Jewish state in Palestine. As a man he directed a bloody resistance campaign against both the British and the Arabs to win it. And now, as Prime Minister of Israel, he is faced with a historic opportunity to gain peace and security for his beloved land.

But there is a catch. To achieve acceptance of the Jewish state among its Arab neighbors, Begin is going to have to give back much of the land captured in the 1967 war. The return of land will have to include at least part of the territory on the West Bank of the Jordan River, an ancient land that Begin still calls by the biblical names of Judea and Samaria. All his life, he has believed that it belonged to the Jews by "natural and eternal right," as he puts it.

There is a touch of the mystical, the messianic, in Begin. Now 64, he is outwardly warm and courtly, a sober dresser and a lover of ceremony. Inwardly he is a hard man, austere in his private life (married 38 years, three children), a stickler for protocol, driven by the vision of Zionism as articulated by one of his heroes, Activist Vladimir Jabotinsky (1880-1940). Though ailing—he was hospitalized twice last year for heart trouble—Begin is determined to move forward.

Determination runs through Begin's life. He was imprisoned by the Russians during World War II for outspoken Zionism. When he was released after a year, he made his way to Palestine and quickly rose to the head of the *Irgun Zvai Leumi,* a violent underground guerrilla group. Despite a $30,000 bounty on his head, he fought the British with the slogan: "We fight, therefore we are." The *Irgun's* most notorious feat was the 1946 dynamiting of the King David Hotel, with the loss of more than 90 lives.

When the war of independence ended in 1948, Begin formed the right-wing Herut (Freedom) Party and was elected to the first Knesset. He spent the next 29 years there as leader of

REININGER—CONTACT

Israel's Prime Minister Menachem Begin
"We fight, therefore we are."

the opposition and perennial loser for the prime ministership. His election last May 1977 as head of the Likud (Unity) coalition was a surprising upset over the long-dominant but now faction-ridden Labor Party.

Begin displayed both his love of the theatrical and his desire for peace when he promptly accepted Egyptian President Anwar Sadat's precedent-breaking offer to come to Jerusalem. But Sadat's demand for the return of all captured land poses a cruel dilemma for Menachem Begin. The West Bank for him is more than 2,270 sq. mi. of rocky hills and desert, populated by 500 Arab communities and 51 Jewish settlements. Its importance to him transcends even the security that the territory provides for tiny Israel. For Begin, Jewish rule over the West Bank is the fulfillment of an ancient quest, the goal of his life.

As early as 1948, Begin said that "the homeland [by which he meant the present-day borders of Israel, including the captured West Bank] is historically and geographically an entity. Whoever fails to recognize our right to the entire homeland does not recognize our right to any of its territories. A line passing through, or drawn by someone, as a separation between a nation's state and a people's country—such an artificial line must disappear."

Could a man who wrote those passionate words now change and return that territory—even for the equally sought goal of peace? After Sadat's dramatic visit and several private talks, Begin told a visitor: "This is a new situation and I have to think it through." In a sudden trip to Washington the week before Christmas, Begin proposed "local autonomy" for West Bankers, but he did not go so far as to offer any territory. If, in the end, he does agree to major withdrawals in return for peace, it will be a stunning accomplishment for a man who has devoted his life to Eretz Israel. — ***Donald Neff, Jerusalem***

---

spond with bombs and vituperation, but they and five militant Arab nations (Syria, Iraq, Libya, Algeria and South Yemen) attempted to counter the Cairo conference by holding a "rejectionist" conference of their own. There they voted to "freeze" their relations with Egypt. Sadat responded by making a full diplomatic break with the rejectionists. Even more moderate states that might have supported Sadat, however, were eloquent by their silence. Jordan said only that it might join in later discussions. Saudi Arabia, which now serves as banker of the Middle East and which subsidized Egypt by $2 billion in 1977, adopted a similar policy of waiting.

After Sadat's initiatives, the next move was clearly up to Begin, and he was ready to make one. On Dec. 15 he arrived in Washington to brief Carter on his plan, then disclosed to reporters that Israel was ready to return virtually all the Sinai desert to Egypt (though there would have to be guarantees of access to the Red Sea). On the more difficult questions of the Palestinians and the occupied territories, Begin said that Israel was prepared to accept some kind of Palestinian "autonomy" on the West Bank. Here again, however, he insisted on the need for Israeli security guarantees, probably including an Israeli military presence in the West Bank. Begin's proposals clearly were insufficient to satisfy even the most moderate Arabs, except as a start toward further negotiations. For that start, Begin and Sadat met again over the Christmas weekend in the Suez Canal city of Ismailia. There, though the talks were cordial, they found themselves still so far apart that they could not even agree on a joint communiqué. They nonetheless professed themselves confident of the future. Said Sadat: "I don't think there is any gap that cannot be bridged." Said Begin: "I am a happy man." With that, they assigned two standing committees to carry on the talks in more detail. It was not the beginning of the end, as Winston Churchill said in a dark time, but perhaps the end of the beginning. — ***Spencer Davidson***

TERRORISM

Mission to Mogadishu

Chancellor Schmidt wins a round against radical guerrillas

About 50 minutes after the takeoff from Palma airport on the Spanish island of Majorca, two Arabic-speaking men and two women whipped out pistols. They quickly seized control of Lufthansa Flight 181 to Frankfurt, Germany, and ordered the pilot to change course. Thus began, Oct. 13, the year's most spectacular battle in the unceasing war of Western democracies against international terrorism.

The Lufthansa skyjackers, who apparently belonged to a hitherto unknown Palestinian commando organization called *Min Beirut,* provided chilling proof that there are now close links among the world's major terrorist groups. In addition to the release of two Palestinian guerrillas held in Turkish jails, the skyjackers demanded freedom for eleven imprisoned West German terrorists. Among them: Andreas Baader, 34, co-founder of the notorious Baader-Meinhof gang (alias the Red Army Faction). The terrorists declared that Baader and his cohort must be given safe-conduct flights to Viet Nam, South Yemen or Somalia, along with $15 million in ransom and $42,000 for each of the eleven. Otherwise, they said, the 82 innocent passengers and five crew members aboard Flight 181 would be killed.

Shortly after the Lufthansa jet was seized, the West German government received a message of support for the skyjackers from a group of Baader's followers who called themselves the Kommando Siegfried Hausner unit of the Red Army Faction. Six weeks earlier, these terrorists had ambushed a guarded car and kidnaped Hanns-Martin Schleyer, 62, a member of the board of Daimler-Benz and one of the country's best-known industrialists.

Following Schleyer's disappearance, West German Chancellor Helmut Schmidt had set up two crisis staffs in Bonn to plan and supervise operations against the kidnapers. Meeting in marathon sessions, Schmidt and his top aides quickly made their decision on the new crisis: no surrender to the skyjackers' demands. In obedience to the frantic orders of the chief skyjacker, who called himself Walter Mahmud, Flight 181 veered eastward across the Mediterranean to Rome, to Cyprus, to Bahrain, to Dubai in the United Arab Emirates, to Aden in South Yemen and eventually to Mogadishu, the capital of Somalia. Tracking the plane's movements, and following a few hours behind it, were two other Lufthansa planes. Aboard were 62 members of an elite antiterrorist unit called *Grenzschutzgruppe Neun* (Border Defense Group 9).

Somalia had long been a haven for Palestinian terrorists, who have even set up training camps there. President Siad Barre, however, was persuaded to cooperate with a West German rescue attempt—possibly by covert promises of Western military aid in his bitter war against neighboring Ethiopia. At dusk on Oct. 18, the Lufthansa jets that had been

Kidnapers' portrait of Schleyer

The identification: "Prisoner for 31 days."

trailing Flight 181 landed at Mogadishu. Just before 2 in the morning—only 40 minutes before the skyjackers' final deadline for release of the imprisoned terrorists—28 of the German commandos crept toward 181. An explosion on the runway momentarily diverted the skyjackers' attention. Blowing open the doors, the commandos hurled in "stun" grenades, warned the hostages to lie flat, and began firing at the skyjackers. The surgically precise operation was over in minutes. Three of the skyjackers were killed, and the fourth, a woman named Suheila Sayeh, 22, was seriously wounded. Although none of the passengers was hurt, the rescue came too late to save Pilot Jürgen Schumann, 37. Walter Mahmud, in a fit of anger, had shot him pointblank during the plane's brief stop at Aden.

The raid at Mogadishu was the most daring exercise of its kind since the now legendary rescue of hostages by Israeli airborne troops at Entebbe, Uganda, on July 3, 1976. Messages from all over the free world poured into Bonn, praising Schmidt and his government for their courage. Cabled Israeli Premier Menachem Begin: "It was indeed a salvation in which all free men rejoice." But then came shocking news. Although they had been in solitary confinement under close guard, supposedly isolated from all contact with the outside world, four of the German terrorists whose release had been sought attempted suicide; three, including Andreas Baader, succeeded.

In a nationally televised address, West German President Walter Scheel pleaded with Schleyer's kidnapers: "The whole world—East and West—is against you. I appeal to you to set your hostage free." Next day came the cruel answer. The leftwing Paris daily *Libération* received a telephone call from someone who claimed to be a Red Army Faction member. "After 43 days," said the caller, "we have put an end to the miserable and corrupt existence of Hanns-Martin Schleyer." His body was found in the trunk of an abandoned green Audi in Mulhouse, France, about ten miles west of the German border. He had been shot three times.

Terrorists' gallery: Murder Suspect Susanne Albrecht; Suicides Andreas Baader, Gudrun Ensslin, Jan-Carl Raspe; Fugitive Friederike Krabbe

Sons and daughters of middle-class homes with a goal that is ruthlessly nihilistic: the destruction of democracy

Schleyer was given a state funeral, and West German police, assisted by security forces of other Western European nations, mounted the largest manhunt in the country's postwar history. As of December, five of the suspects had been arrested. Few West Germans believed that they had seen the last of the Red Army Faction, which has been responsible for at least 18 murders in the past five years. Still at large, West German authorities estimate, are about 120 committed terrorists, who can count on anywhere from 1,200 to 5,000 radicals to provide them with money, food and safe houses.

The West German terrorists, in their flamboyant leftist rhetoric, claim to speak for the oppressed working class. In fact, most of these urban radicals are university-educated sons and daughters of middle-class homes, and their goal is ruthlessly nihilistic: the destruction, by any means, of a prosperous democracy whose constraints and balances, ironically, allow them the freedom to preach and practice their radicalism. In fighting terrorism, West Germany is damned if it does, damned if it doesn't: increasing police powers and toughening laws against radical activity—necessary though they might be—would raise both at home and abroad the specter of the authoritarian Germany that the world hoped had died with Hitler. — *John T. Elson*

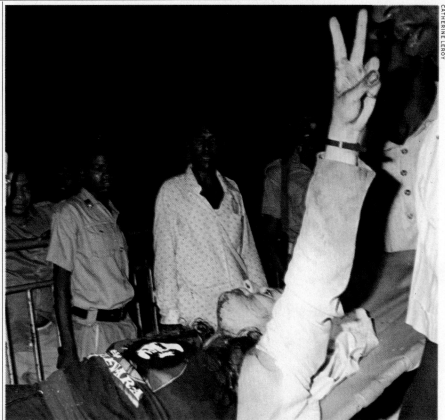

Wounded Skyjacker Suheila Sayeh, 22, proclaims victory sign after capture at Mogadishu
Germans' crackdown won praise: "A salvation in which all free men rejoice."

Catalogue of Crime

International terrorism has no frontiers, and no shortage of self-styled freedom fighters to carry out its cruel strategies. One U.S. expert estimates that there are no fewer than 140 terrorist organizations active in the world, ranging from the Marxist Montoneros of Argentina to the Irish Republican Army Provos in Ulster to the Basque Separatists of northern Spain. Among the major incidents perpetrated last year by bands of revolutionary leftists:
▶ In The Netherlands, South Moluccan terrorists last June seized 164 hostages—54 passengers aboard a Utrecht-Groningen express train and 105 children and five teachers at a primary school in Bovensmilde. The Moluccans, radical vanguard of about 40,000 East Indian exiles who live in The Netherlands, want the Dutch government to help them set up an independent republic in their homeland, an archipelago of 1,000 or so islands that are now part of Indonesia. After 19 days of negotiations, during which the terrorists were persuaded to release the children unharmed, Prime Minister Joop den Uyl ordered army commandos to mount a dawn assault on both train and school. Six Moluccans and two hostages were killed; one terrorist, two commandos and nine prisoners were wounded. Seven of the terrorists were later convicted on assorted criminal charges; their dead comrades were mourned by the stateless Moluccans as martyrs to a cause that clearly lives.
▶ In India last September, five terrorists of the fanatical Japanese Red Army skyjacked a Japan Airlines DC-8 bound from Paris to Tokyo shortly after the plane left Bombay. Landing in Dacca, the capital of Bangladesh, the terrorists demanded the release of nine imprisoned Japanese radicals and $6 million in ransom. In contrast to West Germany's Schmidt, Japan's Premier Takeo Fukuda eventually decided "we have no choice but to comply." For one thing, the country's Self-Defense Force, which would have been charged with a rescue attempt, is constitutionally forbidden to operate outside Japan; for another, Tokyo's relations with the unpredictable Bangladesh military regime are distant. In exchange for 60,000 hard-to-trade U.S. $100 bills, the terrorists released some of their 156 hostages and ordered the skyjacked plane flown to Algeria; the rest of the hostages were set free along the way. In Algeria, the gunmen were given asylum.
▶ In the U.S. last October, three homemade bombs touched off fires in two stores in midtown Manhattan and frightened pedestrians near the main branch of New York's Public Library. A letter found in a nearby phone booth, calling for "a war of nerves" against *"Yanki-imperialism,"* indicated the source of the explosives: the Puerto Rican independence movement known as Armed Forces of National Liberation of Puerto Rico (F.A.L.N.). Although it has only a few hundred members at best and little support in the island commonwealth, the Cuban-inspired F.A.L.N. has set off at least 60 bombs in U.S. cities over the past three years—including one that nearly destroyed New York's historic Fraunces Tavern in 1975, killing four people and wounding 53.

Even when left- or right-wing extremists take credit for it, terrorism is not always political. Last year there were 71 kidnapings in Italy (219 since 1974), most of them by criminal gangs in search of easy loot. A few days after Hanns-Martin Schleyer's death, wealthy Dutch Businessman Maurits ("Maupi") Caransa, 61, was seized by kidnapers; several telephone calls seemed at first to link them to the Red Army Faction. Caransa was eventually released after paying $4 million to his kidnapers who, Dutch police believe, were simply ordinary—but nonetheless skillful—criminals.

DISASTERS

"Oh, God, Take Me! Take Me!"

Freak collision on a runway brings aviation's highest toll

For nearly three hours, the 380 passengers aboard the Pan Am 747 had been good-natured about the diversion caused by a false bomb scare. They had whiled away the time chatting and sipping drinks provided as solace by cheerful flight attendants scurrying down the aisles, but finally they were beginning to stir restlessly. The group was largely composed of elderly couples from California who were eager to get on with the charter flight that had brought them to the Canary Islands for the start of a two-week cruise in the Mediterranean. Their giant jet was now sitting on a fog-shrouded runway on one of the islands called Tenerife. Waiting for the clearance that would send them on to Las Palmas, where their ship was docked, some passengers tried to take pictures of the blue and white KLM 747 that was parked nearby. Then the KLM aircraft trundled down the runway and into the mists, and shortly afterward Pan Am Captain Victor Grubbs, 56, announced: "We're taking off now." There was applause, even a few cheers.

At the controls of the KLM jet was one of the airline's top pilots, Jacob Veldhuizen Van Zanten, 51, who not only had 25 years of experience but was considered by his superiors to be so dependable that he spent half his time training others. Indeed, Veldhuizen Van Zanten's picture appeared in a KLM magazine emphasizing the airline's "reliability"—a well-earned reputation. Waiting at the far end of the runway, Veldhuizen Van Zanten could not see the other plane through the fog, but conditions nonetheless were above flight minimums, and he had the authority to decide whether to go or not. He decided to go. "We are now on [or at] takeoff," radioed the KLM plane.

"Stand by for takeoff clearance," replied the tower. "I will call you back."

Captain Grubbs and his flight crew heard the exchange, spoken in English —the international language of flight operations—as they eased their jet up the same runway. They could not see the KLM jet but they were not unduly worried. They were sure they had time to follow their orders, which were to turn off the runway at a ramp about two-thirds of the way down, in plenty of time to let the Dutch plane flash by. After the KLM radio message, someone in the Pan Am cockpit said reassuringly: "He's not cleared for takeoff."

But Captain Veldhuizen Van Zanten apparently thought he was. Ponderously at first, and then with growing speed, the KLM began to roll. Aboard the Pan Am jet, Captain Grubbs and First Officer Robert Bragg noticed some lights blurred by fog ahead of them on the runway. At first they thought they were stationary, but then they saw to their horror that they were growing larger—and coming straight at the Pan Am plane. "Get off! Get off!" yelled Bragg. Grubbs gunned his engines and frantically tried to swing the 300-ton 747 left.

At about the same instant, the Dutch pilot must have spotted the Pan Am jet. He yanked back on the controls so sharply that the tail of his aircraft slammed down and gouged a streak in the runway. The nose began to lift. For another agonizing second or so, the two veteran pilots struggled to inch their enormous planes out of each other's path. They almost succeeded. The nose of the KLM jet actually cleared the Pan Am aircraft, but the low-slung engines and huge undercarriage did not.

With a scream of tearing metal, the side of the Pan Am jet was ripped wide open. The KLM plane, which had been moving at 165 m.p.h., crashed onto the runway 600 yds. away and exploded in a roar of flame. Captain Veldhuizen Van Zanten and every other person on the aircraft—a total of 248—died in the wreck.

Aboard the Pan Am plane most of the passengers in the tourist section, where the main impact occurred, died quickly, strapped into their seats, their drinks spilled onto their laps. Sheets of flame flared, and explosions sent pieces of the fuselage screeching through the air. There was a smell of burning flesh.

Dorothy Kelly, 35, the purser on the flight, managed to jump free and found Captain Grubbs on his hands and knees, mumbling incoherently. She grabbed him by his shoulders and was dragging him away when an engine exploded. She recalls: "There were horrible shrieks and screams from inside the cabin." She managed to haul Grubbs to safety, and then went back for others. One survivor was so badly burned and hurt that he was crying, "Oh, God, take me! Take me!"

Jim Naik, 37, a cruise official, was sitting with his wife under the first-class dining area when a man fell on his head. Says Naik: "I don't know if he was dead or alive. I suppose I pushed him off me, I don't recall." Naik managed to get his unconscious wife out of her seat, and was tug-ging her toward a hole in the plane's side when there was an explosion. "We were thrown back. It was all smoke and fire. I had ashes all over my face." Once again, Naik got to the top of the wreckage when there was another explosion. This time he was blown out of the plane, but his wife was thrown back inside.

Staggering to his feet, Naik stared about him in disbelief. "The whole plane was burning. It was all yellowish red inside, and my wife was still in there. I couldn't get back up on the wing to go in to get her. There were people leaping off the plane, their clothes and flesh burning, flesh just hanging from their legs.

"I saw some of the crew leap from the cockpit. One yelled at me, 'Get out of there, it's going to blow!' I staggered about 40 yds. away." Suddenly there was a third explosion, and bodies came hurtling out of the wreckage. A huge aircraft tire flipped high into the air. When the smoke cleared, Naik saw someone lying under the plane with a white shirt like his wife's. Despite the danger of more explosions, Naik dashed underneath the plane and found his wife. She was unconscious and her clothes were burning. He dragged her away and she survived.

But 334 persons on the Pan Am flight did not. The combined casualty list of 582 persons killed made the crash the worst in aviation history. —*James D. Atwater*

The gutted shell of Pan Am 747 after collision with KLM jet on fog-shrouded runway in the Canary Islands. Below, dazed and injured Pan Am passengers scramble away from wreckage of burning plane.

DIPLOMACY

New Pressure for Human Rights

Carter condemns oppressors—but does anyone benefit?

One working premise of Henry Kissinger's *Realpolitik* was that American morality—or at least moralizing—ought to stop at the water's edge. It was too volatile, too distorting an influence, he (and many others) believed, to play any major part in the diplomacy practiced among the political powers of the

about human rights offenses committed by allies like South Korea, the Philippines and Iran?

"It is a new world that calls for a new American foreign policy," Carter declared at the University of Notre Dame in May. All year, in his own style, Carter sought to affirm the tradition of Wilson,

MICHAEL CHESNEY—SIPA/BLACK STAR

Soviet Physicist & Nobel Peace Prizewinner Andrei Sakharov
Pressure on dissidents is "unbearable," he told Carter, and "our duty is to fight."

real world. Jimmy Carter, however, campaigned for the presidency with a good deal of rhetoric about "decency, honesty and compassion." No sooner had he entered the White House than he launched a worldwide campaign for human rights —and thus injected a complicating new element into U.S. foreign relations.

It gave new hope to Soviet dissidents, for example, yet infuriated the Kremlin, even to the point of seriously threatening the policy of détente. It raised difficult questions about the extent to which the U.S. can or should criticize other nations' internal affairs—and the extent to which those nations can be made to conform to the standards of a wealthy Western democracy. Finally, Carter's almost Evangelical appeals left his Administration open to the charge of hypocrisy: How could the U.S. excoriate adversaries in Eastern Europe while doing very little

Roosevelt and even John Foster Dulles; all of them, in very different ways, had insisted that U.S. foreign policy should be based on moral purpose. Carter thought the need especially urgent in this era— post–Viet Nam, post-Watergate. It was possible, Carter almost suggested, that the human rights policy was demanded as much by Americans' need to think well of themselves as by the sufferings and deprivations endured by political victims in other countries. The U.S., after so much bitterness and self-accusation, needed to stand for something good in the world. In any case, the human rights campaign reflected some of the best—and the most complicated—aspects of Jimmy Carter. He pursued his good intentions with a persistence that left many allies baffled and the Soviets, among others, near apoplexy.

Early in the year, Carter received a letter from Andrei Sakharov, the Soviet

physicist and 1975 Nobel Peace prizewinner, who wrote of the "hard, almost unbearable situation" of dissidents in Eastern Europe and argued that "our and your duty is to fight for them." More than a year earlier, Gerald Ford had refused, at Henry Kissinger's suggestion, to receive Alexander Solzhenitsyn after the novelist, heroically unbending, was exiled from his own country. Now, astonishingly, Carter replied to Sakharov with a personal letter that the Russian received at the American embassy in Moscow. Wrote Carter: "We shall use our good offices to seek the release of prisoners of conscience, and we will continue our efforts to shape a world responsive to human aspirations."

The State Department, meanwhile, broke a long-standing taboo against strong comment on the internal policies of other countries. It denounced Czechoslovakia for its arrest of dissident intellectuals in violation of the 1975 Helsinki accords, which had promised "respect [for] human rights and fundamental freedoms, including the freedom of thought, conscience, religion or belief, for all." It also warned Moscow that any attempt to intimidate Sakharov "will conflict with accepted international standards of human rights." Soon afterward, Carter invited exiled Human Rights Activist Vladimir Bukovsky to the White House for a ten-minute meeting.

The Soviets probably spent a fair part of 1977 trying to figure Carter out. They were angered by him, but also puzzled. After the Sakharov and Bukovsky episodes, they counterattacked. *Pravda* published an acidulous account of the Bukovsky meeting: "J. Carter of the United States received yesterday Bukovsky, a criminal-law offender from the Soviet Union who is known as an active opponent of the development of Soviet-American relations." In Geneva, at the U.N. Commission on Human Rights, U.S. Delegate Allard K. Lowenstein proposed that the organization request information from the Soviets on the arrest and detention of dissidents. Soviet Delegate Valerian Zorin replied with an hour-long diatribe against the American's "illegal abuse of the commission's authority." He warned that "inventing pretexts for defending human rights is not conducive to the positive development of Soviet-American relations." In both instances, the Soviets seemed to be signaling Carter not to jeopardize important matters—arms-limitation talks and expanded trade—by posturing too extravagantly on human rights.

When 35 nations gathered in Belgrade in October for the first review of the 1975 Helsinki accords, both East and West at first seemed determined to avoid a fight over human rights. But Chief U.S. Delegate Arthur Goldberg launched a frontal attack on the Russians for their arrests of dissidents like Physicist Yuri Orlov and Poet Alexander Ginzburg. Furious, his Soviet counterpart, Yuli Voron-

Poet Alexander Ginzburg

Physicist Yuri Orlov

Activist Anatoli Shchransky

tsov, replied with an hour-long excoriation of the U.S. for what he called "massive violations of human rights." He claimed that Americans use child labor on a large scale and that "thousands of Americans are imprisoned because of their race." By year's end the conference was still at work on the drafting of a communiqué, due early in 1978.

One of the most disturbing questions about the human rights campaign is whether it helps or hurts political dissidents around the world. Publicity has undoubtedly enabled certain dissidents, such as Roy Medvedev and Solzhenitsyn, to spend their time in exile instead of in jail. Dissident Anatoli Shchransky insisted: "World opinion is what keeps us going, what keeps us alive." One month later, however, he was arrested. Indeed, as if in defiance of Carter, the Soviets deliberately tightened a few screws last year after the new President's sermons rose in volume. One of those arrested, Physicist Orlov, had been the chief of the unofficial Helsinki monitoring committee.

The same policy applied in all of the East bloc. The Czechs arrested or harassed many of the nearly 500 signers of a manifesto calling for compliance with the Helsinki human rights accords. In Rumania, President Nicolae Ceauşescu denounced dissidents as traitors and warned of long jail sentences and possibly even death. East Germany expelled two dozen leading intellectuals and artists.

For a time, Washington's allies worried that Carter was endangering the structure of relations built up over the Kissinger years. In midsummer, French President Valéry Giscard d'Estaing claimed that "Carter has compromised the process of détente." West German Chancellor Helmut Schmidt complained that Carter "acts like a faith healer." Yet the Administration remained fairly confident that both Soviets and Americans were able to dissociate the human rights issue from progress on issues like SALT. That would be a reversal of the old Kissinger

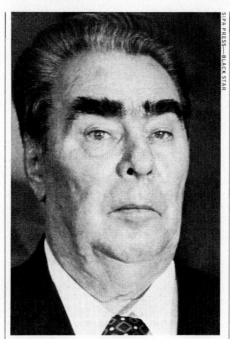
Soviet Leader Leonid Brezhnev
He tightened a few screws.

theory of "linkage," wherein various problems were worked out as an interrelated series. Said a French Foreign Ministry official: "The human rights argument would not be acceptable to the Soviet Union if it came from a less powerful country. Since it comes from the U.S., the Soviets know they must be realistic about it." Meanwhile, a TIME poll in April showed that 55% of Americans supported Carter's rights efforts.

After its opening bursts at the Soviets and their Eastern allies, Carter's Administration took pains to broaden his human rights policy. Said Carter: "Our policy [on human rights] is addressed, not to any particular people or area of the world, but to all countries equally. Yes, including our own country." Secretary of State Cyrus Vance did confess the awkwardness of dealing with U.S. allies like Iran, whose geography and oil

are crucial to American interests but whose secret police have committed offenses similar to those of the KGB. Sometimes, Vance admitted, considerations of human rights would have to be secondary to strategic necessity.

In an effort to demonstrate its evenhandedness, the Administration surveyed all nations receiving U.S. aid. It recommended reducing the aid budget to Argentina, Uruguay and Ethiopia because of their repressive policies (but it exempted South Korea from a similar cutback for strategic reasons). The State Department even released a report on the state of human rights in 82 nations. That prompted Brazil to serve notice that it was dissolving the 1952 U.S.-Brazil Military Assistance Agreement and refusing the planned $50 million in U.S. aid. Argentina, Guatemala, El Salvador and Uruguay also rejected all American aid. Nonetheless, when Rosalynn Carter went on a tour of seven countries in the Caribbean and Latin America last summer, she made it a point to meet with two U.S. missionaries in Brazil and to publicize their stories of imprisonment and torture.

Whatever the serious arguments against it, the Carter policy on human rights has become a significant moral force in the world. Sometimes it cannot be more than a gesture—perhaps a meddlesome one. But at best, it can keep up a hard moral pressure on governments to resist their uglier impulses.

On the other hand, a year of criticism and rebuffs has inclined Carter to mute somewhat his preachments on human rights—which has led one Czech dissident to complain: "Carter started the year with a bugle call to which we all responded one way or another. But in the end there was nothing but the bugle call." Without dangerously inflating the expectations of dissidents and political victims, therefore, Carter still confronts the problem of persuading oppressors that the U.S. does take seriously the worldwide hunger for individual freedom. — *Lance Morrow*

DISARMAMENT

A Major Deadline Missed

SALT I expired, but there are new hopes for SALT II

At the stroke of midnight on Oct. 2, the interim Strategic Arms Limitation Treaty expired. No longer were the numbers of U.S. and Soviet nuclear-tipped intercontinental missiles restricted by a formal ceiling. Although the deadline passed uneventfully—factories did not start spewing out massive quantities of new rockets, for instance—the expiration dramatically symbolized the uncertain pace of arms control.

This was far from the near euphoria that marked the signing of SALT I in 1972. Then President Nixon and the Soviets' Leonid Brezhnev froze the existing levels of offensive strategic weapons for five years. They figured that this would provide enough time to negotiate a more comprehensive limit. But little progress was made until the 1974 Vladivostok summit, when Brezhnev and President Ford agreed that SALT II should allow each side 2,400 strategic missile launchers, of which 1,320 could be armed with the cluster-warheads known as MIRVs.

As clear as these guidelines may have seemed originally, they soon became mired in controversies. The U.S., for instance, insisted that the ceilings cover the U.S.S.R.'s new Backfire bomber; the Soviets rejected this on the ground that it was not an intercontinental bomber. In turn, Moscow argued that all U.S. aircraft firing cruise missiles be counted against the MIRV quota. Here the U.S. balked. A number of critics complained, moreover, that the ceilings would require almost no cut in the superpowers' atomic inventory.

In an attempt to break the stalemate, President Carter sent Secretary of State Vance to Moscow on March 26 with a set of bold proposals. The Administration called for a "deep" (up to 25%) slash in the Vladivostok ceilings on missile launchers, a sharp limit on testing new weapons and a ban on mobile land-based intercontinental missiles (spy satellites that verify compliance with the treaty cannot keep track of such launchers).

Brezhnev took one look at Vance's package and proclaimed a loud *nyet*. The rebuff plunged U.S.-Soviet relations to their lowest point in years. Not until May did the superpower chill start thawing. Meeting with Vance in Geneva, Soviet Foreign Minister Gromyko agreed to consider formulas for amalgamating some of Carter's new proposals with the Vladivostok guidelines. A joint communiqué after the talks declared that "the differences between the two sides ... have been narrowed." But Gromyko cautioned that "major and serious difficulties remain." To resolve these, the Administration reactivated the so-called back-channel that former Secretary of State Kissinger had found very useful in concluding SALT I. Bypassing the relatively low-level teams of Geneva-based arms negotiators, exchanges on key points began taking place in Washington, where Soviet Ambassador Anatoli Dobrynin met with top U.S. officials.

After some back-channel progress, Gromyko flew to Washington in late September to consult with Carter and Vance. The intensive high-level talks convinced a number of U.S. officials that the long-awaited "conceptual breakthrough" had been achieved. Among the principles accepted by both sides:

▶ The Vladivostok ceiling of 2,400 launchers will be lowered by about 10% for the eight-year life of the treaty.

▶ Some 1,320 launchers will still be allowed to be armed with MIRVs, but only 1,200 of these launchers can be ballistic missiles; the rest could be planes carrying cruise missiles.

▶ Restrictions on the range of air-launched cruises will not be set by the main body of SALT II, but by a separate protocol, running for about three years.

▶ The number of Soviet monster rockets (like the SS-18, which soon may be accurate enough to destroy U.S. missiles in underground, concrete silos) will be kept at the SALT I levels (about 310), despite U.S. attempts to cut it.

▶ Testing and deployment of new strategic weapons will be sharply curtailed for at least three years.

Despite the "breakthrough," disagreements over details again slowed the SALT process, and at year's end, experts estimated that a SALT II signing would not be likely in the early part of 1978. Once negotiated, moreover, the accord will face intense scrutiny from the U.S. Senate, where a two-thirds vote is required for ratification. Senator Henry Jackson, a Washington Democrat whose views on arms control are widely respected by his colleagues, will almost certainly oppose the treaty if he feels that the U.S. has conceded too much to the Russians. He is worried, for instance, that the accord may fail to impose sufficient restrictions on the testing and deployment of new weapons and on the number of monster missiles permitted the Soviets.

Until a new treaty replaces the lapsed SALT I, there are no formal restraints on development of new strategic weapons. The Soviets have already begun testing four types of advanced missiles. By the time SALT II is signed, it may be too late to stop deployment of the newest arms systems—a dramatic demonstration of technology's ability to outpace diplomacy. ∎

Secretary of State Vance (left) confronts Soviet Leader Brezhnev and Foreign Minister Gromyko at SALT talks in Moscow

The technology of destruction may outpace the diplomacy aimed at restricting it.

Italy's Enrico Berlinguer, Spain's Santiago Carrillo and France's Georges Marchais exchange greetings at Madrid press conference FLORES—EL PAIS

COMMUNISTS

Roadblocks on the Way to Power

But 1978 could still be a triumphant year

Throughout 1975 and 1976, the movement known as Eurocommunism, a Communism that proclaimed its independence from Moscow, seemed to be sweeping irresistibly toward power along the Mediterranean. Last year, the movement ran into a few roadblocks in all three of its main centers. Items:

▶ France's Union of the Left seemed to have broken apart, largely because the Communists were unhappy at the prospect of having to play a supporting role in an alliance dominated by their old foes, the Socialists.

▶ In Italy, the Communists seemed fearful of taking power during the current economic crisis. But in the face of mounting rank-and-file impatience, the party at year's end began calling for a formal role in the government.

▶ Spain's Communist Party, legalized only last April, quickly swelled its ranks to 100,000 members but drew only 9% of the vote when the country held its first free national elections in 41 years in June.

If the Eurocommunists were slowed, however, they certainly were not stopped. Their brand of Communism has had a significant impact, and in 1978 the French and Italian Eurocommunists may well resume their drive toward power.

FRANCE. In last spring's municipal elections, the Socialist-Communist *Union de la Gauche* won an impressive 45% of the vote—and seemed to be in a strong position for the parliamentary balloting scheduled for March 1978. In all, the leftists gained control of 153 of the 221 French municipalities with populations of at least 30,000. Communist mayors were elected in 72 of these cities.

With victory in its grasp, however, the 600,000-member Communist Party apparently began to have second thoughts about serving as junior partner to the stronger Socialists in a new government. Communist Leader Georges Marchais demanded that the left's common program, drafted when the alliance was formed in 1972, be drastically revised.

The Communists proposed a 50% boost in family allowances, a 27% rise in the minimum wage and other increases that would have sent France's budget ballooning from $66 billion in 1977 to an estimated $160 billion. Even touchier were the Communists' demands for further nationalization of French industry and business. State-run companies (including major banks; the leading automaker, Renault; and *Electricité de France*) already account for more than one-tenth of France's gross domestic product; this is roughly the same percentage as in Britain. The 1972 common program proposed nationalizing nine key companies in major sectors such as mineral resources, armaments, pharmaceuticals and chemicals; this would have brought roughly one-fourth of France's gross domestic product under government control. To this already formidable list the Communists insisted on adding France's four biggest steel companies, its biggest oil company, its second biggest automaker (Peugeot-Citroën) and more than 1,000 subsidiaries of the nine key firms.

When this far-reaching program was published in the Communist daily *L'Humanité,* it inevitably started a row. At a rally in southern France, President Valéry Giscard d'Estaing said the Marchais proposals proved that the left aimed "to impose on that half of France which does not want it a brutal change of society."

François Mitterrand's Socialists got the Communists to budge a little, but not nearly enough. Evidently, said Socialist Mayor Gaston Defferre of Marseille, the Communists were interested in "a popular democracy of the type Czechoslovakia has to endure."

The result of the rift was a plunge in the left's prospects in the 1978 elections. An October sampling by the weekly magazine *Le Nouvel Observateur* gave Giscard and his center-right allies 246 seats in the 487-seat National Assembly to 241 for the parties of the left. Other polls taken in late November forecast a majority of the popular vote for the left next March, but a minority of seats.

ITALY. The 1.8-million-member Communist Party, Western Europe's biggest by far, suffered no comparably dramatic setback, but it did have problems. In the June 1976 parliamentary elections, the Communists polled 34% of the vote, only 5% less than the long-ruling Christian Democrats. All told, the Communists held control of 45 of Italy's 94 provinces and the mayoralties of major cities such as Rome, Bologna, Florence and Naples.

In the Chamber of Deputies, the Christian Democrats can rule only with Communist support, but the Communists still remain outside the Cabinet. Nor, with inflation running at 15% and unemployment more than 8%, did they seem in any hurry to demand the responsibility for setting Italy aright. Nor were Party Leader Enrico Berlinguer and his colleagues pushing for radical change, as were the French. Said Communist Economist Eugenio Peggio: "We don't need further nationalization."

Christian Democratic Premier Giulio Andreotti signed a six-party accord that gave the Communists a formal role in the governing process. The compact gave them virtual veto power over major legislation but still kept them below the executive level. The party's

43

readiness to cooperate with the Christian Democrats caused a lot of grumbling in the ranks and even inspired thousands of students and young workers to a series of demonstrations in Bologna. Said one of the protesters to the Communists: "You've given up fighting to change the system. You only want to save it." In December, Berlinguer responded to such pressures by denouncing the six-party accord and demanding the creation of an emergency government with the Communists as full partners.

The U.S., for its part, was less strident in its warnings about Eurocommunism than it had been during Henry Kissinger's stewardship of the State Department. Nonetheless, when Andreotti visited Washington in July, one State Department official made a point of noting that President Carter hoped the Christian Democrats would do "everything they can to keep the Communists out."

In placing its hopes on the determination and resilience of European non-Communists, the U.S. last year gained support in a surprising quarter: the traditionally anti-American French intelligentsia. There suddenly appeared, on TV and in fashionable bookstores, a whole array known as the "New Philosophers," some of them apostates from Marxism, all of them skeptical about political ideologies of any kind. As Bernard-Henri Lévy, one of the group's best-known members, put it: "Between the barbarity of capitalism, which censures itself much of the time, and the barbarity of socialism, which does not, I guess I would choose capitalism."

The Eurocommunists sought to reassure critics that they were a breed apart from the Soviets. Just read the declaration of principles issued in 1975 by Marchais and Berlinguer, they urged. "All freedom resulting from the great bourgeois democratic revolutions," says the declaration, "should be guaranteed and furthered." The manifesto goes on to catalogue those liberties, ranging from freedom of speech to "the right of opposition parties to exist and to act." Aware of the West's deep concern that a Communist Party would never yield power if voted out, the declaration concluded with a bow toward "the possibility of democratic alternation."

By way of further proof that they are no longer slavishly bound to the Soviets, the Eurocommunists also engaged in public disagreements with Moscow. Even Marchais, whose French party is still full of old-line Stalinists, denounced the Soviets for their treatment of dissidents. For his part, Italy's Berlinguer, speaking at Kremlin ceremonies marking the 60th anniversary of the Bolshevik Revolution, declared that each Communist Party "must follow roads that correspond to the peculiarities and concrete conditions of every country." The Soviets, apparently tired of hearing such sentiments, barred Spain's Santiago Carrillo from delivering his speech at the Moscow meeting.

Despite the signs of independence, the Eurocommunists' biggest problem continued to be a lack of credibility—a suspicion among Western Europeans and others that they were still totalitarians despite their new democratic look. Lenin, after all, once declared that the true revolutionary must be prepared "to resort to all sorts of stratagems, artifices, illegal methods, to evasions and subterfuges" in pursuing his goal. And the goal has always been the same: power. ∎

Walking a Tightrope

A shaky economy, with horrendous problems of inflation and unemployment. A fourth of the country's 35 million people clamoring for autonomy. A plethora of political parties—nearly 160 of them—clawing for power. A disgruntled and uncertain police force, trained to repress civil rights, now being called upon to defend them. Above all, a heritage of violence as the way to settle arguments.

This was Spain at the start of 1977, just emerging from almost 40 years of totalitarian rule. It hardly seemed the most fertile soil for self-government. Yet it was Spain that gave the world its most heartening lesson in democracy in 1977.

The two men most responsible were both products of the long, arid reign of Generalissimo Francisco Franco. King Juan Carlos de Borbón y Borbón, 39, grandson of Spain's last King, Alfonso XIII, had not even been born when the civil war erupted in 1936. Prime Minister Adolfo Suárez, 45, was seven years old when *El Caudillo* seized power. One was thought to be a malleable sportsman-prince, the other an obscure if efficient bureaucrat.

When Juan Carlos acceded to the throne just after Franco's death in November 1975, he had a mandate of one: the Generalissimo himself. Conservatives preferred him to his more liberal father, Don Juan, but the far left loathed him. Most Spaniards were ready, however, to accept Juan Carlos as the right man for a difficult moment. After a hesitant start, Juan Carlos reshuffled his government in July 1976, brought in the smooth, darkly handsome Suárez as Prime Minister and, with him, embarked on a policy of *"reforma sin ruptura"*—reform without a break.

A prudent politician, Suárez also moved cautiously at first, then with increasing boldness. One of his early measures was to strip from the military one of its more significant, and repellent, powers: the right to try civilian political offenders in military courts. It was not until last April, however, that Suárez felt ready for his most dramatic step: legalizing the Communist Party. By his reckoning, there was

King Juan Carlos
Right man for a difficult time.

a real threat of paralyzing strikes and street demonstrations had the ban been continued. He also legalized Spain's trade unions, reinstated the right to strike, and restored diplomatic relations with Eastern Europe.

When Spain's first free parliamentary elections in 41 years were held in June, 6,000 candidates were seeking 557 parliamentary seats, and the potential for a clouded outcome was great. With 20 million of Spain's 22 million eligible voters casting ballots, two blocs emerged with substantial strength. Suárez and his Democratic Center Union, a coalition of 15 centrist parties that campaigned on the slogan THE SAFE ROAD TO DEMOCRACY, won 34% of the popular vote and 165 of the 350 seats in the Congress, the lower house of the Cortes. The Socialist Workers Party, headed by Labor Lawyer Felipe Gonzalez, 35, won 28.5% of the vote and 119 seats; the Socialists thus established themselves as Spain's biggest single party. The Communists polled slightly more than 9% and the far right only 8.2%.

Confirmed in power, Suárez has had to struggle with intractable problems—severe unemployment, a 30% inflation rate, violent regional separatism. Already, he has devalued the peseta by 22%, promised autonomy to the Catalans, Basques and other ethnic minorities, and set about drafting a new constitution that calls, among other things, for separation of church and state. In much of this he has had support from an unexpected quarter: Eurocommunist Leader Santiago Carillo. Suárez compares his job to that of a tightrope walker, except that "someone is always oiling the rope." So far, he has proved an accomplished aerialist. ∎

New triumvirate: Vice Premier Teng Hsiao-p'ing, Chairman Hua Kuo-feng and Defense Minister Yeh Chien-ying

CHINA

A Return to Reason

Peking's post-Mao leadership shows it is tough and pragmatic

As China confronted the Year of the Snake, 1977, its situation appeared desperate. Its two superheroes, Chairman Mao Tse-tung and Premier Chou En-lai, had recently died, and the Communist Party leadership was chaotically divided. By the leaders' own admission, the economy was in a state of "semianarchy." The masses of people were disillusioned over the intense top-level power struggle that had gone on for ten years. The new Chairman and Premier, Hua Kuo-feng, was an inexperienced and unknown official who hardly seemed capable of restoring order.

As it turned out, the Year of the Snake brought an impressive restoration of reason in China. A new collective leadership emerged that now seems more stable than any top grouping in the past decade. Decidedly pragmatic policies have replaced the erratic and ideological programs of Mao's last years. Despite the persistence of major problems there was plenty of justification for Chairman Hua to proclaim at the 11th Congress of the Communist Party in August: "We are now able to achieve stability and unity and attain great order across the land."

Much of Hua's success can be traced back to his stunning 1976 purge of Peking's troublesome radical faction, the small group of top leaders surrounding Mao's extremist wife Chiang Ch'ing, who are now branded the evil Gang of Four. Hua declared last January that the purge of the radicals' followers in China's provinces was the most important task for 1977, and he pursued it with systematic zeal. Dozens of provincial and lower-level officials lost their jobs. There were even reports of executions. By August, when the leadership felt strong enough to convene a party congress, fully one-third of the 201-member Central Com-

mittee was replaced. A refurbished Politburo, headed by veteran bureaucrats, was named.

The new party chairman is widely viewed as a kind of front man for a group of old party stalwarts—many of them targets of attack during the chaotic Cultural Revolution of 1966-69—who strongly reasserted their power as soon as Mao was safely dead. One key member of this group is China's venerable Defense Minister, Yeh Chien-ying, 79, whose support for the overthrow of the Gang of Four was crucial. Another is the diminutive but hard-as-nails Vice Premier Teng Hsiao-p'ing, 74, a man who had been twice thrown into disgrace by his radical enemies, and who in July made still another triumphal return to power. Together with Hua, a relatively youthful 56, they make up a ruling triumvirate. "The people in power now," says one analyst, "are the old boys who were on top in China when Hua was a mere errand boy. They form a collectivity which has agreed that Hua will be their spokesman."

The new collectivity has lost little time in putting its very pragmatic stamp on the country. In particular, it has put economic growth and technical expertise ahead of campaigns for ideological purity. Scientists are being urged to spend most of their time in their laboratories, doing research rather than reading the Maoist classics. University entrance examinations, once considered a bourgeois relic, have been reinstituted on a nationwide scale. And, in a clearly welcome move, more than half of China's workers (who receive salaries of between $20 and $40 a month) got their first pay raises in well over a decade, despite Peking's traditional disdain for "material incentives."

Though Mao remains officially a

demigod—his preserved body was installed in a new mausoleum in the middle of Peking in September—it is clear that the new rulers have undertaken a marked departure from many of his most cherished policies. Mao's concept of people's war—with its slogan "men are more important than weapons"—has given way to an urgent program of modernizing the country's ill-equipped armed forces. Even in Mao's treasured domain of art and culture—one that he entrusted to his zealot wife—there has been a relaxation. Movies, plays and operas long banned by the radicals are being performed once again. Singers and actors disgraced during China's long period of political extremism have returned to the stage.

China's problems remain staggering. Even today, the basic essentials of life, like rice and cotton cloth, are carefully rationed, with many people getting only subsistence supplies. Despite its claims, China remains very poor and gray, even by comparison with some of its neighbors in Asia. No less a person than Hua Kuofeng admitted this in his much publicized report to the 11th party congress. "The life of the people is far better than before liberation," he concluded, "but the standard of living is still low."

In such circumstances, there is some danger that the stability achieved by the new leadership may be threatened. Only weeks after the 11th party congress seemed to cement the new leadership in place, there appeared wall posters attacking at least three members of the Politburo. All of the targets, not coincidentally, were known to have quarreled bitterly with Teng Hsiao-p'ing in the past. At the same time, another three officials newly named to the Central Committee by the party congress have already been purged from their posts. It all suggests a new dispute within the leadership. Still, China enters 1978 in far better shape than it began '77. As one senior analyst puts it: "The time of high drama is finished. At least, for the sake of China, I hope so." ∎

INDIA

The Fall of Indira Gandhi

A seemingly safe gamble turns into a stunning election loss

The announcement caught all India by surprise. "Let us go to the polls," Prime Minister Indira Gandhi told her country's 620 million people in a nationwide broadcast, "with the resolve to reaffirm the power of the people and to uphold the fair name of India as a land committed to the path of reconciliation, peace and progress." Thus last January, after more than 18 months of emergency rule that had caused worldwide concern about India's abandonment of democracy, Mrs. Gandhi suspended such repressive measures as direct press censorship and detention without trial. In their place she promised a free and fair campaign for the country's postponed national elections.

The gamble seemed safe enough. At the time, few doubted that Mrs. Gandhi, then 60, a shrewd and politically gifted tactician who had governed India since 1966, would once again lead her Congress Party to victory. After all, Congress had won every national election since India became independent from Britain in 1947. Besides, despite rumblings of disaffection, India appeared to be in better economic shape. Food-grain stocks were at an alltime high. Foreign exchange reserves, at $3 billion, had tripled in two years. The Prime Minister could also point to new laws abolishing rural debts and bonded labor, and to the jolt she had given the bureaucracy. "Anyone can see," she remarked confidently, "that today the nation is more healthy, efficient and dynamic than it has been for a long time."

What she failed to take into account was the ability of her political opponents, many of whom had languished in detention for months, to forge an effective opposition and win the support of the dissatisfied populace. Despite ideological differences as broad as the Ganges, the four leading opposition parties—the na-

tionalist Hindu Jana Sangh, the conservative Indian People's Party, the Socialist Party and the Old Congress Party —united under the single banner of the newly formed Janata (People's) Party.

They were soon joined by one of Mrs. Gandhi's most senior Cabinet members, Food and Agriculture Minister Jagjivan Ram, the acknowledged leader of India's 90 million Untouchables. The opposition worked out a common platform that evoked Mahatma Gandhi's popular ideals of rural development and decentralization. It denounced not only the emergency measures but also such authoritarian tactics as the forced removal of tens of thousands of urban poor to barren

India's unexpected Prime Minister Desai

Indira Gandhi campaigns for re-election

Jubilant Janata (People's) Party supporters celebrate their surprise election victory over Mrs. Gandhi

Her abuses finally united the squabbling opposition "with bars of steel."

country plots miles from their jobs. But for millions, the single most important issue was the government's aggressive sterilization program and the abuses that resulted from enforcing it. All these combined in popular opposition to the high-handed rule of Mrs. Gandhi (including the growing power of her son, Sanjay, 31, as leader of the Congress youth wing). Said one of the recently imprisoned founders of the opposition: "She has forged us together with bars of steel."

In four days of balloting last March, Indian voters produced a stunning upset, a victory for the Janata coalition, which won 298 out of 542 seats in the new Lok Sabha (Lower House). The Congress Party won only 153 seats (v. 355 in the previous Parliament). Mrs. Gandhi lost even her own well-nurtured constituency in Uttar Pradesh by 55,000 votes. Also defeated in an adjoining district was son Sanjay, who was making his first bid for office.

Mrs. Gandhi at first accepted her defeat "unreservedly and in a spirit of humility." She turned over the reins of government to the Janata's choice for Prime Minister, Morarji Desai. Desai, 81, is an eccentric ascetic who had served in earlier Gandhi governments as Deputy Prime Minister and Finance Minister before the Congress Party split of 1969. But if the opposition had won it had not forgotten; the new government launched a series of civil and criminal investigations into the Gandhi government.

Among the first to be charged was Sanjay, who was haled into court for alleged business misdealings. Then came a number of Mrs. Gandhi's former aides, including four former Cabinet ministers, on charges including the theft of Congress Party funds. Finally, on Oct. 3, senior police officials showed up at the former Prime Minister's residence, arrested her on two charges of corruption, and took her into custody. Next day, however, the court ordered her release, calling the government's case against her weak. Nonetheless, her popular appeal, after a brief resurgence, is waning. On a political tour of South India, Mrs. Gandhi's entourage was assailed by rocks and jeers. The Congress Party flatly rebuffed her bid to resume her leadership. In desperation, she once again split the Congress Party and set up a small party of her own.

The Desai government has found it as difficult as its predecessors did to cope with India's myriad problems. Squabbling over patronage delayed the filling of many posts. After much haggling, the party unveiled a vague but idealistic economic policy to end unemployment by concentrating on small-scale industry and agriculture. The government also has formulated a comprehensive bill governing the country's stormy industrial relations. It now is organizing for the long haul, which means addressing the perennial problems of caste, backwardness and, above all, population growth. If it fails, the alternative is not likely to be Indira Gandhi but something far worse. ∎

Under the Lash

That's now the penalty for playing politics

The ruin of Pakistan Prime Minister Zulfikar Ali Bhutto, like that of India's Indira Gandhi, began with an election—an election, however, that he won too well.

Bhutto, who came to power with army support after the disastrous 1971 war in which East Pakistan broke away and became Bangladesh, called the election in March to legitimize his regime. Despite a certain amount of discontent and regional strife, few doubted that Bhutto's Pakistan People's Party (P.P.P.) would win a narrow victory. But when the P.P.P. swept 155 out of 200 seats in the National Assembly, the opposition Pakistan National Alliance cried foul. In subsequent weeks the Alliance presented convincing evidence of widespread electoral fraud and demanded new elections.

Bhutto resisted. Instead, he clapped major opposition leaders in jail and arrested thousands of lower-ranking political opponents. Their supporters took to the streets, and in clashes with the police and army more than 300 were killed, thousands more injured. Finally, after lengthy negotiations with the opposition, Bhutto agreed to hold new elections in October. Shortly after, however, the military decided to intervene. In the early morning hours of July 5 the army arrested not only opposition leaders but also Bhutto and several members of his Cabinet. That evening it was announced that Pakistan's new leader was General Mohammed Zia ul-Haq, 53, a career officer who had been appointed army chief of staff by Bhutto the year before.

Zia vowed that the military's reign would be brief and was designed only to ensure fair elections. And would Bhutto himself be free to participate? Certainly, said Zia. "I hope he will come back and stand for election." But within weeks, Zia's regime pressed murder charges against Bhutto, alleging that in 1974 he had ordered the Federal Security Force to assassinate Ahmed Raza Kasuri, a onetime political ally. Kasuri had escaped unscathed when gunmen sprayed his car, but his father had been killed. Protested Bhutto, 49, still the suave Oxford-educated lawyer: "I've been framed. The whole plan is to get me out of the way so that my political leadership is not available to the country."

It did seem so. No sooner was Bhutto released on bail than he was rearrested on a host of new charges. Zia announced that he was canceling elections until the charges had been disposed of. In the meantime, all political activity is banned. Violators can get 15 lashes at a public flogging, one of the punishments revived in accordance with the new regime's adherence to Islamic law. ∎

Former Prime Minister Zulfikar Ali Bhutto

New Leader Mohammed Zia ul-Haq
A charge of murder.

SOUTH AFRICA

Forward over the Cliff

Vorster rallies his White Tribe to fight for apartheid

It was said, and not merely in jest, that South Africa's Nov. 30 general election will be remembered as the one in which Prime Minister John Vorster ran against Jimmy Carter—and won handsomely.

In fact, he could hardly have lost. Throughout the year, South Africa had been under rising pressure from both Britain and the U.S. to moderate its policy of apartheid. In October, following a crackdown by the Vorster government on dissident individuals, organizations and newspapers, the U.N. had voted a mandatory arms embargo on South Africa for the first time, and both the U.S. and Britain had supported the move. For the present, South Africa is virtually self-sufficient in the production of arms. But the boycott was a signal to Pretoria that the U.N., and particularly the West, was determined to take a firmer line with South Africa from now on.

Seizing on the issue, Vorster called on his Afrikaner constituents, sometimes known as the "white tribe of Africa," to fight for their birthright against the whole world if necessary. Said he: "There are those in the world outside who believe they can bring South Africa to its knees with a mandatory arms boycott. I tell them they have another guess coming." Opposition M.P. Helen Suzman derided Vorster's call for South African whites to march forward together. "It will be for-ward together over the cliff and into the sea," said she, "like a lot of lemmings." But the strategy proved exceedingly effective. In the biggest victory in the 29 years it has ruled South Africa, the National Party won 134 of the 165 seats in the new Parliament (an increase of 17) and 65% of the popular vote. The puny opposition led by the Progressive Federal Party elected a mere 17. Significantly, Vorster's party increased its support among English-speaking whites from 18% in 1974 to more than 30% this time. As usual, South Africa's blacks, Asians and mixed-race coloreds—who make up 85% of the nation's population—were not allowed to vote at all.

The election gave Vorster what he considered a mandate to proceed with his plan to preserve white rule. That plan features the abolition of the present Westminster-style parliamentary system and its replacement by three communal "parliaments"—one each for the 4.3 million whites, the 2.5 million coloreds and the 750,000 Asians. These, in turn, would nominate representatives to a Council of Cabinets, which would choose the President (presumably Vorster) and make national policy. Since the council would have an entrenched white majority, the coloreds and Asians would have a voice in the government but no real power.

At the same time, the government was proceeding with its grand design of establishing nine "independent" tribal homelands for the nation's 18.6 million blacks. The first of these homelands, the Transkei, was granted its nominal independence in 1976 (no nation officially recognizes it except South Africa); the second, BophuthaTswana, followed in December 1977. Under the homelands scheme, all blacks would eventually be assigned citizenship in one of these remote territories, even though half the blacks live permanently in "white" South Africa. If every black in the country were to move to his ancestral homeland, 70% of the population would be packed into 13% of the land, much of it arid and unprofitable. In reality, urban blacks would stay right where they are—except that they would be permanently written out of the country's political system.

Vorster's 1977 campaign slogan was the same as it had been in 1974: "He made South Africa safe. Keep it that way." But that safety seems increasingly uncertain. The student-inspired riots that broke out in June of 1976 in the sprawling black township of Soweto, near Johannesburg, have continued sporadically, taking more than 600 lives. Throughout much of 1977, hundreds of thousands of black students boycotted their classes.

Vorster's police struck back hard. The pre-election crackdown involved 60 arrests and the closing of two newspapers. In September, Black Consciousness Leader Stephen Biko, 30, died mysteriously in a South African prison. At first the government implied that he had died from the effects of a hunger strike; later, that he had bumped his head against a wall while scuffling with security police. An inquest in Pretoria, which took on the appearance of a political trial, turned up ample evidence that Biko had been mistreated while in police custody. "There is indisputable evidence," declared the eloquent attorney for Biko's family, Sydney Kentridge, "that on the morning of Sept. 6 Mr. Biko went into the interro-

Campaigning Prime Minister John Vorster

Stephen Biko's coffin being carried by angry supporters
The court ruled that no official could be singled out for blame.

gation room alive and well. On the morning of the 7th he came out a physical and mental wreck." Testimony also disclosed that the mortally injured Biko, naked and manacled, had then been driven 750 miles to a prison hospital on the day before he died. Nonetheless, the magistrate, Martinus Prins, ruled that Biko's death could not be attributed to "any criminal act or omission by any person."

The one inescapable change since Prime Minister Vorster took his stand against change has been the disappearance of the buffer regimes that once stood between South Africa and black Africa. Angola and Mozambique now have left-ist black governments, Rhodesia is crumbling, and even Namibia (Southwest Africa), which Pretoria acquired under a League of Nations mandate in 1920, is destined for independence, possibly in 1978. Is South Africa's white leadership capable of adapting to the new realities? Many South Africans are skeptical—and worried. Said Leon Rousseau, a leading Afrikaans publisher in Cape Town: "Three years ago, I hoped for a national change of heart, a spirit of repentance ... There was no miracle, and we may well be doomed. I foresee a very long period of near warfare, which South Africa could never win." ∎

RHODESIA

The Hour Is Late

The question is no longer whether—but when

"**N**o one can deny that Rhodesians are united," declared a jubilant Ian Smith. In snap elections that the Rhodesian Prime Minister had called for Aug. 31, the virtually all-white electorate gave his Rhodesian Front Party a resounding victory. The Front received 86% of the popular vote and won all 50 of the parliamentary seats reserved for the country's 268,000 whites (the 6.4 million blacks have 16 seats).

Smith's purpose in calling the elections was to head off a challenge by the right-wing Rhodesian Action Party, which had been formed earlier in the year by a dozen M.P.s who defected from the Front. The new party accused Smith of preparing a "capitulation" to some sort of black majority rule. In the old days, that sort of campaign would have worked magic with the Rhodesian voters. But times have changed; the Action Party drew only 9% of the vote. The hour is late in white Rhodesia, and the voters decided to stick with the man they still refer to as "good old Smithy" to the end.

If nothing else, the vote showed that most white Rhodesians had at last accepted the fact that the solution to the country's continuing crisis lies in some kind of negotiated settlement—and not in an intensification of the five-year-old guerrilla war. "I believe Rhodesians are prepared to [make a] move," declared Smith, "but not in the direction of a sellout."

What Ian Smith had in mind was an "internal solution"—meaning a multiracial compromise between the whites and some of the more moderate African leaders, notably Bishop Abel Muzorewa and the Rev. Ndabaningi Sithole, both of whom had returned from exile and were again living inside Rhodesia. Muzorewa may well be the country's most popular black leader, but he has no guerrilla faction to reinforce his position. Both he and Sithole were afraid of being branded as traitors to the African cause, and both said they would refuse to join the "broader based" Cabinet that Smith proposed as a first step toward settlement.

What Smith was most anxious to avoid, if he could, was any participation in the new government by the Patriotic Front, headed by Robert Mugabe and Joshua Nkomo, whose supporters are waging guerrilla war from bases in Mozambique and Zambia. Both Britain and the U.S. argued that the guerrilla groups, whose fighting had brought Rhodesia to the point of crisis, would have to be included if the negotiations were to work.

In late August, the U.S. and Britain proposed a new plan calling for a ceasefire and a six-month transition toward the creation of a black-ruled Zimbabwe, the African name for Rhodesia. During this period, the country would revert to its legal status as a British colony. A London-appointed administrator, Field Marshal Sir Richard Michael Carver, would organize a constitutional conference and would oversee elections based on universal adult suffrage. A U.N. peace-keeping force would help maintain order during the interim. Finally, a development fund of at least $1 billion, contributed partly by the U.S. and Britain, would help finance the new government.

Though Ian Smith did not reject the new plan immediately, it was far from the settlement he wanted. Then, in late November, he suddenly announced that he was now prepared to accept black majority rule, based on universal adult suffrage, in return for some sort of constitutional guarantees for whites under a future black government. From his base in Zambia, Joshua Nkomo said angrily: "As far as we are concerned, the war continues." But Moderates Muzorewa and Sithole were pleased with Smith's concession and agreed to attend preliminary talks.

Within hours, however, the mood changed as black leaders learned that Rhodesian armed forces had struck a severe blow against guerrillas operating out of neighboring Mozambique, killing 1,200 guerrillas. Mozambique officials said that nearly 100 women and children died in two bombing raids. Bishop Muzorewa immediately denounced Salisbury's military operations as "abhorrent massacres" that would "adversely prejudice" the talks. He also proclaimed a week of mourning for the raids' victims, whom he described as

Rhodesian trooper conducts interrogation under a midday sun
"No Rhodesian worth his salt will run away."

"mostly men, women and children who fled from the land of their birth to seek asylum." For the moment, at least, that ended Ian Smith's chances of securing a quick settlement.

In the meantime, a white exodus was continuing. Thousands of whites packed up, sold their houses for whatever they could get, and joined what Rhodesians called "the chicken run" to South Africa or Europe. In 1974, Wickus De Kock, then the Minister of Security, had declared: "No Rhodesian worth his salt will run away from the terrorist cowards." Three years later, disapproving of Smith's negotiations toward black rule, De Kock himself took the chicken run to South Africa. "I have certain convictions," he said. "I also have a life to lead." ∎

UGANDA

Faces in the Freezer

When people disappear, it means they are dead

In the house of Uganda's President for Life, Field Marshal Idi Amin Dada, 49, there is said to be a freezer that contains the heads of Daddy's most distinguished victims: a chief justice, an archbishop, a wide assortment of cabinet ministers. From time to time, the story goes, Amin walks over to the freezer, opens it and lectures his frozen audience about the evils of their ways. Apocryphal though it may be, the story reveals the state of terror that exists today in that beautiful East African country beside Lake Victoria.

"I finally fled," said a high-level Ugandan civil servant who sought refuge in nearby Kenya, "not because I was in trouble or because of anything I did, but out of sheer fear. People disappear, and when they disappear, it means they are dead."

Killer and clown, buffoon and martinet, Amin created crises of various kinds throughout most of the year. In February, he staged a giant rally in Kampala, the Ugandan capital, at which several "suspects" in the latest alleged plot against Amin's government were ordered to read their "confessions." Suddenly one of the suspects implicated three of the distinguished members of the audience: the Most Rev. Janani Luwum, 53, the Anglican Archbishop of Uganda; Internal Affairs Minister Charles Oboth-Ofumbi; and Land and Water Resources Minister Erinayo Oryema. The Archbishop shook his head in astonishment as he heard himself described as an agent of the exiled President A. Milton Obote, whom Amin deposed in a 1971 coup. Soldiers cried, "Kill them," but Amin righteously insisted that the accused be given a "proper military trial."

The three were never seen alive again. Next day Radio Uganda announced that they had been killed in an automobile accident while trying to escape. The accident, said Amin, was "a punishment of God." Some of the facts became known later in the year after Amin's Health Minister Henry Kyemba fled to Britain. In reality, said Kyemba (who subsequently published a fascinating account of his experiences in Amin's Uganda, *A State of Blood*), the Archbishop and the two ministers were killed by Amin's secret police; their bodies were riddled by bullets, said Kyemba, who saw them the following day. In a clumsy effort to conceal the truth, Amin forbade the families of the dead men to inspect their bodies before burial, and posted guards at their graves thereafter.

The news of the Archbishop's mysterious death led President Jimmy Carter to remark, at a Washington press conference, that the recent events in Uganda had "disgusted the entire civilized world." Furious, Big Daddy struck back: he ordered the 200 Americans living in Uganda—most of them missionaries, along with a few oil company and airline employees—not to try to leave the country. Then he sent his soldiers out to round them up, together with their "chickens, goats, pigs or any other animals."

As Big Daddy had hoped, the U.S. blinked. The State Department set up the usual operations center; the Pentagon sent warships to stand by off the East African coast. Amin let it be known that he merely wanted to meet the Americans to "reassure them that nothing will happen to them." As a leading Ugandan exile in Tanzania observed: "He always acts the same way. He threatens a group of foreigners; then he says everything is O.K.

Uganda's Field Marshal Idi Amin Dada, President for Life
He makes foreign governments dance back and forth.

ABBAS—SIPA, BLACK STAR

Then he threatens them again; then he says everything is O.K. The foreign government dances back and forth—and everyone forgets about the thousands of Ugandans who are dying."

As reports of Amin's atrocities continued—estimates of the number of Ugandans who have been killed since Amin came to power run as high as 300,000—the British government wondered nervously whether Amin would insist on attending the Commonwealth Conference in June. Finally Prime Minister James Callaghan bluntly wrote Amin that his presence there would be "inappropriate" because of the continuing bloodshed in Uganda. But Amin would not take that. Of course he would attend, declared Big Daddy, and he would bring a retinue of 250 people, including his "Heartbeat of Africa" dance troupe. Amin winked to reporters and told them that he was actually on very close terms with the Queen. In fact, said Amin, smacking his lips, "We knew each other even before Philip knew her. I know her better than anybody."

On the eve of the conference, Radio Uganda announced that Amin had left for London in "an aircraft loaned by a friendly country"—and that the 240 British residents would not be allowed to leave Uganda until the President had safely returned. For three days there were jittery reports that Amin's plane was about to land—in Rome, Lille, Dublin, Brussels. Several of the countries concerned announced that they would ban the unwanted visitor. Then Radio Uganda said he had arrived "secretly" in Britain and expected to be carried on his hosts' shoulders, "the way the black slaves were made to carry the whites in the colonial era." Sure enough, Big Daddy had been in Uganda all along.

The jokes continued sporadically. When Amin disappeared for two days, there were rumors of an attempted coup against him; but then his government announced that the President had merely been off on a "belated honeymoon" with his fifth wife Sarah. In September, there were reports that he had gone into a coma following surgery. "It looks serious," said an aide. Amin had undergone minor surgery that took three minutes to perform. But once again there was method to his apparent madness. The "coma" served to distract world attention from the execution of twelve Ugandans for plotting to overthrow him. "He is sane, very sane in some respects," remarked a prominent Ugandan who chose to go into exile during the year. "The important thing to him is to survive—and thus to eliminate all opposition." ∎

Rebel troops in Eritrea advance against Ethiopian government forces

Soviet Setback

Gored on the horn of Africa

The leftist junta in Ethiopia, which overthrew the late Emperor Haile Selassie in 1974, is in the unenviable position of being on the losing end of the two hottest wars in the world today. After ten years of fighting for independence in the arid northern province of Eritrea, a force of some 25,000 insurgents has gained control of more than three-quarters of the province—almost everything, in fact, except the provincial capital of Asmara and the port cities of Massawa and Assab. In the Ogaden desert, which is officially ruled by Ethiopia but inhabited almost solely by ethnic Somalis, some 5,000 to 7,000 guerrillas backed and armed by Somalia to the east have captured virtually everything except the Ethiopian strongholds of Harar and Dire Dawa. Their goal: to merge the Ogaden into Somalia.

If Ethiopia is defeated in both its desert wars, it will lose nearly half its territory, its access to the sea, and 6 million of its 28 million people. Faced with the possible disintegration of the Ethiopian empire, the unstable junta in Addis Ababa hastily began last spring to recruit a ragtag, 200,000-strong "people's militia." For weaponry the Ethiopians turned to a newly found friend, the Soviet Union, which responded with $100 million worth of jet fighters, heavy artillery, rocket launchers and other arms. Eventually that equipment could well affect the outcome of the war.

Inevitably, the price the Soviets had to pay for their generosity to the Ethiopian junta was their 15-year friendship with Somalia, a much smaller (pop. 3.2 million) though strategically placed ally. In November, the angry Somalis renounced their friendship treaty with the Soviet Union. They demanded that the Russians vacate the Soviet-built naval base at Berbera on the Gulf of Aden, and they expelled the last 1,500 Soviet military and civilian advisers out of a force that had once numbered 4,000 and threatened to dominate the horn of East Africa. That left just seven Soviet diplomats in Somalia—the exact size of the Somali embassy staff in Moscow. Explained a Somali official: "Our brothers were being killed by bullets supplied by people who said they were our friends." ∎

Nobel Prizes

Did one come too late?

When the Nobel Peace Prize Committee in Oslo announced in 1976 that it would give no prize, Norwegians were prepared. An alliance of newspapers and civic groups had already begun a campaign for a "People's Peace Prize." Donations of $324,000 were awarded to Betty Williams and Mairead Corrigan of Belfast, the Catholic founders of the Community of Peace People who had stirred the world with their pleas for an end to sectarian bloodshed in Northern Ireland.

The Nobel Committee had not overlooked the women; their crusade had not begun until August 1976, long after the deadline for nominations. Last fall, accordingly, the committee announced two peace prizes. Corrigan, 33, and Williams, 34, were named winners of the $140,000 prize for 1976. The $146,000 prize for 1977 went to Amnesty International, the London-based human rights organization dedicated to freeing political prisoners and ending the use of torture around the world. Northern Ireland has been one of AI's many targets.

While AI has grown steadily in numbers and reputation, the Community of Peace People lost rather than gained visibility during the past year. Ciaran McKeown, an ex-journalist who became the chief ideologue of the movement, switched its emphasis from massive peace marches toward projects of "community democracy" aimed at healing the hatreds between Northern Ireland's 900,000 Protestants and its nearly 600,000 Roman Catholics. "When the movement started, it was only emotion," Corrigan observed. "Now it is hard work." Among projects McKeown favors are efforts to find housing and jobs to dissuade people from terrorism.

The two peace women also point out a heartening statistic: since their crusade began 17 months ago, violence in Northern Ireland has been cut in half. But it is by no means gone. By Christmas, 68 civilians and 43 security force members had died at the hands of terrorists in 1977. ∎

Clash at DMZ

After 24 years, it's still lethal

The helicopter flight was a routine mission from Camp Humphreys, a U.S. base 40 miles south of Seoul, to a supply depot near the eastern edge of the Demilitarized Zone (DMZ) in South Korea. Somewhere near its destination, the unarmed, twin-engine CH-47 Chinook went astray. The helicopter's four-man crew, Presidential Press Secretary Jody Powell later said, apparently made "a navigational mistake" that carried it over the DMZ into North Korean airspace.

Apparently confused, the pilot, Chief Warrant Officer Joseph Miles, 26, continued on, landed briefly in North Korean territory, then started to take off. North Korean troops, approaching the aircraft, shot it down. Miles, Sergeant Robert Haynes, 29, and Sergeant Ronald Wells, 22, were killed. The sole survivor, Chief Warrant Officer Glenn Schwanke, 28, was captured by the North Koreans.

Thus, last July, began another tense confrontation in a series of border skirmishes that have long plagued the DMZ. In 24 years, 54 Americans and more than a thousand North and South Koreans have died in border incidents. In contrast to some past alarums, however, Washington's reaction to the downing of the Chinook was low-key. "Any penetration of North Korean airspace," said Powell, "was unintentional and regrettable."

The North Koreans responded with uncharacteristic restraint. Survivor Schwanke and the bodies of the three dead crewmen were forthwith turned over to the U.S. The North Koreans' behavior was clearly dictated by Pyongyang's concern that no incident disturb President Carter's plan to pull out the last remaining 30,000 U.S. ground forces from South Korea by 1982. The U.S. Second Division's crack front-line units are now deployed all along the DMZ.

Critics have warned that a pullout invites invasion. Indeed, Major General John Singlaub, third-ranking U.S. officer in Korea, was ousted by Carter last May for issuing just such a warning. The warnings may have had their effect, however. By the year's end Carter had postponed plans to withdraw two brigades until 1982, and Congress has been opposing the removal of any troops at all. ∎

Ice sheathes car after water-main break in Detroit

At the Mercy of the Elements

Arctic winds and blizzards mark the coldest winter in years

"We should not start worrying about an ice age," a climatologist at Columbia University's Lamont Observatory remarked. But in the Great Winter of '77 the long view did not seem especially reassuring. The environment had suddenly turned hostile, and in the Midwest, the Northeast and even the once sunny South, many Americans thought they knew only too well what the cutting edge of a new ice age might be like.

One day in January, for example, in Fort Walton Beach, Fla., an astonished judge named Clyde Wells stopped a trial so that prisoner and jury alike could enjoy a once-in-a-lifetime view of white flakes floating down from the sky. Floridians are not used to snow. Nor to the cold—as low as 32° F. in Miami Beach —which froze a third of the state's orange crop and increased the price of frozen orange juice up North by a third.

In the North, where nobody thinks of nature as benign, and everybody is familiar with antifreeze, snow tires, frostbite and the cold glare of heating bills, most people had never seen—or felt —anything like it. In the Midwest and Northeast January of 1977 was the coldest month on record since the Federal Government began collecting such statistics in 1870. Penetrating cold, day after day, ate up fuel supplies and played hob with the economy, turning busy waterfront piers into grotesque, ice-caked headlands where no ships moved, transforming urban-ghetto buildings into frozen grottoes where men and women sometimes

died for want of food and fuel. Wave on wave of snow kept piling up, burying cars, isolating homes, blocking the routes of buses and ambulances and fire trucks, closing schools and businesses and factories for days at a stretch. Hardly had the deep chill struck when the state of Connecticut discovered it had already used 48,000 tons of road salt—half of the

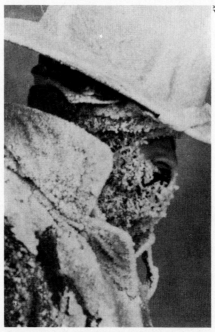

Fireman in subzero Indianapolis
Nature's prelude to a new ice age?

winter's supply—and by the middle of January. When it was over, hardy New Englanders totted up and found they had paid out an average of $182.70 more for oil per household than ever before, just to keep from freezing.

In Chicago the temperature dropped to −19° F., the coldest weather that cold city had endured in 100 years. The broad, brown, meandering Mississippi froze, blocking shipping for hundreds of miles at a stretch. So did the Ohio. On the Great Lakes, where boat traffic all but stopped, the ice was a foot thick eight miles out from shore. Buffalo, a windy city beside Lake Erie, found itself buried for days in back-to-back blizzards. Snow lay 14 ft. deep on the level, and where fierce north winds had sculpted it, sometimes swooped up to drifted peaks as high as 30 ft. After one blizzard, 17,000 workers were trapped for the night in their offices unable to go home. Some 5,000 cars disappeared under drifts. Twenty-two people froze to death. It took a presidential order and Army units, airlifting in snow blowers and trucks from as far away as North Carolina, to dig Buffalo out.

The cold clung with devastating tenacity, just at a time when the nation was in the process of slowly digging itself out from a deep economic recession. It struck in the midst of a fuel shortage that had first set in during the 1973-74 oil embargo and threatened to be with America for decades. Dependence on an intricate, advanced technology, and on foreign fuel, made America's cities all the more vulnerable. Eleven states became "disaster areas." "The weather," a Senate energy expert observed, "is going to be to the natural gas industry what the Arab embargo was for oil."

Some companies began to switch to coal—even the sulfurous kind now barred by antiair-pollution laws—just to stay open. Others were cut back to a rationed 50° F. of heat, or simply had to close down, laying off their share of the 200,000 men put out of work by the weather. Ohio was among the hardest hit. The Cincinnati Gas and Electric Company alone had nearly 4 million gal. of needed fuel marooned for days on barges that remained frozen in the Mississippi and the Ohio.

Sharing hardships, Americans were often kinder to one another. A utility company in Rochester actually gave all its 153,600 regular customers a $10 rebate on their soaring fuel bills. In cold and sickness and isolation, families fell back on one another and often found a new warmth, a deeper knowledge of inner resources. That, plus the clear message that the whole country is at the mercy of the elements, and in a kind of economic bondage to the chronic energy shortage, seemed to be a useful legacy of the Great Winter of '77. ■

In Summer Comes Drought

Lack of rainfall in the West damages crops, kills cattle

"**M**aybe Mother Nature is trying to tell us something," commented University of Nebraska Political Scientist Robert Miewald as he contemplated the extremes of weather in 1977. But if there was a message, it was hard to decipher. While the freezing citizens east of the Rockies were busy praying for winter to let up, those west of the Rocky Mountains were longing for snow in the hills.

In some Northwestern states as much as three-quarters of the year's water supply—and 15% of local hydroelectric power as well—comes from the spring runoff from mountain snow. In 1977 little snow fell in the West. By February, on Oregon's Mount Hood the customary 143 in. of snow at 6,000 ft. stood at only 21 in. The average runoff proved 40% to 60% less than usual. The West was notably short on rainfall, too. So when spring came, while the Eastern half of the country was drowning in runoff floods from heavy snows, the West was already in the grip of a costly and debilitating drought that deepened as the summer wore on.

Drought and freeze alike were due to a single meteorological quirk, an unusual high-pressure, warm air mass that lingered off the California coast for weeks at a time. Just by being there, it diverted the high-level westerly winds—including the jet stream—which normally carry winter weather in a direct west-east flow across the continent. Blocked by the high, they swept north toward Alaska, then back south again, to move diagonally south and east, freezing the rest of the country. On their way, they crossed the Rockies so far north that most of the Mountain States failed to get a normal share of snow and storms—and water.

Millions of acres of Western land grew parched and unfruitful. By March, from Nebraska down to the Texas panhandle, the worst dust storms in 20 years billowed dry particles of earth 12,000 ft. in the air, turning the skies a dark, sullen yellow, cutting visibility so sharply that highways were closed off. In Colorado such blasts swirled across the land at speeds up to 90 m.p.h., tossing drought-parched topsoil into the air—as much as five tons of it off a single acre during one fierce 24-hour blow.

In some states, the lack of moisture and a light covering of snow set back the winter wheat crop badly. In others, cattlemen seemed hardest hit. Grazing land turned to dust, forcing farmers to sell thin stock at low prices or to fatten them on expensive, trucked-in grain. Prices stayed low. "We're practically giving away cattle," one farmer complained. In Washington 25 of the state's 39 counties were designated disaster areas. In parts of Oregon water holes shrank to muddy pits, where cows bogged down and died when they tried to drink.

The greatest threat to crops was expected in California, for the state uses nearly 85% of its water on agribusiness. Partly as a result, it grows 40% of the country's fresh fruits and vegetables. In the spring, as the chronic drought deepened and no rain fell, a loss of more than $1.5 billion in the state's $9.5 billion-a-year output was predicted. In fact, less than a $750,000 loss occurred. Despite the lack of water, Californians skillfully managed to grow almost as many edibles as usual, resorting to long-established drought-defying techniques—like the systematic reprocessing of waste water and the orchestration of irrigation programs.

They also practiced a kind of painful person-to-person conservation. By August Los Angeles and 67 other cities were on mandatory water rationing. With volunteer efforts helping, too, domestic water use was cut 23% in Los Angeles alone. Zealots dropped the use of ice cubes. Horticulturists urged folks to abandon beautiful but moisture-guzzling flowers like gardenias and camellias in favor of the prickly but economy-minded cactus. Especially in Marin County, the overpopulated and underwatered part of northern California, citizens became experts at calculating, and avoiding, water-costly habits: a full bathtub (36 gal.), a lavish shower (25 gal.), an average sloppy family dishwashing (up to 30 gal.), a flushed toilet (7 gal.). And anyone who went over his normal allotment found himself billed for any extra water used at $50 to $100 per cu. ft. One small Marin County ice-cream parlor received a two-month water bill for a cool $2,400.

Climate experts are now about divided as to whether the earth will soon (say in 20,000 years) get a degree or two colder —the first sign of a new ice age—or a degree or two hotter, which will start melting the polar icecap faster and might eventually drown much of the world. But experts reassuringly agree that neither trend had much to do with the fire and ice of 1977. Meanwhile, woolly bears and weathermen have stayed busy predicting yet another supercold start to 1978. ■

Dried-up marina at edge of receding Folsom Lake near Sacramento typified drought conditions in much of the West

With water rationed, some Californians gave up ice cubes while others swapped camellias for cacti.

53

Protesting diabetics arrive in Washington aboard the "saccharin special"

Bittersweet Blow

Debate rages over a saccharin ban

"**A**nybody who says saccharin is injurious to health is an idiot." That harsh assessment, made 70 years ago by Theodore Roosevelt during an earlier debate over the artificial sweetener, was loudly echoed by many Americans last year. The reason: The Food and Drug Administration's announcement on March 9 that it intended to ban saccharin, the last noncaloric sweetener still available in the U.S. since cyclamates were outlawed in 1970, as a suspected cause of cancer. Angry protests flooded into Congress, ranging from beverage bottlers to drug and cosmetic firms (which use the stuff in lipsticks, mouthwashes, cough syrups, toothpaste), from diabetics to dieters.

Confronted by this clamor, Congress postponed the ban until 1979. During this 18-month period of further testing, all products containing saccharin that are shipped in interstate commerce will have to carry a cancer warning.

The FDA has long been concerned about saccharin, a coal-tar derivative. In 1972 it actually removed the product from its "generally recognized as safe" list and warned manufacturers to limit its use. But the clincher finally came in March with the completion of a study by Canadian health authorities. For three years, they had fed rats daily doses of saccharin equivalent to 5% of their diet by weight. In the first generation, three out of 38 male rats developed malignant bladder tumors; in the second, eight of

45. Citing a 1958 law known as the Delaney Clause, which prohibits any food additive that causes cancer in animals or man, Acting FDA Commissioner Sherwin Gardner announced that "science and law dictate that saccharin be removed from food."

Critics were quick to dispute the importance of the animal tests, noting that humans would have had to drink 800 cans of diet soda a day from birth to match the rats' consumption of saccharin.

Only a few months after the Canadians' animal study, they produced more impressive human findings. In a survey of men with bladder cancer, they found that the incidence of the disease was 1.6 times greater among those who had used saccharin. On the other hand, several recent studies, notably those by the American Health Foundation and Johns Hopkins, have found no statistical relation between bladder cancer and the use of saccharin.

Many doctors, while acknowledging the possible risks in saccharin, argued that a ban might produce even worse results, not only among the nation's 10 million diabetics but also among many other Americans as well. If they were forced to satisfy their craving for sweets by sugar products alone, these critics contended, more people would become overweight, and there would be an increase in obesity-linked diseases, and in the nation's No. 1 killer, cardiovascular ailments. ∎

Laetrilemania

Victories—and setbacks—for the anticancer nostrum

Laetrile, a concoction derived from apricot pits, is considered a piece of quackery by virtually the entire medical establishment. Yet under intense lobbying pressure no fewer than 13 states (pop. 50 million) legalized the substance by the end of 1977 as an anticancer drug. Several federal court judges also endorsed the Laetrile campaign, allowing terminally ill cancer patients to import it from abroad, even though it was banned from interstate commerce by the Food and Drug Administration.

Over the years, there have been numerous animal tests of Laetrile, including a 4½-year study completed in 1977 at Manhattan's Memorial Sloan-Kettering Cancer Center. Scientists have found no acceptable evidence whatsoever that Laetrile or its major ingredient, amygdalin, a chemical containing cyanide and found in fruit pits, has any effect against tumors. Yet an estimated 75,000 Americans now are using the drug. Available in pills, capsules or injections, Laetrile is sold under various names—including vitamin B-17 —through a nationwide network of health food shops, pharmacies and a handful of dissident doctors as well as by the flourishing Laetrile clinics just across the border in Tijuana, Mexico. Typical prices: $20-$30 a shot.

Why the continued fascination with a substance so thoroughly discredited? In part, the answer lies in the very stubborn nature of cancer, a disease that now kills some 400,000 Americans a year. Even when it is successfully contained, the costly treatments—powerful drugs, radiation and sometimes mutilating surgery—seem to many people as bad as the disease itself. By contrast, Laetrile is portrayed as painless and cheap.

The enthusiasm for Laetrile also reflects a disturbing new mood in the U.S.: a deep-seated suspicion of all officially proclaimed wisdom, including what many people perceive as medicine's arrogant doctor-knows-best attitude. This mood helped to create a strange alliance of Laetrile supporters—John Birchers and civil libertarians, food faddists and cancer victims, who have joined under the evangelizing slogan, A FREEDOM OF CHOICE IN CANCER THERAPY. In Illinois, hundreds of Laetrilists besieged the state capitol with blue-and-white bumper stickers that read LAETRILE WORKS! YOU BET YOUR LIFE! In Massachusetts, lawmakers found themselves inundated with 40 shopping bags filled with the pleas of more than 12,000 people who demanded the drug's legalization.

Yet even as the pro-Laetrile forces scored their victories, the Government began counterattacking. In a 45,000-word report, the new FDA chief, Donald Kennedy, not only challenged the idea that Laetrile could help cancer patients, but also strongly disputed the idea that it was a harmless placebo. On the contrary, the FDA noted, several people had been poisoned by the cyanide in the drug. It also found that Laetrile imported from Mexico was sometimes contaminated.

Backing up the Government's new tough posture, U.S. marshals seized Laetrile and caches of apricot pits in five states. At one suspected plant in Wisconsin, they seized 12 tons of the stuff. And, as the year ended, the legislative tide began to turn. Though Illinois legalized Laetrile in late November, the drug had already encountered a major setback in the nation's two most populous states. New York's Governor Hugh Carey, whose wife died of cancer in 1974, successfully vetoed a Laetrile bill, calling the substance quackery. In California, a state where the Laetrile movement has been particularly strong, a Laetrile bill died in committee. The Laetrilists also ran into trouble on Capitol Hill. At a hearing convened by Massachusetts' Senator Edward Kennedy, whose son Teddy lost a leg to cancer, Laetrile leaders—among them Ernst T. Krebs Jr. of San Francisco, who with his late father first proposed the drug—could not even agree on the formula for the compound or how it worked.

In spite of these setbacks, Laetrile's supporters got a powerful year-end assist from the federal judiciary. In December, U.S. District Court Judge Luther Bohanon concluded that the Federal Government had no power to ban Laetrile from interstate commerce or deny patients the right to use it. The FDA announced it was appealing Bohanon's ruling. Thus at year's end one thing was clear: the battle over Laetrile would continue into 1978 and perhaps beyond. ∎

Laetrile Promoter Krebs
He wasn't sure how it worked.

The Fastidious Bug

Legionnaires' disease is traced to a mystery microbe

The rolling hills were already wrapped in their bright autumnal yellows, browns and reds, and the tourists were arriving by the carload. But at the Medical Center Hospital of Vermont in Burlington there was no time to take notice of the spectacular fall foliage. Doctors and nurs-

Legionnaire who survived Philadelphia outbreak giving blood sample
Some doctors believe the microbe may have killed 6,000.

es were struggling with an unaccountably large number of puzzling pneumonia cases. Chief of Medicine Dr. Harry Beaty recalls: "The patients looked as though they had bacterial pneumonia, but we could not isolate the organism that was causing it."

On a hunch, he sent off some blood samples to Atlanta's Center for Disease Control (CDC). There, his suspicions were soon confirmed: the ailing Vermonters proved to be suffering from Legionnaires' disease, the same ailment that had struck down hundreds of people—and caused 34 deaths—at a state American Legion convention in Philadelphia a year earlier.

At least 17 people died and a dozen others became gravely ill in the most serious known episode of Legionnaires' disease since Philadelphia. Yet the New England cases were hardly isolated. By year's end the CDC counted 231 victims of Legionnaires' disease spread over 34 states, with a loss of 55 lives.

These statistics underscored a startling discovery made earlier in the year: the dread fever was not an isolated, rare or even new ailment, but an existing form of pneumonia—inflammation of the lungs—that had somehow escaped earlier detection.

Trying to identify the disease, the CDC's detectives had considered everything from food poisoning to tiny micro-organisms called rickettsia (the cause of typhus and Rocky Mountain spotted fever). All to no avail. Then Microbiologist Joseph E. McDade had an inspiration. Re-examining some microscope slides of infected tissue that he and his colleagues had already studied, he spotted a cluster of unfamiliar rod-shaped micro-organisms. Culturing the bugs from preserved lung tissue in lab animals and eggs, he found that they were indeed infectious —and killers.

Turning to still other blood samples —some of them preserved from unexplained earlier outbreaks—the scientists discovered that the same lethal bug had apparently been at the root of a mysterious, pneumonia-like disease that killed at least 12 people at St. Elizabeths psychiatric hospital in Washington, D.C., in 1965. It also seems to have been the cause of a puzzling fever at a Pontiac, Mich., health center in 1968. Most remarkably, the bacterium had also apparently struck a 1974 Odd Fellows convention in the same Philadelphia hotel (since closed) where the Legionnaires met.

Doctors now know that erythromycin is the most effective antibiotic against the still-unnamed microbe. But they still do not know how it spreads (fortunately, it does not seem to move easily from person to person), where it lives in nature, or why it is so lethal. Says McDade: "It is a fastidious bug: hard to grow, but then hard to kill." One thing seems certain: it has been around a long time and done considerable damage. In fact, CDC Chief Dr. William Foege estimates that it may be the cause of as many as 6,000 deaths a year in the U.S. alone. ∎

Fears of Frankenstein

Perils and promise of DNA research

Ever since scientists first "cracked" the genetic code and determined the structure of life's master molecule, DNA, many have feared that science could misuse that knowledge. Some believed that genetic research should actually be forbidden. Others, recognizing that experimentation was inevitable, conjured up Faustian visions of scientists creating monsters in their test tubes.

Such worries were once purely theoretical, but they acquired a focus in the early 1970s, when researchers began planning to take snippets of DNA—from humans, other animals and plants—and slip them into the genetic material of a bacterium known as *Escherichia coli*. The bacteria would then obligingly treat the new DNA as if it were their own, following its instructions and producing whatever it directed. Advocates of such recombinant DNA research insist that their work could ultimately lead to a better understanding of the whole process of cell growth and result in new ways to produce the drugs and hormones used in the treatment of such diseases as diabetes and hemophilia. Critics are not convinced. Noting that *E. coli* is a common intestinal organism, they are concerned that researchers might inadvertently create new and possibly dangerous forms of life against which humanity might have no resistance.

This concern first came to a head in the scientific community in 1971 when Robert Pollack, then at New York's Cold Spring Harbor Biological Laboratory, learned that researchers at Stanford Medical Center planned to insert a monkey virus into *E. coli*. He and others called the Stanford researchers to express their concern about the potential risks of such an experiment. Their questions led the Stanford team to cancel its plans. But other work continued. By 1974 worry about recombinant DNA research had become so widespread that a group of experimenters asked the National Institutes of Health to establish guidelines on the issue. NIH accepted the assignment and drew up a strict set of standards designed to safeguard researchers and the public. But its action did not prevent the debate from spreading. Newspapers that had previously paid little attention to the story erupted with scare headlines like MAN-MADE BACTERIA COULD RAVAGE EARTH.

In 1976, Mayor Alfred Vellucci of Cambridge, Mass., convened his city council and proposed a two-year ban on

All Aboard for Space

Traveling to space will probably never be as easy as catching a commuter train, but the dream has moved a step closer to reality. NASA's new space shuttle—a DC-9-size bird designed to be launched like a rocket and landed on a runway like an overweight glider—proved its airworthiness. Next year, if all goes according to schedule, the shuttle will take an even greater step and make its first round-trip flight to space.

The shuttle program got a go-ahead in 1972 when President Nixon approved a plan to build up to five airplane-like orbiters, each of which could fly at least 100 missions before being retired. But the program really got into gear early last year when Rockwell International completed the first such orbiter, a 122-ft.-long delta-winged craft christened *Enterprise* after the ship in the popular television series *Star Trek*.

Enterprise started its own star trek slowly. In January the completed craft was hauled across California's Mojave Desert from the Rockwell plant in Palmdale to NASA's Dryden Flight Research Center at Edwards Air Force Base, a 36-mile journey that took all day at the stately speed of 3 m.p.h. There it was "mated" to its carrier ship, a converted Boeing 747, and given six months of preliminary tests. By August the *Enterprise* was ready to fly on its own. Shortly after dawn, the 747 raced down the runway and took off with its burden—containing Pilot Fred Haise Jr. and Co-Pilot Charles Gordon Fullerton. Then, at 27,000 ft., the 747 flew over an imaginary hump and nosed downward to pick up speed. As it did, Haise triggered the three explosive bolts holding the ships together. While the 747 pulled down and to the left, *Enterprise* rose buoyantly up and to the right.

The stubby-winged orbiter weighs as much as 40 Chevrolet sedans, and it was completely powerless, as it will be on its return from orbit, but the maiden flight went beautifully. After a couple of maneuvers to evaluate *Enterprise's* handling characteristics, Haise and Fullerton executed two 90° turns to align their ship with the runway, then brought it in. Two minutes later, *Enterprise* touched down at a speed of 210 m.p.h. and rolled more than two miles down the dry lake bed to a gentle stop. "It flies like a good fighter," said Fullerton. "It was very crisp and stable."

NASA officials are even more excited about the shuttle, which could revolutionize the way the U.S.—and the rest of the world—uses space. At present, satellites and other payloads must be put into orbit by means of expensive rockets that are themselves consumed in the process. But the shuttle should change this practice. "This is a space transportation system that will allow us to put things in and out of space easily and relatively inexpensively," said Donald ("Deke") Slayton, a veteran of the 1975 Apollo-Soyuz U.S.-Soviet spaceflight who is the approach-and-landing-test manager for the shuttle. "It's an all-purpose truck to haul things into space."

The *Enterprise* will spend most of 1978 at Marshall Space Center in Huntsville, Ala., undergoing further vibration tests. Then, according to the schedule, one of *Enterprise's* sister ships will take its first flight into space. As early as March 1979, the orbiter could rise from Cape Canaveral attached to two solid-fuel booster rockets and a tank of liquid propellant. Twenty-eight miles up, the boosters will fall into the Atlantic, where a tugboat will recover them. A few minutes later, just short of orbit, the liquid fuel tank, which will not be recycled, will also separate and plunge into the ocean, leaving the shuttle on its own.

The shuttle is not expected to stay in space long on its first flight, which may be as short as two or three revolutions of the earth. On its second flight, the orbiter will carry six experiments designed to be performed in space. On its fifth, it might rendezvous with Skylab, which has been empty since early 1974, and affix a rocket to the space station. That would boost the station into a higher orbit and prevent it from falling back to earth and burning up in the atmosphere. By the mid-1980s, say NASA officials, the shuttle should be flying into space at a rate that will eventually reach one trip a week. The flights, for which reservations are already being taken, should open up space to everybody. It takes only two to fly the orbiter, which contains accommodations for seven. Any man or woman in reasonably good health could occupy one of the other five places. ∎

recombinant DNA research at Harvard and M.I.T. "Something could crawl out of the laboratory, such as a Frankenstein," warned Vellucci. He later backed off and suggested a three-month moratorium so the problem could be studied. The two institutions agreed to halt certain types of experiments while an eight-member review board studied the issue.

The Cambridge city council was not the only governmental body to consider regulating DNA research. The Health Subcommittee of the Senate's Committee on Labor and Public Welfare had also begun holding hearings in 1975 to determine what Congress could do to protect the public. As expected, critics like Biophysicist Robert Singsheimer argued that DNA research was potentially hazardous and could lead to the accidental development of uncontrollable organisms. But most witnesses insisted that the risks of such research were exaggerated, and a National Research Council panel supported them. Said an NRC study: "The body of evidence acquired or adduced over the past few years clearly indicates that recombinant DNA research, when performed under the NIH guidelines, presents no real risk to public health."

More important, there are indications that recombinant DNA research is on the verge of producing some real benefits. While testifying at hearings before the Senate's Subcommittee on Science, Technology and Space in November, National Academy of Sciences President Philip Handler revealed that California researchers had not only succeeded in splicing a man-made gene into a bacterium, but had actually used the altered microbe to make a copy of a mammalian brain hormone that could act biologically in humans.

An important step in this direction had already been taken last spring when scientists at the University of California at San Francisco succeeded in transplanting a rat insulin gene into the DNA of a strain of *E. coli* bred especially for such research and incapable of living outside the lab. The microbe then multiplied into duplicate bacteria, each containing the insulin gene though not able to make insulin. In the work announced in November, teams led by Microbiologist Herbert Boyer of the University of California at San Francisco and Biochemist Arthur Riggs of the City of Hope Medical Center near Los Angeles synthesized copies of the gene for somatostatin, a mammalian brain hormone that inhibits the secretion of pituitary growth hormone and insulin. Then they chemically inserted the genes into the DNA of *E. coli,* which multiplied and began manufacturing somatostatin, which may eventually prove useful in the treatment of diabetes.

The accomplishment was cited by proponents of DNA research as demonstrating its future benefits, and hailed by Handler as a "scientific triumph of the first order." There is no question about that, or about the hope that the development of this technique raises for producing less expensive hormones. The researchers who first isolated somatostatin needed nearly half a million sheep brains to produce 5 mg. (.00018 oz.) of the substance. Using their recombinant DNA method, the Californians produced the same amount with two gallons of bacterial culture. ∎

*ce orbiter **Enterprise** takes off aboard 747, separates from plane, lands safely*

Mixture of Growth and Unease

Expansion continues—so do inflation and unemployment

New York Stock Exchange suffering its sharpest downturn in 18 months
The market worried about taxes, interest, energy—and about worry itself.

By many standards, if not most, 1977 was a highly prosperous year for the U.S. The gross national product rose to a record $1.9 trillion; that increase, discounted for inflation, was a healthy 5%. Total personal income climbed 11%, and corporate profits after taxes were up by 12%. Yet in the midst of all this prosperity there were equally strong signs of doubt and anxiety. That was clear enough in the stock market, which dropped by roughly 17%, and on international currency exchanges, where the value of the dollar sank.

These contradictions threaded through the entire year, leaving policymakers as uncertain at the end as at the beginning. The chief novelty—in many key indicators—was the lack of novelty. At the end, as at the start, consumer spending was strong—witness a 12% jump in Christmas sales over the 1976 season—but business investment in new plant and equipment was still lagging. Consequently, after more than 2½ years of recovery from the 1973-75 recession, the unemployment rate was still painfully high. At 6.9% in November, it was about a point lower than a year earlier —but all the drop occurred in the early months of 1977; the rate hardly changed at all after May. Nor was there any substantial improvement in the basic rate of inflation. Despite ups and downs, it was still around 6% to 6½% a year.

So the Carter Administration was caught in the same maze in which the Nixon and Ford Administrations had found themselves imprisoned: wanting to stimulate the economy to more job-creating growth but afraid that too much stimulation would only increase inflation. In the last months of 1977, Jimmy Carter and his aides were again debating exactly the same question that preoccupied them a year earlier: how big a tax cut should they recommend, and what kind? In January, they had settled on a proposal for a $50-per-person tax rebate, but that was hastily withdrawn in mid-April, when the economy seemed momentarily to be spurting ahead with almost too much vigor. This time they have decided to ask for permanent cuts in individual and corporate taxes totaling $25 billion a year, largely at the urging of Treasury Secretary W. Michael Blumenthal.

Will that do the job? The question is difficult because the answer involves not just economics but psychology. Carter must not only provide more spending money for consumers and corporate investors, he must overcome a spreading mood of unease among both businessmen and the general public.

Part of the unease came from what in the '50s would have been called "rolling readjustment"—while some industries went up, others went down. Some of the hardest-hit were those suffering from cut-price foreign competition: shoes, textiles, TV and electronics—above all, steel. As imports at times captured almost 20% of the U.S. market, steelmakers laid off 60,000 workers. Bethlehem Steel Corp., the nation's second largest producer, reported in the third quarter the worst three-month loss ever suffered by an American corporation: $477 million.

But for every disappointment there was a more-than-offsetting gain. Automakers pushed sales for the 1977 model year to nearly 11 million cars, not much under the 1973 record. General Motors joined A T & T as the second corporation ever to earn $1 billion profit in a single quarter. Homebuilding, which had only a moderate recovery in 1976, broke into an all-out boom. The annual rate of housing starts in six months topped 2 million, nearly equal to the best years of the early '70s. And though the unemployment rate remained high, payrolls rose by nearly 4 million people; the number of Americans holding jobs crossed the 90 million mark in the spring for the first time.

By standards of most other industrial countries, the progress of the U.S. economy in 1977 was enviable. Western Europe, for example, is struggling with lower growth rates (generally under 3%), and higher inflation rates (around 10%, on the average). That, indeed, is a major reason why the U.S. in 1977 ran a trade deficit of around $28 billion, nearly five times more than in 1976. Slower growth in other countries held down U.S. exports and gave Europeans and Japanese an extra incentive to sell in the American market.

Yet the malaise, the lack of confidence, is undeniable. The value of the dollar dropped steadily in foreign markets, falling more than 22% against the Swiss franc, for instance. The stock market, beset by worries about inflation, interest rates and potential problems resulting from new energy and tax proposals, dribbled down week after week. From a 1976 close of 1004.65 the Dow Jones industrial average fell more than 20%, to a November low of just over 800. Among the general public, a majority of people questioned in a Harris poll in October thought the U.S. is actually in a recession.

Why the pessimism? One reason is a perfectly justifiable feeling that the progress of the economy just is not good enough. Conservatives are dismayed that the inflation rate has not budged much since falling from more than 12% in 1974 to 6% by 1976. Liberals complain that two years of recovery from recession should have pushed the unemployment rate lower than 6.9%. In the words of Arthur Okun, a Brookings Institution senior fellow, "We have a single-size recovery from a double-size recession."

Another reason for unease is a fear

Former Federal Reserve Chairman Burns
Symbol of the fight against inflation.

that even the unsatisfactory recovery is heading for a slowdown. Not a new recession: economists can see no signs of the imbalances—swollen inventories, shortages, speculative excesses—that usually precede an actual downturn. But there is some worry that the growth rate of real G.N.P. in the second half of 1978 will drop to about 3%. If so, unemployment would surely start to rise again from its already too-high level.

Behind that fear lies a simple assessment: consumers are spending, but business is not. Consumers, so goes the theory, cannot reasonably be expected to increase their purchases of cars, houses and other goods much more rapidly than they are already doing; indeed, auto sales took a worrisome drop from mid-November on. If the economy is to get a new lift, it must come from business expansion and modernization of production capacity. But business spending for new plant and equipment started rising only about half as rapidly as in past periods of expansion. In 1977 it was going up at an annual rate of about 8%, discounted for inflation—still short of the 10% or more that is required. And a survey late in the year found executives planning only a slightly higher expansion rate for 1978.

Businessmen have many reasons for saying no—or wait. Inflation has made

them doubt that they can accurately assess future costs. The energy crisis that followed the 1973 Arab oil embargo causes them to worry whether they can find fuel to power a new factory, and at what price. Environmental regulations are diverting investment dollars from projects that could increase capacity into equipment to clean up the air and water around existing plants.

Another factor, and a major one, is that businessmen—like many other Americans—fear that the Carter Administration has shown a very unsure touch in dealing with the economy. There is considerable evidence to support that view. Take, for example, the Administration's waffling on inflation. Carter has disavowed wage-price controls or even guidelines, a stand that businessmen and labor leaders approve. Unfortunately, that leaves him with not much of a policy, and his case-by-case decisions on other matters are likely to make the inflation worse. The President has, for instance, signed into law a 45% increase in the minimum wage by 1981, increased farm-price supports, and negotiated "orderly marketing agreements" limiting the import of low-priced color-TV sets from Japan and shoes from the Far East; he also has raised tariffs on imported sugar. All these moves please powerful political constituencies, but all will raise living costs further.

On the tax front, the President promised an overall reform, then postponed it. As for specific steps, he has so far proposed a wellhead tax on crude oil and persuaded Congress to enact a huge boost in Social Security payroll taxes starting in 1979. Whatever the merits of these moves in promoting conservation and building up the depleted Social Security trust fund, they will drain billions in purchasing power out of the private economy, which needs more, and add to inflation as well.

Unfortunately, the problems of the economy today are complicated by factors that resist analysis. For example, the

DOW JONES
Industrials

1977 WEEKLY CLOSINGS

980
960
940
920
900
880
860
840
820
800
780
760
0

J F M A M J J A S O N D

TIME CHART BY NIGEL HOLMES

Federal Reserve Board, for reasons that few people seem fully to understand, has been unable to keep the nation's basic money supply from expanding far beyond its target range of 4% to 6½% a year. During a three-month period last summer the annual rate averaged 12%—a pace that, if continued, would have been highly inflationary. The Fed has been trying to throttle back by pushing up borrowing costs; the "prime" rate on bank loans to business has risen from 6¼% at the start

Treasury Secretary Blumenthal
How big a tax cut—and what kind?

of the year to 7¾%. Liberals—and the White House—fear that further increases could choke the very business growth that a tax cut would be designed to promote.

At year's end, Carter decided to dump Fed Chairman Arthur Burns, 73, who had become to conservatives a revered symbol of stubborn resistance to inflation, and to replace him with G. William Miller, 52, chairman of Textron Inc., one of the nation's first and most successful conglomerates. It was an adroit political move: liberals hailed the sacking of Burns, while many of Burns' business admirers welcomed Industrialist Miller as one of their own. But that does not solve the dilemma; Miller, whose views on monetary policy are largely unknown, must decide whether to let money supply go on increasing swiftly or push interest rates higher still.

Assuming a tax cut, the best that most economists can foresee for 1978 is an expansion of real G.N.P., starting out at about this year's rate and then slowing; a continuation of inflation at about the present 6% pace or a trifle faster—through sheer momentum, more than anything else—and a very gradual decline in unemployment, to perhaps 6.4% by year's end. That would make 1978, like 1977, a year of progress, though not altogether satisfactory progress.   — *George J. Church*

Obstructing Free Trade

New curbs in the U.S. and Europe

Free trade is supposed to benefit both trading partners by allowing them to complement each other's strengths. But during times of economic trouble, just the opposite of what should happen, happens. That is the case now.

Having never fully recovered from the 1973-75 recession, the world's industrialized economies are tilting away from free trade toward protectionism as a means of shielding domestic industries and jobs from foreign competition. While there may be some short-term gains, trade experts worry over the long-range impact. If the flow of goods across international boundaries really does slow significantly, they are convinced, unemployment and economic stagnation will worsen.

As of now, no nation has erected anything like the nearly insuperable import barriers that blocked trade during the Great Depression of the 1930s. However, many of them have established curb after curb to restrict trade in specific products. The nine-nation European Community, with more than 6 million jobless, has established higher minimum prices for imported steel and tighter quotas for foreign textiles. The U.S. has struck deals limiting imports of shoes and television sets, and the hard-hit U.S. steel industry has pleaded for, and got, some restrictions on Japanese and European imports that at times account for 20% of all steel sold in U.S. markets.

The Common Market—built on the idea of free trade, at least within its own borders—is entertaining other far-reaching protectionist schemes and labeling them with Orwellian euphemisms. One is "organized free trade," coined by French Premier Raymond Barre. It means negotiating import quotas during hard times. A U.S. variant of that idea is the "orderly marketing agreement" (OMA), which is emerging as one of the Carter Administration's responses to protectionist clamor. An OMA already exists for Japanese color television sets, limiting imports to 41% of the 1976 level. That action, announced last spring, did not help Zenith Radio Corp., the largest U.S. maker of TV sets. It plans to lay off 5,600 U.S. employees during the next year, because of competition from imports, and to transfer much of its color-set production to Taiwan and Mexico.

The Carter Administration is committed to free trade and is reluctant to impose more than a modicum of import restrictions. Foreign imports of cheaper autos, steel and textiles keep the pressure on domestic industries dominated by a

German steel being unloaded in Chicago

few large companies to become more efficient and more competitive. At the same time, cheaper imports help keep domestic inflation down and give low-income Americans more buying power. Any severe restriction on foreign goods could boost the inflation rate, says Economist Arthur Okun, a Brookings Institution senior fellow and chairman of the Council of Economic Advisers under President Johnson.

Yet pressures are mounting for the Administration to resist the import surge and try to lessen the nation's deepening trade deficit, which, overloaded by oil imports, now stands at a record $28 billion for 1977. Even some old-line free traders, like Representative Charles Vanik of Ohio, have called on Carter to give U.S. manufacturers some protection against imports. Vanik and others warned that if the President did not take some action, especially with steel, Congress might enact tough protectionist measures of its own.

Foreign steel producers got the message and last fall offered to voluntarily limit steel shipments. But that was not enough for the protectionists, who continued to cry for help. U.S. companies increased their suits under antidumping provisions of existing trade laws, which prohibit foreign manufacturers from selling below cost in U.S. markets. Other products either currently or likely to be involved in dumping cases include television sets, microwave ovens, Citizens Band radios and motorcycles. Some of these products, contend the U.S. manufacturers, sell for as much as 60% less than in Europe or Japan.

But steel is the biggest worry. With 60,000 steelworkers laid off partly because of competition from cheap imports, the steel industry has accused Japanese steelmakers of dumping metal on the U.S. market at an average of 38.2% below cost. The Japanese deny this, saying they are simply producing steel more efficiently. In December the Administration came up with a complex remedy. It proposed setting so-called reference prices—minimum prices—on 40 to 60 principal categories of imported steel. Any steel entering the U.S. at rates lower than these reference prices would be subjected to heavy antidumping penalties. Steelmen reacted cautiously to the plan.

These protectionist moves will not endear the U.S. to such economic powers as Japan and West Germany—which Washington is simultaneously urging to buy more goods from less prosperous countries, thus giving a lift to global economic recovery. But the Administration's rather tepid moves so far—affecting only a handful of the thousands of products imported into the U.S.—seem a far more acceptable way of saving import-threatened U.S. jobs than the stiffer protectionist measures that have been tried in the past. ∎

American consumer compares prices of Japanese and American TV sets

A rising clamor for protection against cheap imports.

Skytrain Soars

Suddenly all's war in airfares

Britain's Freddie Laker is a big (6 ft. 1 in.), ebullient self-made millionaire of 55 with a small fleet of planes (13 jets) and a giant-killer's dream. For six years he battled the aviation officialdom on both sides of the Atlantic for a chance to try out his Skytrain idea: an air shuttle that would offer travelers flying between New York and London a no-frills, first-come, first-seated service at rates far below those charged by the big scheduled airlines. To do battle successfully with those "sacred cows," he said, "you have to get the public on your side, and the way to do that is to give the public what it wants."

What Laker offered was a rock-bottom New York–London round-trip fare of $236. The price would not include meals (up to $5 extra), but it would be a lot cheaper than any of the existing New York–London fares, which ranged in cost from $1,312 and $626 for regular first class and economy to $382 for the cheapest group-tour plan. In June, Laker finally got what he wanted: the Carter Administration, which shares his ideas about opening up air travel to more competition, approved the Skytrain, and British authorities followed suit. Finally, on Sept. 26, Skytrain took off.

At London's Gatwick Airport, where a huge sign above a hangar read LOOK OUT, LOOK OUT, FREDDIE LAKER'S ABOUT, a 346-passenger DC-10 bearing Laker Airways' bright red trim and logo

Freddie Laker jumping for joy at U.S. approval of Skytrain

Down with "sacred cows," says he. "Give the public what it wants."

roared into the air to inaugurate the new service. Hours later, the same DC-10 took off from New York's Kennedy Airport for London. Its passengers represented what has become a typical Laker crowd: long-haired youths with backpacks, older couples and whole families—some from as far away as California and Canada —who had camped overnight at the Laker terminal in Queens to be sure to make the flight.

Since then, few Skytrain flights have been filled to capacity. The average Skytrain takes off with only 281 of its 346 seats occupied. Yet Laker says he needs only 264 passengers per flight to break

even and claims to have been clearing a profit of $79,000 a week. Confident of a big upturn next April, when he will be allowed to expand from seven flights weekly to 14, he has ordered four new planes (including two DC-10s) for his airline. He has also applied for permission to begin daily Skytrain service between London and Los Angeles at a round-trip fare of $453—less than half the regular economy rate.

Already Skytrain has had an enormous impact on the air-travel industry. To meet the Skytrain competition, the six scheduled lines on the New York–London route—Pan Am, TWA, British Airways, Air India, Iran Air and El Al—all began

Biting the Big Apple

"Today we take our first real bite of the Big Apple, and we expect it to taste very sweet indeed." So said Edmund Dell, Britain's Secretary of State for Foreign Trade, after he had arrived at New York's Kennedy Airport on Nov. 22 aboard the British Airways Concorde that inaugurated supersonic service between New York and London. The slender, 100-passenger, 1,340-m.p.h. jet, which made the trip in just 3 hrs. 25 min., about half the standard time, touched down at Kennedy a few minutes after an Air France Concorde that had screamed in from Paris in equally fast time.

The landings marked the end of a long struggle by the British and French to get New York landing rights for the planes, on whose development they had spent 15 years and $3 billion. Waiving federal noise restrictions, the Ford Administration had granted permission for Concorde flights out of Washington's Dulles Airport and New York's Kennedy for a 16-month test period. But the trial program was

quickly blocked in New York, where residents near Kennedy raised a howl of protest against the Concorde's noise. By last March, as New York officials continued to dither over the Concorde issue, the French and the British began lofting charges of a "conspiracy" against their plane. France's President Valéry Giscard d'Estaing went so far as to promise "a very grave crisis" if the Concorde was not allowed into Kennedy. Finally, in October, the U.S. Supreme Court ruled that the Concorde must indeed have its New York trial.

U.S. noise regulations have been waived only for the 16 Concordes already built or under construction. So far the planes have proved no noisier than other jets operating out of Kennedy. What is less certain is whether, as Air France and British Airways hope, the Concorde will attract enough passengers willing to pay 20% above standard first-class one-way fares—$793 to London, $820 to Paris—to persuade other cities around the world that they cannot get along without supersonic service. If not, the first Concordes will also be the last.

Air France and British Airways Concordes taxiing to their gates after inaugural commercial flights to New York

setting aside some seats on their regular flights to be sold at competitive fares ($256 round trip) under various advance-booking and stand-by schemes. Meanwhile, other airlines went on a fare-slashing binge. KLM introduced a bargain fare on flights out of New York to The Netherlands. Alitalia dropped its New York–Rome economy ticket from $565 to just $460. Pan Am has proposed a budget-type service for its Pacific routes.

All this price cutting has posed a grave problem for the International Air Transport Association (IATA), the organization of 109 airlines (60% of them government-supported) that has been regulating international airfares since 1946. At their annual meeting in Madrid in November, IATA members voted to undertake a complete reappraisal of their fare structures next June. Also under consideration is a drastic step: opening all North Atlantic routes to free competition on fares and service for an experimental twelve-month period.

Actually, bargain fares of all kinds have been chipping away at the cost of air travel for some time: of the nearly 14 million passengers carried on North Atlantic flights in 1976, almost 80% flew aboard charters or on one of various cut-rate plans offered by the scheduled lines; a decade earlier, the percentage of passengers traveling on such fares was just 54%. In September, the Carter Administration approved yet another bargain tariff: the Super APEX, which for a low, low fare ($290 for a New York–London round trip, for example) allows a traveler to go on the flight and date of his choice as long as he buys his ticket 45 days before departure and spends 14 to 45 days at his destination.

Reflecting the unhappiness of many foreign governments, which have fought to keep ticket prices high, IATA Secretary General Knut Hammarskjold blames the proliferation of cheap fares on the "disruptive" ideas of the Carter Administration about relaxing regulation of air travel—foreign and domestic—to allow more competition. Most IATA members charge that this will lead to price wars that will hurt the traveling public: airlines will become even more strapped for cash than they already are and thus less able to buy new equipment and more likely to scrimp by cutting down on the number of flights they offer and points they serve.

Laker, a seaman's son who made his first fortune operating old transports during the Berlin airlift, disagrees. He argues that instead of trying to keep fares high to meet rising costs, the airlines should fill their new wide-bodied planes by bringing fares down within reach of a vast untapped market of budget travelers who would fly if they could. "What about the poor bugger who hasn't got much money?" Laker asks. "If it weren't for people like us, he'd never fly." ∎

Fiduciary Fandango

Scandal hits Switzerland's banking system

No one had to tell Ernst Kuhrmeier, 57, that the rules of the Swiss banking game were changing. Manager since 1962 of a Crédit Suisse branch in the Italian-speaking Ticino canton of Switzerland (pop. 265,000), Kuhrmeier had seen the local banking industry transformed over the years from a modest group of staid institutions to a gaggle of 254 firms, large and small, locked in ever more frenzied competition. Their main quarry: huge sums of capital smuggled across the border by wealthy Italians, who were growing steadily more edgy about Communist political advances and double-digit inflation at home. Somehow Kuhrmeier always managed to gather in his share of those loose lire and then some—until auditors uncovered a billion-dollar scandal that shook the world-renowned Swiss banking system to its roots.

To prevent sudden shifts in the value of its prized currency, Switzerland since 1975 has discouraged large nonresident deposits that are guaranteed in Swiss francs by imposing a 10% quarterly "negative interest" charge on such accounts. Bankers quickly learned how to continue attracting foreign deposits anyway: they were legally registered as "fiduciary" (trust) funds, which are not subject to the confiscatory government tithe. The catch is that neither can such deposits be secured in Swiss francs, a provision that

forces any prudent trustee to reinvest fiduciary funds in low-yield Eurodollars.

Kuhrmeier's gambit was risky. He simply failed to report to his superiors in Zurich about $1 billion in major new deposits by foreigners. But to his customers he offered a far better deal than the unsecured trust arrangement used by competitors: a promise in writing that the Crédit Suisse, Switzerland's third largest bank, with assets of $20 billion, stood firmly behind their deposits (and thus was liable to losses if the Italian lira declined). For good measure, Kuhrmeier also dangled the guarantee of a return of up to 4% higher than that offered by other banks, a commitment that forced him to plunge into riskier investments.

The one he concentrated on was called Texon Finanzanstalt, a highly speculative, Liechtenstein-based holding company with operations ranging from resort hotels to wine production and plastics manufacturing. Over the years, Kuhrmeier sank the unreported $1 billion of Crédit Suisse deposits into Texon—a company that he just happened to have personally founded in 1961.

The ruse started coming apart in March, when a suspicious Crédit Suisse auditing team found that Kuhrmeier's branch in the border town of Chiasso was keeping two sets of books. Over the next

Schwarzenbach Aeppli von der Crone Jeker

New Credit Suisse Chairman Oswald Aeppli addresses worried stockholders in Zurich

It could no longer be assumed, said one expert, that every banker was a gentleman.

few months there followed a bout of ax-wielding unprecedented in Swiss banking. Kuhrmeier and five business associates were arrested and charged with "disloyal management," the Swiss equivalent of business fraud; Crédit Suisse President Heinz Wuffli, 50, and two other top company officials resigned in disgrace. In November, it was announced that Kuhrmeier's customers may be liable for as much as $29 million in negative interest payments. Crédit Suisse was required to withhold enough to cover those payments but otherwise made good on Kuhrmeier's guarantees to "bona fide" depositors.

More important, the scandal forced some new regulatory controls on one of the world's few remaining honor-system industries. Under a new industry code, Swiss banks were forbidden to assist in the transfer of any funds illegally exported to Switzerland—including not only flight capital but also known tax-evading cash and Mafia loot. In addition, there is considerable pressure to beef up the Bern-based Federal Banking Commission, which has exactly twelve employees to keep track of Switzerland's banking assets of nearly $140 billion. Said Swiss National Bank President Fritz Leutwiler, who has long pressed for such reforms: "We are no longer assuming that every banker is a gentleman and that, if he is a gentleman, he observes the rules." ∎

The Legacy of Howard Hughes

A classic legal scramble for a dwindling empire

He became the world's most legendary hermit—a man so eccentric, so capricious, so secretive, so mysterious that only his death proved he had actually been alive. Yet since Howard Robard Hughes died of kidney failure at age 70 aboard an ambulance jet streaking from Acapulco to Houston on April 5, 1976, his legacy has created an even bigger mystery than the final years of his life. Did the fabled recluse leave a will? Who are the rightful heirs to his estate—once estimated to be worth as much as $2.3 billion? And of what does the estate itself consist?

The definitive answers to such questions are not likely to emerge for years. But for now, Hughes' relatives, former business associates and two states are scrambling for a share of his financial empire. With 200 lawyers buzzing around the remains of the steadily shrinking estate, and legal struggles under way in Nevada, California, Texas, Louisiana and Delaware, the Hughes case is already becoming a classic battle.

Childless and twice divorced, Hughes left no immediate family—and apparently no will clearly designating what he wanted done with his fortune. Though a personal aide has testified that Hughes once mentioned that he had drafted a handwritten last testament, investigators have sifted through the billionaire's belongings, including old flight bags, map cases and safe-deposit boxes, and failed to turn up any uncontestably valid will. So far, 40-odd alleged wills have surfaced, but most were immediately dismissed as fakes or practical jokes.

Yet one is being taken seriously. Nicknamed the "Mormon will" because it appeared mysteriously at the headquarters of the Church of Jesus Christ of Latter-day Saints in Salt Lake City three weeks after Hughes' death, the handwritten, three-page document divides the estate among such beneficiaries as the Mormon Church, the Howard Hughes Medical Institute and ex-Wives Ella Rice and Jean Peters. Eight handwriting experts have authenticated the scrawl and signature as Hughes'—in spite of several uncharac-

Artist's version of Hughes at 70
Where is all the money going?

teristic misspellings ("cildren" for children, for example, and "revolk" for revoke). But there are two highly suspicious entries: 1) named as a beneficiary is a former Utah gas-station operator named Melvin Dummar, who claims he once picked up Hughes on a desert road in southern Nevada and gave him a lift into Las Vegas; 2) the will names as executor Noah Dietrich, 88, a onetime Hughes lieutenant who bitterly split with his boss 20 years ago. Though Dummar has admitted his story was false, Dietrich contends the will is genuine, and his lawyer went to court in Las Vegas in November to prove it.

Contesting the Mormon will on behalf of himself and Hughes' 22 other living relatives is the billionaire's cousin, William Rice Lummis, 48, a Houston lawyer and court-appointed co-administrator of the estate. Lummis wants one-quarter of the fortune to go to his mother and the rest to be distributed among the family. Meanwhile, California and Texas are each claiming to be the official place of resi-

dence of the peripatetic Hughes at the time of his death, in order to collect inheritance taxes (Texas officials, for example, hope to collect at least $150 million).

But that could all turn out to be academic if Chester Davis gets his way. Former chief counsel of Summa Corp., the umbrella organization formed in 1972 to oversee Hughes' patchwork empire of airline companies, hotels, casinos and real estate, Davis has gone to court to argue that Hughes intended to leave his entire fortune to the tax-free Howard Hughes Medical Institute in Miami, which happens to be run by Davis and Summa Chief Executive Officer Frank William Gay.

Regardless of who finally gets Hughes' money, the controversy has disclosed fascinating details of how the tycoon lived and worked. While he was alive, Hughes used his wealth and power to conceal his eccentricities, but legal investigators now are discovering that he was a near lunatic who spent his tormented last years in a self-imposed prison. Dazed by tranquilizers and codeine, he refused to deal with Summa executives face to face and rarely even telephoned them.

As the billionaire hermit was wasting away, so, apparently, was his fortune. Shortly after Lummis took over Summa as chairman of the board in August 1976, he was stunned to discover that the company had lost $132 million in less than six years. Worse, though Hughes had sold off properties worth $650 million between 1966 and 1976, Summa had only $94 million left as of last March. Merrill Lynch, Pierce, Fenner & Smith has assessed the Hughes empire (excluding the Hughes Aircraft Co., which was turned over to the tax-free medical institute in 1954 to bankroll its research) to be worth no more than $168 million.

Where did it all go? According to tax reports and other Summa documents revealed in the Las Vegas court in November, Hughes was evidently not a very good businessman during the last decade of his life. Many ventures, including mining claims and helicopter investments, either failed to turn a profit or simply lost millions. And while other Nevada gambling operations cruised along in the black, Hughes' seven casinos and hotels were gobbling much of Summa's wealth. A major reason: the company's executives were novices at running casinos and thus unable to compete with Vegas sharpies. Trying to block the flow of capital with some "spigot-turning," Lummis suggested several economy moves but met with staunch opposition from Davis and the rest of the Summa Old Guard. Lummis' tough response: he sacked Davis, who then retreated to the medical institute to pursue the Hughes legacy in the courts.

Yet by the time the courts manage to untangle the Hughes case, and the armies of lawyers working on it collect their fees, there may be no legacy left. Indeed, California lawyers are already worried the Hughes estate may be billed for inheritance taxes that exceed its assets. ∎

On the Labor Front: Battle Cries

Strikes afflict coal, steel, aircraft and docks

Labor relations in the U.S. were supposed to be peaceful during 1977—and much of the time they were. During the first ten months, 30,517,000 man-days were lost through strikes *v.* 38,126,000 in 1976. But it was all too good to last. As the year drew to a close, that relative peace seemed no more than a cease-fire.

Some of labor's fiercest battles were fought within the unions themselves, notably among the 1.4 million United Steelworkers of America. Union Presidential Candidate Lloyd McBride, 61, backed by the U.S.W. Establishment, found himself challenged by scrappy Ed Sadlowski, 39, a third-generation "mill rat" who claimed that the leadership was entirely too chummy with management. Sadlowski cam-

ments for increased production, similar to those granted 85,000 steel-mill workers. That seemed a money issue, inside the no-strike zone under the E.N.A., but the union argued that it was really a local issue. Big Steel rode out the strike for 20 weeks on its ore stockpiles, but by year's end the companies more or less had come around, granting an incentive-pay plan to at least 75% of the miners.

In October, International Longshoremen's Association members from Maine to Texas quit unloading containerized ship cargoes. They wanted higher wages and benefits, but most of all they wanted port employers to ante up more money for their 13-year-old guaranteed-annual-wage agreement (New York City mini-

dustry. Lately it has been more industry-wide famine than feast: employment has declined from 738,000 production workers in 1968 to some 428,000 at the beginning of 1977. Said newly elected I.A.M. President William W. ("Wimpy") Winpisinger: "We've never licked Boeing, but this may be the year we find out how long it takes to do it." Nope. After 44 days, the 24,000 workers who struck Boeing accepted a 13% wage increase over three years and additional guarantees of job security for some senior employees. At Lockheed, workers turned down a similar money offer because seniority-protection provisions were judged inadequate, and most picketers remained off the job at year's end.

The biggest strike of the year loomed in the coal industry in December. United Mine Workers President Arnold Miller, 54, reelected by only a minority of the union's 277,000 members in June, may have dug the ultimate pit for himself with a demand that any contract give each U.M.W. local the right to strike over local issues. The locals hardly need that encouragement: from January through August the industry lost more than 2.3 million man-days through wildcat strikes. Last summer, during an eight-week wildcat that spread from West Virginia to Kentucky and Ohio, Miller himself could not persuade the miners to return to work. Coal productivity in U.M.W. territory has declined from 16 tons per man-day in 1969 to nine tons last year. The coal operators are in no mood to legitimize what they see as anarchy. Says one: "There's one thing we're unanimous on: getting a no-strike clause in the contract."

Coal miners in West Virginia ready to go out on strike
Their union may have dug the biggest pit.

paigned mainly against the union's Experimental Negotiating Agreement with the steel companies: a four-year-old pact banning strikes over money by steelworkers when their contracts expire. McBride wanted to give the E.N.A. another chance during 1977's spring bargaining; Sadlowski denounced it as "contrary to my concept of the trade union movement." McBride won the election by a margin of almost 3-2, and the steelworkers settled a new contract calling for a 30% wage-and-benefit increase over three years.

That contract took effect in August, but when it did, more than 14,000 Great Lakes iron-ore miners walked out. It was the first substantial strike in any segment of the basic steel industry in 18 years, affecting 90% of U.S. ore production. The miners' big demand was incentive pay-

mum: $16,640). The container revolution in shipping has left thousands of longshoremen with little or nothing to do, and the guaranteed wage is part of a deal that has frozen union membership. The strike lasted 60 days before an agreement was reached raising the guaranteed pay rate in New York by 30% over three years —the largest increase ever. Other ports also moved their guarantees upward.

Three days after the longshoremen struck, some 43,000 members of the International Association of Machinists and Aerospace Workers formally began downing tools at Boeing Co., and soon afterward at Lockheed Aircraft Corp. A major issue for many was a desire to protect job security for the aging (average: 46 years) membership *v.* the companies' wish for flexibility in a feast-or-famine in-

The miners walked out on Dec. 6, but coal consumers had plenty of supplies on hand, and they also have access to Western strip mines, where the U.M.W. is virtually unrepresented. Indeed, the union's share of U.S. coal production has declined to less than 54% from the 74% it mined in 1970. The big danger is that the national union might be torn to shreds —and then real anarchy would reign in the Eastern coal fields.

However the individual battles were being decided, organized labor was having real trouble remaining relevant in modern American society. Its share of the U.S. labor force was only 25% last year, and the unions have failed to gain a strong foothold in the burgeoning service sector of the economy. Politically, labor has made few advances under the first Democratic Administration in eight years. As if to underscore that unexpected isolation, President Jimmy Carter rebuffed an invitation to attend the biennial convention of the A.F.L.-C.I.O. in December. Many concerned labor sachems feel that the movement needs new leadership. Yet at that same Los Angeles convention, A.F.L.-C.I.O. President George Meany, 83, successfully steamrollered to another two-year term. ∎

Merger Wave

Wall Street's roster shrinks

Plagued by changing regulations, cut-rate commissions and a listless stock market, Wall Street's brokerage community kept shrinking. Mergers and tales of proposed mergers swept the Street, linking some of the oldest and biggest names in U.S. finance. The number of New York Stock Exchange member firms now is at 475, v. 681 in 1961. Twenty-five brokers account for two-thirds of the revenues.

With the notable exception of Merrill Lynch, Pierce, Fenner & Smith, the nation's largest broker (revenues: $1.1 billion), very few major brokers' nameplates read the same as they did a decade ago. Commas were added and dropped, ampersands shifted. Bache Halsey Stuart Shields Inc., formed in July, consolidates what once were four firms. Hornblower & Weeks–Hemphill, Noyes became Hornblower, Weeks, Noyes & Trask after taking over Spencer Trask in May, and the combined company is now forming a joint venture partnership with Loeb Rhoades. Paine Webber took over Mitchell, Hutchins. Two old-line investment-banking houses, both founded in the 19th century, united late in the year to form Lehman Bros. Kuhn Loeb Inc. At year's end stockholders approved a merger of Reynolds Securities and Dean Witter & Co. that would create the nation's second largest brokerage firm, without, so far, drawing any Justice Department protest.

Trustbusters, in the view of many Wall Streeters, have no grounds to complain, because it was Government action that produced the sorry state of the securities industry—and thus the merger wave. In May 1975 the Securities and Exchange Commission abolished the vestiges of the antiquated and anticompetitive fixed-commission system, which had lavished riches on many brokers. In its place came a system of negotiated rates under which investors could haggle over how much they would pay brokers. The typical commission on 10,000 shares of a $10 stock fell from about $1,200 to roughly $500. Small investors got no such price break: in many cases, they pay more in commissions now than before.

Brokers face still another problem that could reduce their numbers even more. That is the decade-old threat by the SEC to establish a nationwide central securities market, bristling with electronics, which would allow investors to get the best price for stocks no matter where they are traded. To that end, the SEC plans to abolish rules that require most trading to be done on the floors of the major exchanges. That would mean more "off board" trading and, in the view of opponents, more business for the big brokers. A price of sorts already is being exacted. A seat on the New York Stock Exchange, which once cost $515,000, now sells for about $45,000. ∎

"Say, buddy, could you spare $3.98 for a cup of coffee?"

Brewhaha

Coffee prices boil over

It was, somebody said, the Great Brewhaha of 1977. As coffee prices began rising—from an average of $2.55 per lb. at the start of the year to a peak of $3.94 per lb. in mid-June—U.S. consumers' tempers began steaming. In a campaign reminiscent of the meat boycott four years earlier, consumer activists urged customers to swear off the bean until prices fell. Chicory, long used in Europe to make coffee go further, enjoyed a revival in the U.S. Manhattan's expensive "21" Club restaurant offered free tea to diners who passed up the traditional postprandial cup; other restaurants simply started charging prices that would have seemed steep even at "21" not that long ago (up to 50¢ per cup).

Cofflation was caused by a succession of freak weather events in the coffee-growing nations of Latin America, notably a 1975 freeze that killed or damaged more than half the trees in Brazil, the world's largest supplier. Since that year's crop had already been harvested, it took more than another year for the lost production capacity to start registering on world markets. When it did, producer countries took a cue from OPEC and drastically increased export taxes, compounding the price increases. Brazil kicked up its levy from 22¢ to $1.67 per lb. Sales of coffee fell off in most supermarkets at the height of the price surge but rebounded when prices came down even a bit (they ended the year at $3.57). U.S. consumption of what used to be called the national beverage has been steadily slipping anyway, from more than three cups per capita daily in 1962 to just above two in 1976. Overall, U.S. consumption declined 4% in 1977. But even in the bad old days of June, a cup of coffee brewed at home cost only about 6.5¢. If, as the old joke has it, the results were not grounds for divorce, neither could most coffee devotees give up the drink that wakes them up and gets them to work. ∎

Soviet Sting

Again, U.S. grain goes cheap

Even among the sharpest of horse traders, there is no disgrace in having been set up—the first time. What is not permitted in the unwritten code of supersalesmanship is a second loss of innocence. By that standard, U.S. grain traders have lost their charter membership in the Club of Hard Bargainers. For the second time in five years the Soviet Union in 1977 secretly bought up large quantities of American grain at bargain prices before Yankee brokers figured out what was going on.

Happily, Soviet Sting No. 2 seemed unlikely to cause the traumatic repercussions that accompanied the Great Grain Robbery of 1972. In that memorable operation Soviet agents working out of New York City's Hilton Hotel cornered close to 30% of the U.S. wheat market at a time of severe world shortages. The result was a sudden crimp in domestic grain supplies that caused irritating increases in the price of bread and grain-fattened beef for American consumers. Last year, by contrast, the Soviets were buying smaller quantities (an estimated 15 million tons of wheat and corn) from stockpiles that were glutted by a record U.S. harvest. Domestic prices went up (cash prices to farmers for corn in Illinois, for example, rose from $1.65 per bushel in August to $2.10 in December), but not by enough to raise food costs significantly in the supermarket. As for farmers, most were glad to get the grain out of their silos even at less than break-even prices.

The main losers were U.S. traders in grain futures, who for much of the spring and summer had been "selling short," i.e., at the prevailing market price of $2.30 per bu.—and ended up having to deliver at a price of $2.80 per bu. after the market had moved up. Agricultural experts estimated that the Soviets would have had to spend up to $100 million more than they did if their buying plans had been known in advance.

Precisely why they were not known was a matter of some embarrassment in Washington. For one thing, under a treaty designed to prevent a repetition of the 1972 chaos, the Kremlin is supposedly required to notify the U.S. if it intends to siphon more than 8 million tons off the U.S. market. It got around that provision —technically—by buying through corporations legally based in Western Europe. The CIA added to the confusion by coming up with an estimate of the Soviet grain harvest that was a crucial 10% too high. Finally, the Soviets misled visiting grain experts as to the projected size of their crop, steering them away from regions that were not producing good harvests. Secrecy and misinformation are two commodities that never seem to be in short supply in the U.S.S.R. ∎

Vladimir Nabokov

A lucid, mad mind

He once translated Lewis Carroll's *Alice in Wonderland* into Russian. In hard times, he eked out a living partly by giving boxing lessons. He delighted not only in solving elaborate chess puzzles but in inventing them. He was a research fellow in entomology at Harvard's Museum of Comparative Zoology, and he discovered a dozen new varieties of butterflies, including one that acquired the name Nabokov's Wood

He hunted for butterflies

Nymph. When he died of a viral infection in Lausanne, Switzerland, on July 2, there were many who believed that the loss of Vladimir Nabokov meant the loss of the world's greatest novelist.

Nabokov wrote voluminously (16 novels, nine plays, seven collections of short stories, an autobiography, and a cornucopia of poems, translations and miscellaneous pronouncements), but since most of his work was in Russian, he spent most of his life in relative obscurity. At the ripe age of 59 he suddenly became rich and famous with the appearance of a brilliant comedy that almost failed to get published at all. Four American publishers rejected *Lolita* as obscene, and it first appeared in Paris under the imprint of Sex Book Publisher Maurice Girodias. Yet Nabokov's stylish tale of a middle-aged intellectual in love with a twelve-year-old nymphet (the word was Nabokov's invention) was not only a romance but also a brilliant portrait of the American highway culture and a rich allegory of innocence and corruption. Nabokov loved such conundrums and complexities. *Pale Fire,* perhaps his best novel, took the form of a pedantic commentary on a 999-line epic poem by a Wordsmith University literature professor who claimed to be the exiled king of a more or less imaginary monarchy.

"I travel through life," he once said of his wanderings, "in a space helmet." He was born in 1899 into the cosmopolitan aristocracy of St. Petersburg and soon became what he called "a perfectly normal trilingual child." An uncle left him $2 million on the eve of the revolution that doomed the Nabokovs to flight. Young Nabokov, who earned his degree in literature at Cambridge, lived in Berlin until 1937, then fled to France with his wife Véra and son Dmitri, then moved on to the U.S. in 1940. The first job he was offered in New York was as a bicycle delivery boy.

For two decades the aloof immigrant supported himself by teaching memorable courses in literature at Stanford, Wellesley, Cornell. Nabokov's courses were remarkable partly because of his methods —he would write out his lectures verbatim, then recite them in a melodramatic style. But his most striking attribute was his fierce judgments of other writers. He ridiculed Dostoevsky and loathed Cervantes. "Many accepted authors simply do not exist for me," he once said. "Brecht, Faulkner, Camus, many others mean absolutely nothing to me." In his denunciations he liked to use the Russian word *poshlost,* which he defined as "corny trash, vulgar clichés, Philistinism in all its phases, imitations of imitations, bogus profundities, crude, moronic and dishonest pseudo-literature." By contrast, he admired Gogol, Tolstoy, Proust, Joyce, and he had little doubt that he himself belonged among the masters. If his endless games and puns and riddles struck some critics as almost hallucinatory, Nabokov agreed. Said he: "I have never seen a more lucid, more lonely, better balanced mad mind than mine." ∎

Elvis Presley

Up the road from Tupelo

From the moment he rocketed to stardom in 1956 it was plain that Elvis Presley had the rare ability to arouse his audiences to an enthusiasm bordering on passion. And when the man who had led American youth into the rock-'n'-roll era died last Aug. 16 at 42, many pop radio stations immediately began dirging the bad news—round the clock—with the incongruously lively refrains of such Presley hits as *Hound Dog, Heartbreak Hotel,* and *Blue Suede Shoes.* Just as quickly, thousands of fans from every nook of the country dropped everything to set out for Memphis. There, only 100 miles up the road from Presley's birthplace in Tupelo, Miss., his musical career began and ended.

He led the way to rock

Elvis Aron Presley took up singing as a child at church meetings. He kept at it after his odd-jobbing farmer-carpenter father Vernon moved the family away from a scratch-hard existence in Mississippi to Memphis. By the time he graduated from L.C. Humes High School in 1953 and took a job driving a truck, he could also chord a guitar.

That summer he went to the local Sun Records studio and paid $4 to have two songs recorded as a gift for his mother Gladys. Result: Sun signed the 19-year-old youth to a contract and issued the first five of Presley's professional discs. They were immediately local hits, and Elvis was on his way. His arrival awaited only the management of Thomas A. Parker, a canny impresario and self-styled colonel. Parker took charge in 1955, put his client on the road as The Hillbilly Cat, soon had him signed with RCA Records. Presley's sensuous singing, his self-assured sneer, his pelvic gyrations, his oily hairdo—all of it outraged the genteel traditionalists and inspired ever-growing audiences to ever-more-feverish adulation.

Presley's private life was not such a fairy tale. His marriage to Priscilla Beaulieu in 1967 ended in divorce six years later. He grieved endlessly over the death of his mother, also at 42. He led, in fact, a rigorously cloistered private life behind the guarded walls of Graceland, the 18-room mansion he owned in Memphis. Only through the tales of former hired intimates did it get about that Presley constantly turned his mood up and down with sedatives and stimulants, some of which were found in his system during the autopsy. Presley died alone on the floor of a bathroom at Graceland, and doctors attributed the death to an abnormal heart rhythm.

Within 24 hours of the star's death, buyers had exhausted the inventories of most record stores. Some customers lugged off as many as 40 Presley albums at a grab. By the end of 1977 Presley's lifetime record sales totaled roughly 700 million, more than those of any other recording star in history. MGM re-released 14 Presley films. Television networks scheduled specials. A memorabilia firm—Factors Etc., Inc. of Bear, Del.—bought exclusive rights from his estate to market Presley souvenirs for five years; the firm immediately made up a million iron-on transfers of a Presley lithograph and expects to gross $10 million this year. One of the owners said, "This way the Presley family will get some money —a lot of money."

By the end of the year the crest of the memorabilia wave had passed, but the special zeal of the Presley fans had not. Late in November, when the public was finally admitted to view Presley's permanent grave—adjoining the new resting place of his mother on the grounds of Graceland—more than 3,000 fans eager to be among the first visitors waited in line, some of them throughout the night, in a freezing rain. ∎

Groucho Marx

The view from upside down

Surname: "Marx. (And if you don't know it by this time, forget it.)"

Christian name: "I haven't met one in years."

Educated at: "Leisure."

Brief descriptions of important positions held: "Vertical and horizontal."

That thumbnail (or hangnail) autobiography is as good as any, for no one could completely describe Groucho Marx—including Groucho himself. Julius

Impudence was a way of life

Henry Marx was a scrupulous autodidact for whom impudence was a way of life. He began that way on the streets of Manhattan's Yorkville, wisecracking to his fellow truants and getting knocked on the jaw for his pains. Julius and his four brothers, Leonard (Chico), Adolph (Harpo), Milton (Gummo) and Herbert (Zeppo), might easily have ended in jail or worse. But hovering over them was a guardian angel, played by their Yiddishe mama, Minnie. When her brother Al made it big in vaudeville as the right half of Gallagher and Shean, Minnie pushed the boys onstage. For twelve years the Marx Brothers played the circuit, polishing their act and their timing. Of the five, Groucho continually got the short end of the shtik until *The Cocoanuts,* written by George S. Kaufman. "Kaufman molded me," Groucho later acknowledged. "He gave me the walk and the talk."

Groucho's manic onslaughts took surrealism out of picture frames and brought it into picture houses. "Do you know that property values have increased 1929 since 1,000%?" he asked in *Cocoanuts.* In *Monkey Business* he made advances to a blonde: "You're a woman who's been getting nothing but dirty breaks. Well, we can clean and tighten your brakes, but you'll have to stay in the garage all night." In *A Day at the Races* he proposed to Margaret Dumont, the Marxes' dowager queen. "Many, many years ago," he confided, gazing at an oil portrait, "I proposed to your mother." "But that's my father!" "No wonder he turned me down!"

Groucho himself admitted that he was getting laughs from other people's wit, people like Kaufman and S.J. Perelman, but among the cognoscenti he gained a reputation as the fastest mouth in the West. It was not until *A Night in Casablanca* in 1946, though, that Groucho decided to get into the ad-lib business. "I was hanging upside down by my knees for a scene," he recalled. "And I said to myself, 'Groucho, old boy—and believe me, you *are* an old boy—don't you think this is rather a ridiculous way for you to be spending your few remaining years?'"

When a quiz showman asked Marx to be a master of ceremonies, Groucho grabbed the mike and never let go. *You Bet Your Life* became one of radio and TV's finest half hours. "Say the secret woid," Groucho commenced in his unique nasal locution, and past his leer walked the world's straightest straight men. Groucho's snipes were classics: "Either this man is dead or my watch is stopped." "I never forget a face, but in your case I'll make an exception." A million ripostes (and perhaps millions of dollars) later, Groucho finally hung up his spites. But even in his 80s, after three wives and innumerable amours, he could not resist making his patented double-entendres on TV talk shows, wearing a wild hat and chanting his old song, *Lydia, the Tattooed Lady.*

Groucho's last months were darkened by a lawsuit in which his son Arthur and his longtime companion, Erin Fleming, 37, fought to be appointed conservator of the debilitated old man's fortune (estimated at $2.5 million). The judge awarded conservatorship to his grandson, but Groucho remained in bed, oblivious to the controversy. It is both kinder and wiser to remember him as the founder of another, perhaps profounder, Marxist theory of looking sideways at a cockeyed world. The secret woid, at his death at 86 on Aug. 19, was regret. Since 1,000%, show business has been diminished. ∎

Robert Lowell

The bright splash of life

His eye, as Norman Mailer once noticed, shone with a grim Cromwellian light. His lines could sound as clangorously dark as a Puritan November. Robert Lowell worked with dense images—his metals were bronze and pig iron instead of gold, his stones were millstones and grave slates, never gems. The lines he wrote for Robert Kennedy seemed appropriate enough for Lowell himself: "Doom was woven in your nerves,

Dark as a Puritan November

your shirt ..." He made intense, alarming poetry out of his periodic swoops into madness: "I hear/ my ill-spirit sob in each blood cell,/ as if my hand were at its throat .../ I myself am hell." Lowell's gaze was inward and often forbidding. Yet when he died at 60 of a heart attack in a New York City taxi on Sept. 12, he left behind a wonderfully vital body of work—twelve volumes of it—that ranked him as probably the best American poet of his generation.

Few poets have written with such passionate control. Even in moments touched by madness, he could rescue the almost embarrassing personal revelation with his always dignified intelligence and with his rich assemblage of classical learning. For his materials, Lowell plundered history, mythology and other poets—from Homer and Horace to his early mentors, Allen Tate and John Crowe Ransom—as thoroughly as he did his own life and psyche. In his 20s he turned from the "cold Protestantism" of the New England Lowells to the Catholic Church, and his motives were aesthetic as well as religious: he found that he loved the sonorities and pageants of Catholicism. "We were kind of religious," he wrote in one poem. "We thought in images."

Lowell managed to give both grandeur and conversational intimacy to his poems; he kept both his private and public lives upon the same stage. He wrote of his patrician New England forebears (who included Distant Cousin Amy Lowell and relatives on his mother's side dating back to the *Mayflower*); his painful relationship with his father, a Navy officer and failed businessman; his parents' devastating quarrels; his own three marriages (to Novelist Jean Stafford, Critic Elizabeth Hardwick and English Novelist Caroline Blackwood). Someone once gibed unkindly: "He writes as if Christ was crucified on the Lowell family tree." A conscientious objector during World War II, Lowell was jailed for five months for resisting the draft. During Viet Nam, he campaigned for Eugene McCarthy and joined the Armies of the Night for the 1967 march on the Pentagon. Tall, stooped, vaguely distracted, he seemed to one critic "an Old Testament prophet in ungodly times." Lowell inspected the century's moral slums with a savage eye: "On Boylston Street, a commercial photograph/ shows Hiroshima boiling/ over a Mosler safe, the "Rock of Ages"/ that survived the blast."

Mortality obsessed him. "Infirmity's a food the flesh must swallow," he wrote, "feeding our minds ... the mind which is also flesh." There was something Elizabethan, sumptuous, in his contemplation of death. He was fascinated as well by love, marriage, madness —and his art, which he tended like a living, sacred thing. He caught the bright splash of life and cessation in a poem published in 1967 called "Waking Early Sunday Morning":

O to break loose, like the chinook
salmon jumping and falling back,
nosing up to the impossible
stone and bone-crushing waterfall—
raw-jawed, weak-fleshed there, stopped
*   by ten*
steps of the roaring ladder, and then
to clear the top on the last try,
alive enough to spawn and die. ∎

Bing Crosby

Singer for all seasons

The sound was always unmistakable. And to most Americans old enough to remember World War II, the voice of Bing Crosby was one of the few enduring delights of popular entertainment. For half a century, from *I Found a Million Dollar Baby (in a Five and Ten Cent Store)* to *White Christmas* and onward to *Silver Bells,* it reached out to listeners with a perfect blend of nostalgia and affection.

Old Groaner, suave and casual

There were more than 3,500 songs recorded, some 400 million records sold. In an age increasingly given over to hype, the man remained a star, and he did it by keeping sentiment fresh. *Suave. Effortless. Casual.* All were adjectives that naturally attached themselves to his style—in music as in life. But there was perhaps a better word: *mellow,* which accurately described the famous theme song (*Where the Blue of the Night Meets the Gold of the Day*) that for years told thousands of fans that the *Kraft Music Hall* was on again, and with it Bing Crosby.

"Der Bingle," "the Groaner," "Old Dad" were nicknames that his countrymen knew well, though Crosby got most of them courtesy of his best pal and frequent colleague, Bob Hope. Humming and hamming, they did touring shows for front-line troops throughout World War II. For a decade or so, too, the pair were traveling companions with Dorothy Lamour and her sarong in a series of celluloid confections that started in 1940 with the *Road to Singapore.* The seven *Road* shows were rummage sales of soft-shoe stuff out of vaudeville, bits of burlesque, marvelously shoddy masterpieces of farce and fantasy stitched together with ad libs and bad puns.

The Road to Bingdom began May 2, 1903 in Tacoma, Wash. His full name was Harry Lillis Crosby. As a boy, he cared more about sports than music, once taking nine first places at a local swimming meet. Baseball was his real love, but he eventually settled for owning 15% of the Pittsburgh Pirates and being a crack golfer (he scored 13 holes in one). He went to Gonzaga University and studied law and even worked part-time in a law firm. But when he saw that he could make more money by singing and playing drums he left school and headed for Los Angeles.

There were none of the usual struggles. At 23 he was singing in vaudeville for $150 a week. Paul Whiteman noticed him, and he joined the King of Jazz. His voice was smooth and rich but light, its unique flavor partly the result of nodules on the vocal cords. Radio found him at just the right time; amplification enabled him to maintain his distinctively conversational style. One of his most beloved movie roles, for which he won an Oscar in 1944, was as the Catholic priest in *Going My Way.* It was a role that Devout Catholic Crosby almost turned down because he felt it was not fitting for a crooner to impersonate a man of the cloth.

A becoming diffidence adhered to Crosby even during the decades of his highest celebrity. He had his troubles at times in his marriage to beautiful but hard-drinking Dixie Lee, who died of cancer in 1952, and again in dealing with four sons with a penchant for getting into mischief. In 1957 he married Kathryn Grant, 30 years younger, and started a new family (three children). Crosby never claimed to be an exemplary singer or an exemplary anything else, and he once attributed his good reputation to the practice of admitting his sins only to "the father confessor."

When he died, there was a shred of consolation in that the way it happened seemed fitting. On Oct. 14, he had a heart attack just as he strode off the 18th green of a private golf course in sunny Spain. He died after carding 85—at age 74—and winning his foursome. ∎

Charlie Chaplin

The crumpled harlequin

Charles Spencer Chaplin, who died Dec. 25 at 88, rose from the darkest of London slums. His father was an alcoholic who disappeared shortly after Chaplin was born. His mother was a vaudeville singer until her voice cracked, and then she sewed blouses for 1½ pence each. Chaplin was consigned at one point to an orphanage, where he was beaten.

He was twelve when he got his first bit part in a touring company version of *Sherlock Holmes.* But it was not until 1914, when he tried on a pair of Fatty Arbuckle's outsize trousers and put some shoes on the wrong feet and painted on a false mustache, that he suddenly became The Tramp. The sad little figure made its creator an international hero. Within three years, Chaplin signed a million-dollar contract to write and direct his own films—among them some of the greatest ever made.

The Tramp, seeking romance

Comedy derives from the Greek *kōmos,* a dance. And indeed, as The Tramp capered about with his unique sleight of foot, he created a choreography of the human condition. In classics such as *Modern Times, The Gold Rush, The Great Dictator,* objects spoke out as never before: bread rolls became ballet slippers, a boot was transformed into a feast. Such lyric moments lifted Chaplin to the most exalted status. He became the friend of kings and critics. Einstein sought him out; Churchill praised him. George Bernard Shaw called him "the one genius created by the cinema."

Chaplin tried several times to explain his creation. He said once of The Tramp's repeated pratfalls that he was "forever seeking romance but his feet won't let him." Despite those pratfalls, The Tramp clung fiercely to his dignity. "No matter how desperate the predicament is," he said, "I am always very much in earnest about clutching my cane, straightening my derby hat, and fixing my tie, even though I have just landed on my head."

In private life, Chaplin married and divorced two teen-agers and earned a reputation as Hollywood's outstanding satyr. Shortly after being divorced by his third wife, Paulette Goddard, he was sued in a splashy paternity case and ordered to pay a young actress for the support of a child he denied fathering. He was also widely criticized in the early years of the cold war for supporting various left-wing causes.

In 1952 Chaplin and his fourth wife, Oona—the daughter of Eugene O'Neill, whom he had married in 1943 when he was 54 and she was 18—learned that he would be barred from re-entering the U.S. unless he could prove himself innocent of "moral turpitude." His new film, *Limelight,* was boycotted on the West Coast. Injured in soul and pocketbook, Chaplin spent most of his last 23 years in quiet retirement in Switzerland, surrounded by Oona and their eight children, awaiting signs of non-belligerency from old enemies. They came at last in 1972, when the cold war was mere scraps of snow, when Hollywood was able to recall that the "disloyal" clown had provided the aesthetic foundation for every film comedian since 1920. The evidence was an Academy Award for "the incalculable effect he has had in making motion pictures the art form of this century."

The lionizing had just begun. Queen Elizabeth II bestowed knighthood on Chaplin in 1975. Afterward, Sir Charles commented, "Life is a marvelous, a wonderful thing, but as you get on, you always think of moments past —and you always think of death." In a sense, Chaplin had always thought of the past; it was the poignancy of his childhood that furnished the comedies with their melancholy undertow. Yet the classic fadeout of the great Chaplin films shows the crumpled harlequin, twitching his little shoulders, setting his head forward and skipping off on the road to Better Times. ∎

Milestones

BORN. To **Evonne Goolagong Cawley,** 25, second-ranked woman tennis player in the world in 1976, and **Roger Cawley,** 27, a British metals broker: their first child, a daughter; in Beaufort, S.C. Name: Kelly Inalla. May 12.

BORN. To **Paul McCartney,** 35, owl-eyed ex-Beatle, composer and pilot of Wings, his high-flying soft-rock group, and **Linda Eastman McCartney,** 35, singer and photographer: their third child, first son; in London. Name: James Louis. Sept. 12.

BORN. To **Princess Anne Elizabeth Alice Louise** of England, 27, and Captain **Mark Phillips,** 29: their first child, a boy; in London. Nov. 15.

MARRIED. Jeanne Moreau, 49, protean femme fatale of French cinema; and American Movie Director (*The Exorcist*) **William Friedkin,** 37; she for the second time, he for the first; in Paris. Feb. 8.

MARRIED. David Cassidy, 26, onetime teeny-bopper heartthrob; and **Kay Lenz,** 24, TV actress; in Las Vegas. April 3.

MARRIED. Julie Harris, 51, the actress who played Emily Dickinson in *The Belle of Amherst*; and **Walter Erwin Carroll,** 54, occasional playwright; both for the third time; in Sterling, Va. April 26.

MARRIED. Lesley Hornby, 27, spindly singer and former model better known as **Twiggy;** and **Michael Witney,** 44, an American actor; she for the first time, he for the second; in Richmond, England. June 14.

SEPARATED. George C. Wallace, 58, Governor of Alabama and three-time presidential contender; and **Cornelia Wallace,** 38; after 6½ years of marriage; in Montgomery, Ala. Sept. 12.

DIVORCED. Edward W. Brooke, 57, junior Senator from Massachusetts; and **Remigia Ferrari-Scacco Brooke,** 58, his Italian-born wife; after 30 years of marriage, nine years of separation, two daughters; in Cambridge, Mass. May 16.

DIVORCED. Bob Dylan, 36, folk-rock hero; and **Sara Dylan,** 34; after eleven years of marriage, five children; in Santa Monica, Calif. June 29.

DIVORCED. Hayley Mills, 31, former child star in Walt Disney romantic sagas; and **Roy Boulting,** 63, British producer-director; after six years of marriage, one son; in London. Sept. 16.

DIED. Robert Anthony Eden, the first Lord Avon, 79; of liver failure; in Wiltshire, England. Jan. 14. Longtime Foreign Secretary (1935-38, 1940-45 and 1951-55), Eden finally succeeded Winston Churchill as Prime Minister in 1955, but had to resign 21 months later after blundering into the Anglo-French-Israeli attempt to recapture the Suez Canal.

DIED. Anaïs Nin, 73; in Los Angeles. Jan. 14. Nin's self-absorbed, incandescent writing (*The Diaries,* six volumes) dissected the female psyche at large in the artistic world of Paris and New York.

DIED. Bernard ("Toots") Shor, 73; of cancer; in Manhattan. Jan. 22. Saloonkeeper Shor was a Falstaffian companion to the celebrities of politics and sports.

DIED. James Jones, 55; of heart disease; in Southampton, N.Y. May 9. A pugnacious and largely self-taught writer, Jones drew upon his own experiences as a soldier for his gritty, powerful novels (*From Here to Eternity, The Thin Red Line*).

DIED. Joan Crawford, seventyish; of a heart attack; in Manhattan. May 10. With the same toughness and determination shown by the heroines she liked to portray (Mildred Pierce, Daisy Kenyon), Crawford rose from chorus girl to *grande dame* of the screen in a career that spanned four decades.

DIED. Robert Maynard Hutchins, 78; of kidney disease; in Santa Barbara, Calif. May 14. Boy wonder of liberal education —he became dean of the Yale Law School at 28, president of the University of Chicago at 30—Hutchins challenged all conventional teachings, pioneered in early college admissions and emphasized the Great Books.

DIED. General Lewis Blaine Hershey, 83; in Angola, Ind. May 20. Director of the Selective Service from 1941 to 1970, Hershey supervised the draft of some 14.5 million Americans in three wars.

DIED. Tom Campbell Clark, 77; of an apparent heart attack; in Manhattan. June 13. Dapper Attorney General under President Truman, Texas-born Clark served nearly two decades as a Supreme Court Justice (1949-67).

DIED. Wernher von Braun, 65; of cancer; in Alexandria, Va. June 16. The German-born pioneer in rocketry designed the deadly V-2 rockets that terrorized London in World War II. Brought to the U.S., he developed the Jupiter-C rocket that launched the first U.S. satellite in 1958, then the Saturn 5 rocket that carried the first men to the moon in 1969.

DIED. Francis Gary Powers, 47; in a helicopter crash; in Encino, Calif. Aug. 1. When Powers' high-flying U-2 plane was shot down deep inside the Soviet Union in 1960, the incident revealed a successful four-year CIA program of high-level surveillance of the U.S.S.R.—prompting Soviet Premier Nikita Khrushchev to cancel an impending summit conference with President Eisenhower.

DIED. Alfred Lunt, 84; of cancer; in Chicago. Aug. 3. Lunt and his wife Lynn Fontanne were Broadway's leading couple for almost four decades (*The Guardsman, The Visit*), delighting playgoers with their sophisticated badinage and consummate craftsmanship.

DIED. Archbishop Makarios III, 63, of a heart attack; in Nicosia, Cyprus. Aug. 3. A leader of the guerrilla campaign for Cyprus' independence from British rule, Makarios was elected as the island's first President, survived numerous plots and threats to rule his turbulent nation for 17 years.

DIED. Ethel Waters, 80; of heart disease; in Chatsworth, Calif. Sept. 1. Born into poverty, the "Queen of Blues" dazzled audiences in Southern black nightclubs with her raw honky-tonk singing and went on to become a Broadway star (*As Thousands Cheer, The Member of the Wedding*).

DIED. Leopold Stokowski, 95; of a heart attack; in Nether Wallop, England. Sept. 13. Audacious and innovative, Conductor Stokowski made the Philadelphia Orchestra into one of the world's most glittering ensembles and brought the classics to millions in the Walt Disney film *Fantasia.*

DIED. Maria Callas, 53; of a heart attack; in Paris. Sept. 16. The most exciting operatic soprano of her time, Callas electrified audiences in such specialities as *Norma* and *Tosca,* also delighted gossip columnists by her public quarrels with impresarios and her protracted romance with Aristotle Onassis.

DIED. James M. Cain, 85; of a heart attack; in University Park, Md. Oct. 27. Cain's two-fisted crime novels (*Double Indemnity, The Postman Always Rings Twice*) won him a reputation for powerful portrayals of thwarted ambition and sexual betrayal.

DIED. Guy Lombardo, 75; in Houston. Nov. 5. For 48 consecutive years Bandleader Lombardo and his Royal Canadians ushered in the New Year with the "sweetest music this side of heaven."

DIED. John L. McClellan, 81; of a heart ailment; in Little Rock, Ark. Nov. 27. As chairman of the Senate Permanent Subcommittee on Investigations and the "Labor Rackets Committee," McClellan, a cotton-country conservative, conducted hard-hitting investigations of labor unions and organized crime that led to the imprisonment of Teamster Jimmy Hoffa.

DIED. Baroness Spencer-Churchill of Chartwell, 92; of a heart attack; in London. Dec. 12. An aristocratic beauty, "Clemmie" was Prime Minister Churchill's wife and constant companion for 57 years and the mother of his five children.

The *Times's* three weekly supplements, which have helped boost circulation by as much as 45,000 a day

High Life at the *Times*

All the news that's fit to print, and then some

Of the 1,811 daily newspapers left in the U.S., none spends so much money (more than $35 million a year) to employ so many journalists (640 at last count) to produce so much news (now 152,000 words of a typical morning) as the New York *Times*. Its earnest editorialists can doom pending legislation with the drop of an admonition, its influential critics can close Broadway plays with the drop of an *aperçu,* and its 4½-lb., 400-page Sunday edition can kill an ox—and did some years ago, when one copy dropped accidentally from a plane over a rural area. No one has ever accused the *Times* of lacking heft.

Thus it came as a surprise to many loyal *Times* readers when the paper introduced three weekly 20-odd-page supplements that have little to do with hard news. The weightless innovations: Living, a Wednesday insert frothy with ads and upbeat articles on food, wine and related pleasures; Home, a similar Thursday celebration of furniture, design and gardening; and Weekend, a Friday guide to entertainment and the arts in the nation's cultural capital. Since the new sections began appearing, the *Times's* daily circulation has climbed from 821,000 to 867,000, the largest gain in ten years.

Living, Home and Weekend are the most elaborate manifestations of a new notion that is creeping across the newspaper industry. Stung by a decline in readership—some 2 million fewer Americans now buy a newspaper daily than in 1973 —publishers have been hiring consultants and conducting reader polls to find out what kind of news people want.

What the polls generally show is that Americans nowadays are increasingly eager for information about food, fashions, home furnishings and other "life-style" concerns, and less interested in national and international news. This preoccupation with the quality of life has prompted newspapers as large as the New York *Daily News* (circ. 2 million, the nation's largest) and as small as the Albuquerque *Journal* (circ. 77,000) to launch life-style supplements similar to those at the *Times.* The inserts often have zippy names like Tempo, Now or Trends. Says Los Angeles *Times* President Tom Johnson: "People do not want a newspaper, they want a 'use' paper."

The conversion of the New York *Times* to a use paper is the latest in a series of changes by Publisher Arthur Ochs ("Punch") Sulzberger. Soon after he took over—in 1963, upon the death of Brother-in-Law Orvil E. Dryfoos—Sulzberger closed the *Times's* hemorrhaging West Coast edition, diversified the paper into more profitable businesses, and replaced aging family retainers with younger, more aggressive executives. In the past couple of years, Sulzberger has ordered the *Times* redesigned to relieve some of the grayness, moved the bulk of its production processes to a more efficient new plant in nearby New Jersey and spun off four suburban editions. After years of seesaw profits, such changes are beginning to pay dividends. The New York Times Co. —which now includes 13 smaller newspapers, six magazines (including *Us,* circ. 500,000, launched last May in imitation of Time Inc.'s PEOPLE), two broadcast stations, two book companies and part of three paper mills—earned a record $18 million for the first three quarters of 1977, on alltime-high revenues of $369 million.

Critics of the new *Times,* many of whom are on the paper's news staff, fear that Sulzberger's growing emphasis on profit will pinch the paper's high editorial quality. They fret that Living, Home and Weekend are at best merely sloppily written fillers for advertising and at worst a courtship of the self-indulgent rich, while the more pressing problems of the city go underreported.

Times editors insist that they have not diminished the amount of space and money they lavish on hard news, and that Living, Home and Weekend—while trivial in subject matter—are up to the *Times's* high standards in execution. "Other papers have added water to the soup," says Executive Editor A.M. (Abe) Rosenthal. "We've added vegetables."

In any case, the three new non-news sections are so successful that Publisher Sulzberger insists they will not change substantially, and in fact are being joined by two others: a Monday sports supplement scheduled to appear Jan. 9 and a Tuesday insert, no firm startup date yet announced. That would just about round out the week for the *Times* and make the paper almost as hefty each weekday as it is on Sunday. ∎

Lord's Hustler

Larry Flynt sees the light

In one of the most startling religious conversions since Paul took the road to Damascus, Skin Magazine Publisher Larry Flynt, 35, announced that he had found God with the help of Evangelist Ruth Carter Stapleton, the President's sister. Flynt added that his *Hustler* (circ. 1.9 million) would be reborn as a "religious" magazine. Said Flynt: "I owe every woman in America an apology."

Flynt's proclaimed change of heart began months earlier, while he was fighting—and eventually losing—a much-publicized obscenity charge in Cincinnati (he now faces seven to 25 years in jail). After a number of meetings with Stapleton, Flynt had what he called a "powerful and awesome" experience while in a chartered jet, somewhere between Denver and Houston. He recalled: "I'm not ashamed to say I cried for God."

The publisher specified only a few of the changes he planned for *Hustler* and its California-based clone, *Chic* (circ. 436,000): vaginal closeups will be eliminated, for instance. Because of long publishing deadlines, however, the new look will not appear until the spring, so Flynt will have time to reflect on the financial losses such a shift might entail. Meanwhile, he assured readers that his magazines would not abandon erotica altogether. "Sex is beautiful and God given," he said. "If they think it's obscene, they should complain to the manufacturer."

Stapleton and Flynt at church rally

"I'm not ashamed to say I cried for God."

Tycoon Invades

And headlines turn shrill

The nation's newest press baron has a fondness for racing news, snappy headlines and photos of pretty girls, as well as a distaste for suede shoes, beards and radicals. He also has the nation's third largest evening daily (the New York *Post*), the nation's largest "alternative" weekly (the *Village Voice*) and the two largest regional magazines *(New York* and *New West)*—all of which he acquired in a six-week spending blitz.

The invader is Rupert Murdoch, an Australian who owns ten major newspapers, 13 magazines and dozens of lesser publications in his native land and Britain. He moved to New York four years ago to launch the *Star,* a weekly collection of tattletales and how-to-be-happier features. Murdoch remained virtually unknown in the U.S. until he bought the ailing *Post* late in 1976 from Publisher Dorothy Schiff for $30 million. Only days later he began a bitter but successful takeover fight for Clay Felker's New York Magazine Co., which includes *New York, New West* and the *Voice.* Estimated purchase price: $14 million.

Despite widespread fears that Murdoch would instantly turn all the publications into copies of his other, often sleazy journals, the changes so far have been confined largely to the *Post,* which grows more Murdochian almost daily. Sample front-page headline: DON'T TURN OFF MY MOMMY'S LIFE MACHINE; I WANT MY BROTHER TO BE BORN. ∎

Murdoch in his office at New York *Post*

"Don't turn off Mommy's life machine."

Capp's Last Strip

For 43 years, Al Capp had been amoozin' but confoozin' the reading public with the antics of Li'l Abner, Daisy Mae and assorted other denizens of Dogpatch. One day in September, the frog-voiced, razor-witted cartoonist casually told an assistant: "You can stop cutting the paper. I'm not going to draw any more."

Capp was uncharacteristically reticent about his reasons for retiring, though his health has been bad, his daughter had committed suicide a few weeks earlier and his cartoons had been losing readers. The last daily strip (see below) appeared in fewer than 400 newspapers, down from 900 at its peak in the late 1960s. Capp was the first comic-strip artist to engage in overt political satire, but his increasingly strident conservatism gradually alienated many young readers.

Though gone from the newspapers, Capp's creations will live on in memory, where Mammy Yokum will always defend her clan from the likes of Evil-Eye Fleegle and his triple whammy, where trigger-happy Fearless Fosdick will shoot unwary gangsters full of holes, and where bachelors will flee on Sadie Hawkins Day from the pursuit of belles like Moonbeam McSwine and Appassionata Van Climax.

D-Day for The Disabled

At last, they get equal rights

Eight-year-old Kimberly is lame and suffers from attacks of epilepsy. Once thought to be beyond training, she still "fades out" occasionally, her concentration lost. Six-year-old Cherise's legs are sheathed in long metal braces, and seven-year-old Lisa navigates the corridors in a wheelchair. Yet all three are successful students in a regular first-grade class at the William Trotter School in Roxbury, Mass. Says Teacher Barbara Fagone: "If they were stuck in a hole somewhere, there's no way they could ever make it."

All too often in the past, the handicapped were indeed stuck in a hole. Educated—if at all—in institutions or at home, many of the disabled then spent their adult lives hidden away from view.

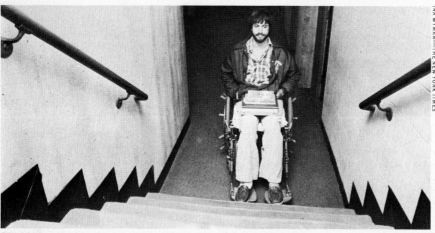

Disabled student confronts stairs at University of Massachusetts
Once the victims had to spend much of their lives hidden from view.

But that is now changing. Determined to have equal access to education and employment, America's 20 million to 35 million handicapped emerged in 1977 as the newest civil rights movement. Last April, after wheelchair demonstrations in ten cities from San Francisco to Boston, Secretary of Health, Education and Welfare Joseph Califano signed regulations to carry out the sweeping Vocational Rehabilitation Act of 1973. Under the act, any program that receives federal funds must admit the physically and mentally handicapped, and all physical barriers such as narrow doors must be corrected within the next three years.

Close upon the regulations victory came the White House Conference on Handicapped Individuals, the largest gathering of disabled people ever assembled in the U.S. Authorized by Congress at a cost of $3 million, the Washington conference drew 2,500 participants, who drafted recommendations to the Federal Government on how best to help the handicapped. Besides the Vocational Rehabilitation Act, the group could hail yet another legislative triumph, this one the Education for All Handicapped Children Act. Passed in 1975, the act decrees that all disabled children be given a free public education, as often as possible by "mainstreaming" them with normal children in regular classrooms. An estimated 8 million of the disabled—12% of all school-age children—will be affected.

The initial stages of the legislation went into effect last October, although school systems are allowed until next September to develop the bulk of their programs. Even as schools such as Roxbury's Trotter successfully integrated handicapped students, however, educators worried about how to finance the new system. While start-up costs have been estimated at $4 billion to $5 billion, funds authorized by Congress total only $775 million for the 1978-79 school year. Some fear that local school districts, already hard pressed financially, will be forced to mainstream even ill-prepared students rather than place them in small, expensive special classes. Equally troublesome is the question of how teachers who lack any background in special education will deal with severely handicapped children. Says Richard Cartwright of the National Education Association: "There's wall-to-wall worry out there."

But at least one educator, Massachusetts Deputy Commissioner of Education Michael Daly, insists that the fears are exaggerated. In his state, a bill that provides equal education for the handicapped has been operating since 1974—and with good results, says Daly. "Local schools were saying to Massachusetts a few years ago: 'It's impossible; we can't do it,'" he says. "But the fact is, we are doing it. Many of those kids are now in school with their brothers and sisters." ∎

An End to the Rubber Diploma

Now it's competency testing

Four years ago, Sam Owen, the folksy, pipe-smoking superintendent of schools for Greensville County, Va., announced that he was fed up with handing out "rubber diplomas" to high-school graduates who could barely read or write. Instead, Greensville decreed that all students must take a standardized exam twice a year to determine whether they had mastered their grade's material. Those who flunked would be forced to repeat the grade and get a heavy diet of basic reading, writing and math. For chronic failures Greensville devised a special Occupational Proficiency Training Course, in which students would earn not a diploma but a certificate that cited their job skills.

The result: Greensville became one of the first school districts in the country to inaugurate so-called minimal competency testing, now the hottest new catch phrase in education. Inspired by complaints about illiterate high-school graduates and criticism that a diploma is little more than a certificate of attendance, 31 states have ordered minimal competency programs (nearly half of them during 1977). In some cases the tests disclosed horrendous rates of failure—42% of the students of Miami's Dade County, for example, proved unable to pass the mathematics section of a competency exam. Now 16 more states are planning similar programs, and Congress has begun hearings on whether competency exams should be tried on a nationwide basis.

Despite its popularity, competency testing poses its own problems. What, for example, should be tested—only reading and math or such "survival skills" as how to balance a checkbook? Where will schools find the money for extended remedial programs? Some fear that minimal competency may turn into maximum competency as well—that teachers will end by teaching mainly the preparation for the test. Others feel that the tests will be so simple that they really will not test much of anything.

There is also the question of whether standardized tests set fair standards for minority students. In Greensville, where 65% of the 3,700 students are black, the N.A.A.C.P. has asked the Department of Health, Education and Welfare to examine the program for fear that black students are being held back disproportionately. Of the 220 students in the occupational-training course last year, 78% were black. Educators fear that further complaints of racial quotas and discrimination are in the offing. ∎

"I was surprised that I was so easy to replace," confessed **Farrah Fawcett-Majors,** noting how smoothly Actress **Cheryl Ladd** became Farrah's fill-in on *Charlie's Angels.* Farrah, who checked out of the top-ten TV show after just one season that made her the celebrity of the year, seems more than ready to wing it alone. Now at work on her first starring role in a movie, she has already lent her frame to more than 5 million pinup posters, and her famous name to plumbing fixtures (a $100 Farrah faucet, in gold), toys (the Farrah Fawcett Foxy Vet), and a catalogue of hair-care products from Fabergé. The latter deal alone, according to Fabergé President **Richard Barrie,** could enrich the former angel by "several million dollars." Gushed Farrah: "It's one of my most favorite things that's happened."

■

To find a new field, he would have to wait until soccer went to the moon, **Pelé** once joked, because "I've already played all over this world." In his 22-year professional career, the star had performed in 88 countries, led Brazil's Santos to three World Cups, and his adopted second team, the New York Cosmos, to the championship of the North American Soccer League. Once declared a "national treasure" by the Brazilian government—lest he be lured away to a foreign rival —Pelé played before a crowd of 76,000 in New Jersey on Oct. 1 in a farewell game televised to 40 countries. At 37, he

Onetime Angel Farrah takes wing toward movie stardom

now plans to do public relations work for the New York Cosmos, make a movie in Brazil and conduct youth-coaching clinics around the world. Although his three-year stint with the Cosmos had helped to double U.S. soccer attendance, the world's most famous athlete retired with characteristic humility. Said he: "Everything I did, inside the game of soccer and outside it, I did with love."

■

"We were programming ourselves for martyrdom. When the '70s came, all of a sudden we had to live our lives." So says **Jerry Rubin,** onetime member of the Chicago Seven. Having beaten a conspiracy rap stemming from riots at the 1968 Democratic National Convention in Chicago, Jerry and most of his co-defendants have been slipping through the '70s like straight men. Rubin, who publicized the "never-trust-anyone-over-30" philosophy, is 39 now, lives in a New York luxury apartment and earns $1,250 per lecture on self-growth psychology. Former S.D.S. Logistician **Ren-**

Brazilian Star Pelé leads the Cosmos to victory

nie Davis, 36, has packed off to Colorado, where he sells life insurance and proselytizes for **Guru Maharaj Ji.** Despite campaign help from Wife **Jane Fonda,** former S.D.S. President **Tom Hayden,** 37, ran unsuccessfully for the Senate last year, and is now lobbying in California for the development of solar energy. One of the few to keep his radical reputation intact is **Abbie Hoffman,** 41, the media-wise Yippie prankster. On the lam because of a 1973 cocaine bust, he has undergone plastic surgery, and is pursuing his politics as an underground fugitive.

■

It was all just a terrible accident, said French-born former Showgirl **Claudine Longet** as she explained how she happened to shoot her lover, Ski Ace **Vladimir ("Spider") Sabich.** Unsympathetic officials in the chic ski town of Aspen nonetheless took her to court last

Claudine Longet on eve of trial

January on a charge of "reckless manslaughter." With former Husband **Andy Williams** on hand for moral support, Claudine testified that she had asked Sabich to demonstrate the use of a .22-cal. pistol in case she ever needed protection. While questioning him about the safety lever, she said, the pistol went off. Longet was convicted of "criminally negligent homicide," a lesser offense, and sentenced to 30 days in the county jail. She is not off the down slope yet. Bitter about the trial's outcome, Sabich's parents filed suit against her for $1.3 million in damages.

People

Margaret Trudeau with Mick Jagger in Toronto

Billy frolics with Margaux Hemingway

"In the freest countries in the world, First Ladies are still prisoners. I'm trying to break that," announced **Margaret Trudeau,** 29, who spent much of the year shattering the stereotype of a politician's wife. In March, Margaret skipped out on the sixth anniversary of her wedding to Canadian Prime Minister **Pierre Elliott Trudeau,** 58, and set off for two days of picture taking and partying with **Mick Jagger** and the Rolling Stones in Toronto. Then came a well-publicized solo jaunt to New York, a brief fling at professional photography and, finally, a formal separation from Trudeau. By August, however, Maggie was back in Canada hoping for "a complete reconciliation" and preparing for a new kind of camera work —as an actress in an upcoming movie thriller titled *Kings and Desperate Men.*

■

To one British official, **Queen Elizabeth's** Silver Jubilee was "the biggest souvenir bonanza since the coronation" a quarter-century ago. The year-long celebration of the Queen's reign inspired mementos ranging from beer mugs to a Jubilee bra-and-panties set, helped attract more than 11 million tourists to the U.K. and sent Elizabeth off on visits throughout the Commonwealth. At the climax in June, Londoners flag-waved through a week-long bash marked by bonfires and pageants, and Parliament eventually softened up and granted the Queen a regal $522,000 boost in her annual allowance of $2,878,-000. Not everyone was pleased by the extravagance, however —or even by the birth of Elizabeth's first grandson to **Prin-**

cess Anne in November. Groused William Hamilton, a Labor M.P.: "How charming. Another one on the payroll."

■

He has given up managing the family peanut business, but First Brother **Billy Carter** is still making hay. Now pulling in $5,000 to $10,000 for every personal appearance, Billy has six-packed off to the Miss Piggy's Pizza Beauty Pageant in Boston, the Golden Ratchet Award ceremonies in Chicago, the Annual World Belly Flop and Cannonball Diving Championship in Vancouver, B.C., and to other corners of his ole

Queen Elizabeth's Silver Jubilee was a year-long celebration—and she got a $522,000 raise

74

The Shah and Empress Farah suffer the effects of tear gas

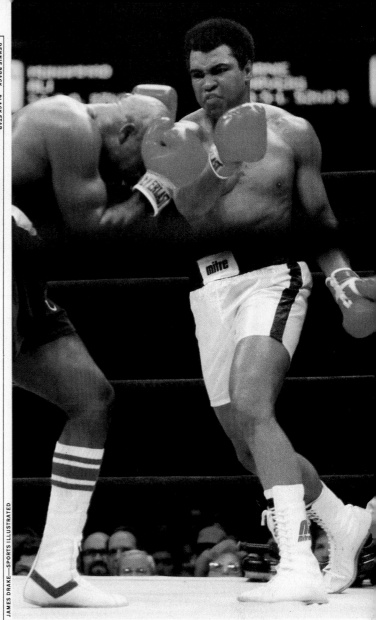

Shavers and Ali, bobbing and weaving all the way to the bank

boy constituency. For those who miss him in the flesh, there are Billy posters, T shirts, belt buckles, iron-on patches and, of course, Billy Beer. According to his agent, Billy turns down 95% of the deals he is offered because they are "too flippant." No matter. This year he earned a reported $500,000 from his Billy business—more than twice the salary of Older Brother **Jimmy.**

■

There were no silver herald trumpets and scarcely a ruffle or flourish when Mexico's President **José López Portillo** came to Washington as **Jimmy Carter's** first state visitor in February. Despite President Carter's yen for stripped-down pomp, the White House welcome mat got plenty of wear last year. Among Carter's visitors: General **Omar Torrijos Herrera** of Panama, Israeli Prime Minister **Menachem Begin,** Egyptian President **Anwar Sadat** and West German Chancellor **Helmut Schmidt.** One of the warmer welcomes went to the **Shah of Iran,** whose visit in November set off a club-swinging fracas near the White House grounds. While the Shah and **Empress Farah** stoically wiped away the effects of police tear gas, nearly 100 supporters and opponents of the Iranian ruler and more than two dozen policemen were injured in the melee. "There is one thing I can say about the Shah," observed Carter afterward. "He knows how to draw a crowd."

■

In 17 years as a professional pugilist, Heavyweight Champion **Muhammad Ali** has been the master of bobbing and

weaving all the way to the bank. Besides starring in his first movie *(The Greatest)* and his third marriage (to **Veronica Porche,** 21), the champ won 15-round victories last year over **Alfredo Evangelista** and **Earnie Shavers** and boosted his lifetime ring receipts to more than $55 million. With two ex-wives, six children and an army of retainers behind him, Ali, now 35, obviously hopes to clinch a few more paydays before giving away his gloves. "People are always asking me when I'm going to retire," he huffed. "Well, I've announced my retirement three times now. I won't say any more about it now because it kills your credibility."

■

"After 14 years at sea, our ship is coming safely into port," **Ted Kennedy** announced happily as he and a clutch of kin broke ground in Boston for the long-planned John F. Kennedy memorial library. For the most part, in fact, the whole crew of Camelot survivors enjoyed fairly smooth sailing throughout the year. Finally free from pressures to run for the presidency, Ted settled comfortably into his role as a

Jackie with Christina Onassis before the $26 million settlement

semi-senior Senate Democrat and new chairman of the powerful Antitrust Subcommittee. A lurid Viking Press novel describing an imaginary assassination attempt on his life led Sister-in-Law **Jackie Onassis** to resign as a Viking editor, but the former First Lady could content herself with a newly negotiated $26 million settle-

ment with the estate of Second Husband **Aristotle** and his heiress **Christina.** Jackie's daughter **Caroline** spent the summer as a $125-per-week copy person at the New York *Daily News,* earned a *Rolling Stone* byline for her coverage of Elvis Presley's funeral, and by fall was at Radcliffe trying out as a reporter for the Harvard *Crimson.* **Joseph,** eldest son of the late Robert Kennedy, considered a race for political office (Massachusetts state treasurer), but opted for some seasoning in a $25,000-per-year job with the Community Services Administration. Meanwhile, Joe's sister **Kathleen Townsend** launched a whole new generation of the family by giving birth in November to a baby girl. **Meaghan Kennedy Townsend** became the first great-grandchild of the family matriarch, **Rose.**

Star Wars: Wise and Childlike

An astronomical take of $200 million with no end in sight

"The force will be with you ... always." These are the last words we hear from Alec Guinness, playing the wise old Jedi Knight, Ben (Obi-Wan) Kenobi, in *Star Wars.* It begins to seem that no truer voice-over was ever spoken, for the picture has turned out to be not just the show-biz success of the year but perhaps even of the decade. The film is not just a hit but a full-fledged mass cultural phenomenon. Its images seem destined to haunt our minds permanently, its phrases are already entering the language, and its merchandise is in our living rooms and playrooms, first stop on the preordained journey to our attics and thence to the nostalgia shops of the future.

The film, as everyone knows, became the alltime domestic box-office champion in a mere six months, surpassing the $200 million mark this holiday season, having passed *Jaws'* rental record (the amount actually returned to the distributor) around Thanksgiving. And most of the world is still virgin territory, though very promising, since the picture broke both the Australian and British records for advance sales this autumn. Box-office figures are made to be broken in these days of high admission prices. *Jaws,* after all, held its title for only 2½ years. It seems safe to assume that something or other will replace *Star Wars* at the top of the all-

time top ten within a similar span. What is going to make it hard to dislodge from its pinnacle as the most profitable piece of celluloid ever to flap through a projector is its merchandisability. The ancillary rights to *Jaws,* for example, pretty much began and ended with some T shirts and rubber fishes, for *The Godfather* with Marlon Brando posters. But practically every frame of *Star Wars* contains something—a monster, a weapon, a vehicle—that you can convert into a toy, a costume, a knick-knack.

The standard spin-offs, the kind of stuff that even flop movies generate, have been boffo. The publisher, for example, has shipped more than 3 million copies of the paperback novelization of the screenplay, while 1.5 million copies of the soundtrack album have been sold. The company making *Star Wars* T shirts claims to have captured 40% of the entire U.S. T-shirt market. And the beat goes on. Some 14 other *Star Wars* books are in preparation, while a new record album, which recounts the story of the movie, has now arrived in the stores.

Meantime, the *Star Wars* calendar may become the new champion in its field, displacing J.R.R. Tolkien's Middle-earthlings; the little firm that makes the $40 masks of the *Star Wars* characters cannot keep up with the demand and is

expanding production; and the people who did the less expensive kid costumes for Halloween are convinced that Darth Vader is going to replace Frankenstein's monster as the ultimate villainous archetype, the one and only guy to dress up as when you want to scare your little sister.

But all of that is just the beginning. Around the world some 30 manufacturers are cranking out the rest of the Star Wares —everything from digital watches to blankets—and nobody can predict what astronomical revenues they may generate. All anyone can say for certain is that they've never seen anything like this before. So they want to imitate it.

In Hollywood, the rush is on. There is something obviously comic-strippish about the *Star Wars* style and so, with *Superman* already before the cameras, producers have rushed to register titles ranging from *Flash Gordon* to *Dick Tracy,* hoping that the secret of success is to be found in resurrecting yesteryear's pulp. Equally obviously, *Star Wars* is a form of science fiction, and so a remake of *Invasion of the Body Snatchers* is now shooting, and the much discussed, off-again, on-again *Star Trek* feature looks to be on again. And, of course, *Close Encounters of the Third Kind* has won rave reviews and large audiences. Indeed, it has generated more commercial optimism than it may warrant chiefly because, like *Star Wars,* it deals with creatures not of this world.

Yet one has to wonder ... Everybody glances at the comics, but except among

buffs they have rarely stirred the kind of massive response that *Star Wars* has created. The same goes for sci-fi; the cult that cares about it is intense but fairly narrow; fans' ardor can keep you from going bankrupt, but it has never made anybody a millionaire either. It's obvious that *Star Wars* had something going for it beyond style or subject matter, something that may in the end prove to be inimitable.

The film's quality is, in fact, a spirit that is at once innocent and knowing, wise and childlike, and it is a true manifestation of the sensibility of a singular individual named George Lucas, whose credits as writer and director of the film somehow fail to express the depth of his creative commitment to the project. At 33, Lucas is a slight, shy, but really quite forceful individual. He is one of those rare people—especially rare in the movie game—who combine genuine sophistication of mind and craft with an uncanny ability to remain affectionately in touch with their own past—and particularly with the subcultural material that dominated their childhood.

What sets Lucas apart not merely from other moviemakers but from just about everyone else who attempts to use this material for artistic purposes is his refusal to apologize for it or to sneer at its continuing influence on all of us. He can and does kid its manner, but there is neither campiness nor commercial calculation in his use of it in *Star Wars* or in his previous success, *American Graffiti*. To indulge in that would be to express a kind of contempt for the folkish art that shaped the man he is today. His calculations —and he spent two years drafting and redrafting his script for *Star Wars*—are those of the artist—that is, of a man who

understands that the best in our popular culture is as deserving of serious contemplation as any Norse saga or Arthurian legend. What he sought in those two years was the animating essence of pop, with which he could remind his contemporaries (and elders) of what was good and useful in their shared past—and introduce youngsters to a tradition of popular culture more heroic and idealistic than that of *Charlie's Angels* and *Laverne & Shirley*.

Stuff of Star Wares—Guinness with quasi-laser (above); Robots See-Threepio, Artoo-Detoo (inset); Imperial and rebel fighters

What Lucas instinctively understands is that there is a difference between a classic adventure comic like, say, Hal Foster's *Prince Valiant* and mental junk food on the order of TV's *The Six Million Dollar Man*. The former is a highly individualized expression—in larger-than-life terms—of certain common beliefs and longings about the nature of heroism; the latter is formula fare derived not from anything resembling the collective unconscious but from the trivializing dictates of commercialized technology.

It is this sense that *Star Wars* is soberly, even studiously derived from good models, that it has an honest moral undertow, that its desire is to respect rather than rip off modern forms of folk expression, that surely accounts for its unprecedented popularity. Even—perhaps especially—a child can see that something authentic, and actually rather delicate, is being expressed here, despite all its technical hoopla, its mad-dash pacing.

But as Lucas was at pains to remind us, there is a dark side to any force, and in the case of *Star Wars,* merchandising may be it. A large staff has done its best to see that the quality of all the *Star Wars* stuff is good. It has so far spent something like $250,000 in protecting its property against unlicensed purveyors of inauthentic and inferior knockoffs. On the other hand, proliferation inevitably cheapens. And wearies. A *Star Wars* lunch box does not really have any mythic resonance to it. Right now the force is too much with us, and one wishes not merely that its imitators would cease and desist but that *Star Wars* originators would resist the impulse to squeeze every last nickel out of their creation.   — *Richard Schickel*

Dance

"What You Need Is Three Legs"

Balanchine reflects on storms and success

The New York City Ballet dancers had not performed *Vienna Waltzes* for months, and they were having trouble with its looping patterns during rehearsal. "No, no," cried Choreographer George Balanchine. "You must all bend the same way—like the passengers on a boat in bad weather. They all bend overboard the same way—to vomit."

The joke works. The dancers relax, shoulders stop pumping, and couples start to glide instead of swoop. Swirling across the stage at Lincoln Center, they are all bending the same way, as always to the will of Balanchine. *Vienna Waltzes,* which had its première during the company's spring season, is a major hit, doing turn-away business at every performance. The work also has a symbolic importance to the company: it brought them out of a bad slump caused by a musicians' strike last January. The New York City Ballet is acknowledged to be America's finest classical troupe. But like every performing-arts institution, it must struggle against a deficit. Such battles are often won on momentum: 1977, which began so badly, ended with 98%-capacity audiences and a $1 million federal grant.

Vienna Waltzes is an opulent, dramatic work created for Balanchine's stars. In the first sequence, led by Karin von Aroldingen and Sean Lavery, couples drift through a moonlit grove to music by the younger Johann Strauss. The women are proud-necked beauties in billowing pink dresses; the men, in formal uniforms, are grave and ardent. They wander off, as if seeking another part of the woodland, and Patricia McBride darts in, accompanied by a band of gauzy dryads. During their brief, exuberant ballet—the only section danced on point—the grove becomes a fairies' arbor. But Balanchine soon banishes not only elegance and enchantment but even the waltz. The forest is filled with local hooligans who bucket around to Strauss's *Explosion Polka.*

For the ballet's last two sequences, the setting is a ballroom. Kay Mazzo, looking limpid and sexy, plays the Merry Widow to Peter Martins' cavalier. The idea is not to mime the plot—the music is Lehar's *Gold and Silver Waltz* rather than an excerpt from the operetta—but to sketch the romantic, mildly decadent spirit of *fin-de-siècle* society. The ballet's finale is set to music from Richard Strauss's *Der Rosenkavalier.* Suzanne Farrell, in a magnificent white ballgown, dances alone. She looks ready for any festivity, but her partner seems to exist only in her imagination. Sometimes a man appears and dances with her briefly, but she drifts away. In the end she leaves, arms outstretched as if to reach into silence. Instead, the gesture calls forth dozens of waltzers who sweep onto the stage, crossing and recrossing it swiftly and boldly like dancers in a 1930s movie musical.

The sequence writes a bravura signature to a ballet that began with chaste young couples courting to quavering zither strains. The work is formal, with classical proportions and balance. It is inviting yet mysterious. When Suzanne Farrell, looking perfect as a lily, glides across the floor alone, the mind tries—like her occasional partner—to go inside her reverie, to anchor her in a situation. But like the ballet, she remains elusive.

Whoever this apparition in white may be, she is not a mystery to her creator. Talking backstage before a recent performance, Balanchine brushed aside the romantic aura that may be the secret of *Vienna Waltzes'* success. "Ah, she would like to have a partner, in an enormous ballroom, in the moonlight," he says. "But it happens in life, you are in a situation and you would like a partner, but you are alone." Lest that sound too redolent of significance: "Probably her partner is simply late. He will come!"

For Balanchine, love of the waltz goes back to childhood in St. Petersburg. He is a vigorous man who speaks rapidly with Russian inflection, punctuating his thoughts with many gestures. "Two legs and three-quarter time," he muses. "What you need is three legs. It must all be calculated. You need room and time to turn in those dresses, but the girls do it well.

The trouble comes with the boys. Maybe they feel it is sissy to be beautiful, to be graceful, to be attentive to one's partner —I don't know."

At 74, Balanchine is a benevolent god moving through his kingdom, creating ballets for his younger dancers, reviving some of his classics for brilliant new casts. During the strike, there were rumors that he might close down everything in New York and start up in Europe. He denies that he regarded the situation even as a crisis. "In America there is always a strike," he says. "Here the musicians, there the elevator operators. It is a disaster, a calamity—no, it is a storm. You get caught in a storm and then you settle—until the next storm. Our dancers all know exactly where they are because they have been with us since they were children at our school."

The company is dancing unusually well right now. There are new stars, like the quicksilver Merrill Ashley, for whom Balanchine has just made *Ballo della Regina,* set to the ballet music from Verdi's *Don Carlo.* The year has been a high point from which Balanchine can survey the past and the future. If his own future is narrowing, he remains serene. "I never worry. Not about now, because I am here. In the future everything will be different anyway. Think of Louis XIV watching the *commedia dell'arte.* He might wonder: what will happen to the *commedia dell'arte?* Why, nothing! It won't exist!"

But, it turns out, that thundering conclusion needs a coda. "Actually," says Balanchine, "as a young man I went to Naples with the painter Pavel Tchelitchew and I saw the last Pulcinella. The very last. She must have been 80. And I learned from her things about the Italian style—things that I have been able to use."

— *Martha M. Duffy*

Dozens of waltzers sweep across enormous ballroom in elegant finale
A bravura signature to a work both inviting and mysterious.

Top: Balanchine directing his dancers. From left: Tomasson and McBride on point; exuberant hooligans; Von Aroldingen in moonlit grove

One major hit gave America's finest classical ballet troupe the momentum for a triumphant season.

Steve Cauthen, at 17, has rewritten the whole record book of Thoroughbred racing

"I've trained more than most jockeys. I've grown up to be a horseman, not just a rider."

JEFFREY E. BLACKMAN

The Kid Wins $6 Million

Horses run kindly for him

Last January he was only 16, an apprentice jockey riding light and lucky, and they called him "The Kid." By the end of the month, though, he had set a single-week record for victories at New York tracks—a total of 23 wins. The measure of his accomplishment: 54 races were run, and Cauthen won nearly half of them. He consistently booted home winners by the handful each racing day. Believers along the rail began calling him "Stevie Wonder."

In May, he took his first serious spill when his horse broke a leg and brought him down. He suffered a fractured wrist, cracked ribs, cuts on the forehead, and the experts said that this would provide the first real test. Next time out, would he have lost, maybe just a little, his nerve? After being sidelined for a month, he made his comeback on June 23 and won with his first horse, Little Miracle. The following week, he surrendered his bug-boy allowance—a 5-lb. weight advantage given apprentice riders—and became at last Cauthen, jockey.

By Christmas, with 477 victories on mounts that won more than $6 million in purses, Steve Cauthen had established himself as top man. At age 17, he rewrote the record book to become the biggest

Reggie Jackson—powerful shoulders and tender ego—slammed four homers in four swings

And that made champions out of "the best players money could buy."

WALTER IOOSS JR.—SPORTS ILLUSTRATED

Glory to Everyone

The Brawling Yanks Triumph

"I never saw a club so tough to handle," said Manager Billy Martin, a man who has gazed often into the eye of a storm, about the 1977 New York Yankees. It was a team full of fascinating conflicts. There was the brooding Reggie Jackson, a player Martin had not wanted to bring to New York, who drew the largest salary in baseball history ($2.9 million for a five-year contract). There was Owner George Steinbrenner, a domineering shipbuilder who sprawled all over his manager and team. There were All-Star players at several positions, some of them sulky about their contracts. And there was Martin himself, a bold, unstable personality, a onetime street fighter who had been fired from his last three clubs.

"Trouble follows me," said the sad-eyed Martin, and from the very start of the season the sullen, gifted Yankees were never out of trouble. Outfielder Mickey

money winner in the history of Thoroughbred racing.

How to explain it? His seat is low, balanced, so perfectly streamlined that his horse seems riderless when viewed head-on, an aerodynamic miracle wrought on the lunging back of a race horse. His memory for the detail of instruction on racing strategy, trainers assert, is computerlike. Says one trainer: "He actually goes out and does what I actually told him to do." Others laud his extraordinary sense of timing, an instinctive knowledge of the moment when a horse must be held back or sent out. Says Cauthen: "I've trained more than most jockeys. A lot of them start training just seven months before they begin riding; others might spend two years at it. I've grown up to be a horseman, not just a rider. I have been around horses all my life, and I've worked my way up." But at its base there remains something mysterious about Cauthen's phenomenal success. It lies beyond explanation in that mute language of animal and special man. "He has great hands," says onetime Jockey Sammy Renick. "Horses settle in and run kindly for him. Few jockeys have this touch. Steve hits the horse at just the right time —which is a feel, a gift that he has."

Cauthen's gifts, honed with unrelenting study and practice since he entered his teens, stood up to the strongest challenges and most skeptical caviling. When he was scorching the track through the bitterest winter in memory, backstretch naysayers noted that the best horses from the top stables were wintering in friendlier climes. The fields on these frozen days were drawn from tired also-rans and

Cauthen was unhurt in this tumble last February, though a fall in May broke several bones

An instinctive knowledge of when a horse must be held back or sent out.

worn-out players, they said, and Cauthen's horses greatly benefited from the weight allowance accorded him. But he consistently met the country's top jockeys —Vasquez, Maple, Turcotte—and ran them down.

Cauthen settled in as a journeyman jockey. He had been without a mount in the glamorous Triple Crown events, where top horseflesh traditionally goes to established riders, not phenoms. Although his celebrity value and skill earned him mounts in a few important California stakes races, the big rides eluded him until August and the Saratoga Meeting. Saratoga's season is short but, for horsemen, sweet, with top jockeys and prime horses, as befits America's oldest racing

fixture. There Cauthen matched up with the best—Willie Shoemaker on three-time Horse of the Year Forego. On a rain-soaked track, Cauthen and Nearly On Time handed Forego his third and worst defeat of the year.

Almost equally notable was Cauthen's Saratoga debut on Affirmed, a stylish two-year-old from prestigious Harbor View Farm and a certain Triple Crown contender. The young colt and its jockey dueled down the other two-year-old favorite, Alydar, eventually running away with the Eclipse Award for the best of the new crop of colts. Firmly up in the irons on the winter-book favorite, Cauthen will not be left behind again when the Run for the Roses begins next May. ∎

Rivers arrived in spring training demanding to be traded. Outfielder Jackson, who drove in a Rolls-Royce and announced that he was "the straw that stirred the drink," was treated like an outcast by his teammates. Pitcher Catfish Hunter, another million-dollar man, and Relief Ace Sparky Lyle griped about the way the manager used them.

The Yankees—whom Steinbrenner described as "the best players money could buy"—lost eight of their first ten games. But they were too good to fall very far behind. Through the spring, with all their bickerings and grudges, the Yankees bumped along within sight of the lead.

At the center of the Yankee turmoil was the hostility between Martin and Jackson. "I'm the hunted one," said Jackson, "on a team that's hunted." The two men pawed the ground and finally, in the middle of June, rammed. "All the players were waiting for it," said the manager, who chose his turf carefully. After Jackson loafed in fielding a hit in Boston—in front of a national television audience —Martin yanked him. When the wounded Jackson cursed the manager in the dugout, Martin attacked him. The brief

Yankee Manager Martin yelling at umpire
Trouble follows him.

scuffle was a burlesque, but Martin viewed it very seriously; he described it as the turning point of the season, the moment when he showed the players who was boss.

Steinbrenner for his part was stunned. At first he wanted to fire Martin, but then

he backed off and decided to risk it with the volatile manager. Steinbrenner did wonder aloud whether the team was headed for a complete collapse. "Dissension is everywhere," he said. At the same time, he must have noticed that the notorious Yankees were on the way to attracting 2 million fans at home and another 2 million on the road.

In the middle of July the owner flew to Milwaukee for a night session with his manager, and an incident occurred that Steinbrenner viewed as the team's true turning point. Shortly after midnight, two of New York's key players, Catcher Thurman Munson and Outfielder Lou Piniella, knocked on the owner's door. Steinbrenner said they told him flatly that the Yankees couldn't win under the erratic Martin, that the majority of the players felt the manager had to be fired. Munson and Piniella recalled the conversation differently: they claimed they demanded that the owner either fire Martin immediately—or get off his back. Suddenly Martin himself was banging on the door, enraged to find his players there. The four men argued until 6 o'clock in the morning and finally agreed to some lineup changes: Reggie Jackson would get his wish and bat cleanup; certain pitchers would be rotated regularly; Piniella would become the permanent designated hitter. At the same time, Martin's shaky contract would be redrafted to give the manager more job security.

In early August, the Yankees at last began to show their expensive muscles; they won 40 of their next 50 games. The lineup changes paid off. Over that period, Jackson drove home 50 runs, Piniella hit .357, the pitchers calmed down and the Yankees reached 100 victories and the division title. Martin, always shrewd, managed his team with renewed skill —but if New York lost the upcoming playoffs to Kansas City, he told a friend, Steinbrenner was sure to dump him.

The Yankees and Royals had a brawling playoff that stretched until the last inning. Just before the final game began, Martin announced that he was benching Jackson; he had decided his slugger was not up to Kansas City's strong lefthanded pitching and its slippery artificial turf. It was a gutty, dangerous decision by the manager, even though Jackson indeed was having trouble with the Royals. In the locker room someone told Martin that Jackson hated him, and the manager replied: "He doesn't know how to hate, not the way I do." Trailing late in the game, though, Martin sent Jackson up as a pinch hitter, and the outfielder came through with a single that helped tie the game. New York roared ahead in the 9th inning and won the game, 5-3.

Now the Yankees seemed really together; even Martin allowed himself to smile as he explained that the owner could no longer hurt him. Said he: "A little Dago like me fixed his ass." The Yanks defeated Los Angeles in the opener of the World Series, but Catfish Hunter was shelled out of the second game. Immediately Martin and Jackson were at each other again. The outfielder told reporters that the manager should never have started Hunter, who was out of action much of the season. Martin fumed and sent a gamy insult flying back. But the Yankees won the next two games in Los Angeles; then the Dodgers won one.

In the sixth and final game Jackson, the man with the powerful shoulders and tender ego, saved everybody—including himself. With three swings, each on the very first pitch, Jackson smashed three home runs out of the park. Since he had hit a homer his final time up in the previous game—also on the first pitch—Jackson had slammed four homers on four successive swings, a record that probably forever would go unequaled. The Dodgers were wiped out (final score: 8-4), and the Yankees had won their first championship in 15 years. Steinbrenner, the busybody executive, was vindicated. Martin's job was saved, and now he seemed a managing genius. Jackson, the outcast, almost the richest loser around, had brought a piece of glory to everyone. ∎

Other Winners

And also-rans

Auto Racing: A.J. Foyt edged out Tom Sneva by 28 sec. to capture the Indianapolis 500 for an unprecedented fourth win. His time: 3:5:57.16. Though he lost the big race, Sneva won the title of USAC National Driving Champion. Winner of the world championship on the Formula I Grand Prix circuit was Austria's Niki Lauda.

Basketball: the Portland Trail Blazers defeated the Philadelphia 76ers by four games to two to capture the N.B.A. championship. The Marquette Warriors won the N.C.A.A. championship by downing North Carolina, 67-59.

Sailing: Ted Turner skippered *Courageous* to four straight victories over *Australia* in the America's Cup.

Football: the Oakland Raiders won handily over the Minnesota Vikings in the Super Bowl, 32-14. At the college level, University of Texas Halfback Earl Camp-

bell earned the Heisman Trophy and led the Longhorns to the nation's only major-college undefeated and untied record in regular-season play (11-0)—and to a showdown with Notre Dame in the Cotton Bowl.

Golf: Tom Watson won the Masters with a 276, two strokes ahead of Jack Nicklaus, and the British Open with a 268, one stroke ahead of Nicklaus. Watson also led in P.G.A. tournament winnings, earning $310,653.

Hockey: the Montreal Canadiens routed the Boston Bruins in four straight in the Stanley Cup.

Soccer: the New York Cosmos, led by Pelé, edged the Seattle Sounders in the N.A.S.L. Soccer Bowl, 2-1.

Tennis: at Wimbledon, Bjorn Borg won his second straight title, defeating Jimmy Connors, 3-6, 6-2, 6-1, 5-7, 6-4. Virginia Wade defeated Betty Stove, 4-6, 6-3, 6-1. At Forest Hills, Guillermo Vilas beat Connors, 2-6, 6-3, 7-6, 6-0, to win the U.S. Open. Chris Evert won her third consecutive women's title by stopping Wendy Turnbull, 7-6, 6-2. ∎

Challenge to Racing Traditions

A Triple Crown winner, history teaches, is a beast that comes along once in a decade. A horse that can triumph over the hoopla of the 1¼-mile Kentucky Derby, the sizzling speed of the 1³⁄₁₆-mile Preakness and the Belmont's torturous mile and a half is a horse for the ages. Only nine had turned the trick in the half-century between Sir Barton in 1919 and Secretariat in 1973. But a bargain-basement colt named Seattle Slew became the tenth Triple Crown winner in 1977, and he did it in a fashion none of his illustrious predecessors could match: unbeaten in every contest from maiden race as a two-year-old to his walkaway triumph in the Belmont Stakes. Jockey Jean Cruguet stood up in the saddle 20 yds. short of the finish line at Belmont, holding a disdainful whip aloft for all doubters to take the measure of this strong dark bay colt.

Bought at auction for the piddling price of $17,500, Slew and his success challenged the traditional Thoroughbred Establishment, which holds that a min-

Seattle Slew racing to victory in the Belmont

imum of three generations of breeders must dream and fret before the fates bestow the Triple Crown on a famous stable. Slew's co-owners—Washington Lumberman Mickey Taylor and New York Veterinarian Jim Hill and their wives—had been involved in the sport only four years when Seattle Slew breezed away with the Crown. Trainer Billy Turner had been widely second-guessed for working the horse too sparingly; Jockey Cruguet, similarly, was criticized as second-rate. The Triple Crown ended all that.

In a radical departure from recent racing practice, Seattle Slew was not put to stud after his three-year-old campaign and will resume his racing career during the Florida winter season. Despite offers ranging as high as $14 million, the Horse of the Year in 1977 will be back to challenge all pretenders in 1978. ∎

Former NOW President Karen DeCrow and Houston delegates hail passage of ERA resolution

Is ERA Doomed?

Despite the push in Houston, time is running out

Jackie Onassis sent her regrets and Pat Nixon was ill. But Rosalynn Carter, Betty Ford and Lady Bird Johnson were all there. So were Gloria Steinem, Margaret Mead, Phyllis Schlafly, Bella Abzug and nearly 2,000 delegates from every walk of life. The National Women's Conference 1977, in Houston in November, was a roaring celebration of women's possibilities—and a nagging reminder that the movement still has far to go.

Tightly run by liberal feminists, the convention endorsed a package of women's issues—including the right to abortion, civil rights for lesbians and the Equal Rights Amendment. Despite fears of disruptive tactics by conservative women—some 20% of the delegates were "pro-family" traditionalists, mostly from the South and West—the meeting proceeded peacefully enough.

For some, the convention demonstrated that feminism is now mainstream Americana. "Houston was a rite of passage," said Eleanor Smeal, a housewife who heads the 65,000-member National Organization for Women. Others pointed to relatively modest gains: new contacts with like-minded women in other regions and racial groups.

It was unclear, however, whether Houston could rescue the Equal Rights Amendment, now the No. 1 issue for feminism and its increasingly vocal opponents. Indiana, which voted yes last January, is the only state to ratify the amendment in nearly three years. Eight states rejected ERA during 1977, leaving the amendment three states short of the constitutionally required total of 38, with only 15 months remaining in the seven-year ratification period set by Congress. To make matters worse, Idaho, Nebraska and Tennessee have voted to rescind their ratification, a legally debatable tactic.

How did ERA go wrong? Lulled by the early success of the amendment (approval by 30 states in two years), many feminists came to view ERA as an obvious issue that would pass without effort. Its text, after all, appears unexceptionable: "Equality of rights under the law shall not be denied or abridged by the United States or by any State on account of sex."

As late as 1975, few politicians saw any political rewards in opposing equal rights for women. Then opponents began descending on state legislatures, offering exaggerated arguments that ERA would force the legalization of homosexual marriage, end the support of wives by their husbands and require use of the same public toilets by men and women. More important, opponents have won followers by insisting that a vote against ERA is a vote against sexual license and radical change. The Conservative Caucus reports that ERA is "a good recruiting tool," and in much of the South opposition to ERA has used the tradition of regard for states' rights. When North Carolina voted no on ERA in March, former U.S. Senator Sam Ervin called it "a great victory for all North Carolinians who want to keep government at home instead of having it transferred to Washington." Says Radical Feminist and Writer Robin Morgan: "I feel personally guilty because I was one of those people who thought, 'The ERA doesn't matter. It doesn't have any teeth in it. So phooey.' But suddenly it matters to the tenth power if it fails."

Feminists have belatedly found a way of exerting economic pressure in behalf of ERA: a boycott of convention centers in the 15 states that have not ratified. The campaign began last February in Las Vegas, and so far has swung about 20 conventions away from cities in non-ERA states—notably Chicago, Atlanta, Miami and Las Vegas. The tactic is promising, but perhaps too late: most conventions are booked at least two years in advance and legally locked into convention sites.

ERA supporters clearly need more time, and are likely to push in 1978 for a seven-year extension of the ratification period. Though the legality of such a move is cloudy, the Justice Department believes Congress can grant the extension by a simple majority vote. The extension may be as controversial as ERA itself. Says Phyllis Schlafly, a leading opponent of the amendment: "It's like changing the rules in the middle of the game."

Without an extension, ERA backers might be down to one last roll of the dice: electing pro-amendment legislatures in 1978 and pushing quickly for ratification early in 1979. Given the strength of the opposition, the odds are hardly good. ∎

Gay Backlash

The squeeze on Anita

"The 'normal majority' have said, 'Enough! Enough! Enough!'" That exultant cry from Singer Anita Bryant capped her successful crusade last spring to repeal a gay rights ordinance in Dade County, Florida.

But that was just the beginning. Gays began organizing a nationwide boycott of Florida orange juice, which Bryant advertises on TV. The Pride Foundation, a San Francisco organization that works for homosexuals' legal rights, sued Bryant and several co-defendants for incitement to murder, claiming that her crusade led to the local slaying of a homosexual last spring. Bryant herself was hit in the face with a banana cream pie in Des Moines. In New York City, NBC reported several threats of violence when Bryant appeared on the *Today* show. Said an overwrought Bryant: "Why don't they just kill us and get it over?"

Actually, though Bryant had to curtail her touring and keep travel plans secret, the gay boycott had little effect, and the Florida Citrus Commission extended her $100,000-a-year contract through August 1979. In fact, Bryant's new book, *The Anita Bryant Story,* is selling briskly, and a Gallup poll showed her following close behind Rosalynn Carter and Golda Meir as most admired woman in the world. ∎

War over Women Priests

Can a barrier of nearly 2,000 years be removed?

It was New Year's Day, 1977, the first day on which the historic action could be taken. At All Saints' Church in windswept Indianapolis, Jacqueline Means, a truck driver's frizzy blonde wife, mother of four, hospital and prison chaplain, was ceremonially clothed in a white chasuble and ordained as the first officially recognized woman priest in the Episcopal Church. Just before the ritual, a layman had risen to denounce the proceedings as "heresy" and "sacrilege," and about a dozen people, many of them in tears, marched out of the church. Afterward Means was more sad than jubilant. Said she: "I've just been so hurt by the whole thing, but God never said life would be easy, and maybe the fabric of the church will be stronger for this."

In subsequent months some 90 other women took advantage of the Episcopalians' new policy of allowing female priests (including New York's Ellen Barrett, who became the denomination's first avowedly homosexual priest). But the 2,000-year tradition of an all-male priesthood did not die quietly. Despite the 1976 decision of the church convention to ordain women,* some Episcopalians refuse to admit that Means and her sisters are really priests at all.

Two months after the convention acted, St. Mary's of Denver became the first parish to quit the Episcopal Church over the issue. Soon other parishes defected in Arkansas, Virginia, Massachusetts, Nevada, then four in the Los Angeles area, then a big downtown church in Oakland, Calif. By September a schism was officially launched, with a barrage of tough talk about apostasy, at a St. Louis rally of 1,750 Episcopalians, including hundreds of male priests.

The dissenters opposed other liberal moves as well—notably, the updating of the venerable *Book of Common Prayer*, which had won preliminary approval in 1976—but the principal target was in fact women priests. The founders of the emergent "Anglican Church in North America" declared that the Episcopal Church and Canada's Anglicans "have departed from Christ's One, Holy, Catholic and Apostolic Church."

The most prominent sympathizer with the schismatics' views on women —though not with their schism—turned out to be none other than the head of the

*That leaves the Lutheran Church–Missouri Synod as the only major U.S. Protestant body to forbid women clergy. There is an unwritten ban on women ministers, however, among the 4 million members of the Churches of Christ. Even in those denominations that do permit female ministers, their numbers remain a tiny proportion of the total.

Episcopal Priest Means before ordination
Maybe the church will be stronger.

Episcopal Church, Presiding Bishop John M. Allin, who attended the St. Louis meeting as an observer. Two weeks after St. Louis, when the church's House of Bishops met at a Florida resort, Allin announced in a low-key Mississippi drawl that he was unable to believe that "women can be priests, any more than they can become fathers or husbands." If his opinion was unacceptable to his brother bishops, Allin said, he would resign. Under polite but pointed questioning from the floor, Allin indicated that although he would support church policy in official actions, he could not personally ordain a woman priest, or even receive Communion from one.

As Allin had hoped, the bishops decided to try to head off the schism by granting considerable leeway to the anti-women faction, including the 27 bishops who had signed a "covenant" of total opposition to a female clergy. The assembled bishops declared that neither Allin nor anyone else would be penalized for conscientious objection.

The women's supporters were furious, but they were forced to settle for a messy compromise in which part of the church refuses to recognize those of its duly ordained priests who are female. To some extent, the compromisers succeeded, for at year's end the number of schismatic congregations totaled only 100, most of them small. The schism may develop further after the schismatics' first three bishops receive "apostolic" consecration in Denver on Jan. 28.

Far more massively opposed to the ordination of women is the Roman Catholic Church. While various branches of the Anglican Communion were moving toward a male-and-female priesthood, Pope Paul directed the Congregation for the Doctrine of the Faith to consider the question. The resulting lengthy decree and "commentary," issued Jan. 27, ruled out Catholic women priests for the indefinite future.

In essence, the Vatican said that the Roman Catholic Church cannot ordain women because it cannot change "an unbroken tradition throughout the history of the church." The commentary said that the ban now has a "normative character," and it is "considered to conform to God's plan." The decree recalled that Jesus Christ chose no female apostles, despite his dignified treatment of women, and that the New Testament church denied the priesthood even to the Virgin Mary. Further, the Vatican argued that since a priest represents Jesus Christ in celebrating the Eucharist, the role "must be taken by a man."

The Catholic hierarchy in the U.S. soon endorsed the statement, but some other Catholics criticized it strongly. In Berkeley, Calif., for example, 23 teachers at the Jesuit School of Theology wrote the Pope's Apostolic Delegate to the U.S., charging that it was a "serious scandal that so decisive a document could be issued whose consultation was so minimal and whose argumentation appears so weak."

The issue of women priests, besides fomenting debate—and schism—is causing considerable difficulty in the ecumenical movement. In the same month that an international Anglican-Catholic negotiating team announced substantial progress toward reunion, the Vatican issued its decree, in effect adding women to the list of items dividing the churches. Equally serious is the hostility to the Anglicans—and the praise of Rome—from the Eastern Orthodox, among whom a female clergy is not even under discussion. If women priests are authorized at the decennial Lambeth Conference of the world's Anglican bishops this coming July and at the subsequent General Synod of the mother Church of England, the Orthodox have threatened that all further ecumenical discussions with the Anglicans will be cut off. ∎

What Is Fair?

Allan Bakke demands equal protection for whites

The case known as *The Regents of the University of California* v. *Allan Bakke,* which reached the crowded chamber of the U.S. Supreme Court on Oct. 12, was widely regarded as one of the most important civil rights controversies to come before the court since the 1954 school desegregation case. Fifty-eight friend-of-court briefs, an alltime record, came pouring in from interested groups, ranging from the N.A.A.C.P. to the Sons of Italy and the United Auto Workers.

At stake was the future of "affirmative action"—a broad and complex series of programs designed to help women, blacks and other minorities to enter and get ahead in higher education and professional careers. To their supporters, these programs are essential to overcome the effects of past discrimination; to their opponents, they are themselves discriminatory, a violation of the basic concept of judging individuals on their merits.

Amid all the arguments, Bakke himself remained something of a mystery. As his case wound through the courts, he avoided press interviews while continuing to work as a mechanical engineer at an aerospace agency near his home in Sunnyvale, Calif. A tall, blond father of two, he had earned engineering degrees from Minnesota and Stanford, and served as a Marine captain in Viet Nam before belatedly deciding that he really wanted to become a physician. When he began ap-

plying to medical schools in 1973, he was 33, and a dozen of them turned him down.

Among them was the newly established Medical School at the University of California at Davis. The school had created a special admissions procedure for "disadvantaged" students, which in practice meant minorities. It reserved 16 out of 100 places for them. Bakke's grades and test scores were superior to those of many who were admitted in the special program. Bakke sued, claiming that he was a victim of "reverse discrimination." In September 1976, the respected California Supreme Court agreed that the special program was unconstitutional.

At the Supreme Court, Harvard Professor Archibald Cox reasoned for the university that any harm done to Bakke must give way to the more important goals of society. Said he: "There is no racially blind method of selection which will enroll today more than a trickle of minority students in the nation's colleges and professions." In response, San Francisco Attorney Reynold Colvin insisted that his client deserved a literal reading of equal protection. Said he: "The ultimate fact in this case, no matter how you turn it, is that Mr. Bakke was deprived of an opportunity to attend the school by reason of his race."

During the argument, Justice William Brennan reminded participants that the Supreme Court usually avoids sweeping constitutional decisions when a case can be decided more narrowly. Indeed, only a few days later, the Justices asked for supplementary briefs on the applicability of an overlooked civil rights law banning race discrimination by recipients of federal funds. No observer expected the

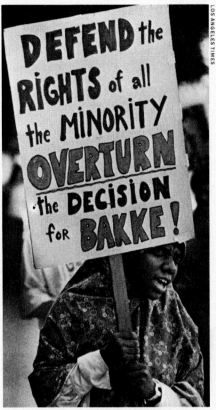

Affirmative-action backer in Los Angeles

Is "reverse discrimination" illegal?

court either to endorse or to strike down all the varied affirmative-action programs. Nonetheless, the court's decision in 1978 will be a vital indication of judicial tolerance for whatever short-term inequities may be required to resolve an enduring social problem. ∎

The Death Penalty Reborn

Gary Gilmore's wish is granted

Gary Mark Gilmore was different from most death-row inmates: he wanted to die. He disavowed appeals on his behalf and so he doomed himself to become the first victim of capital punishment in nearly ten years.

The prospect attracted reporters from all over the world to the bleak state prison at Point of the Mountain, Utah. Somebody wrote a Gary Gilmore song, and somebody produced a Gary Gilmore T shirt, and TV producers bid for the rights to his life story. When a series of unauthorized legal appeals delayed the date of execution, Gilmore showed his displeasure by twice attempting suicide in his cell.

At last, a firm date and place were set: at dawn on Jan. 17 in an abandoned tannery called the slaughterhouse. Gil-

Gilmore after learning date of execution

First capital punishment in ten years.

more, 36, freshly shaved and wearing a black T shirt, wrinkled white pants and red, white and blue sneakers, was led manacled to a raised platform and loosely strapped to a mahogany office chair. Twenty-six feet away, behind a sailcloth partition with five narrow slits, stood five anonymous marksmen armed with .30-.30 deer rifles; one rifle contained a blank. After Warden Sam Smith read the death sentence for the shooting of a motel man-

ager, Gilmore peered around, then said: "Let's do it." A Roman Catholic priest administered last rites, a target was pinned over Gilmore's heart, and a black corduroy hood was slipped over his head. Then, at a hand signal from Smith, the marksmen fired. Two minutes later, at 8:07 a.m., Gilmore was declared dead.

Although some civil libertarians feared that wholesale executions would soon follow once the moratorium had been broken, that proved to be false. By year's end, 18 months after the U.S. Supreme Court authorized resumption of capital punishment, 402 men and 5 women were awaiting death in 23 states, but various legal defenses managed to keep all alive. (Seeking to provide a "more civilized and humane" form of death, Oklahoma and Texas legislatures during the year adopted laws mandating execution by lethal injection of chemicals.) Those postponements could not go on forever, though. Warned David Kendall of the N.A.A.C.P.'s Legal Defense Fund: "It may be a year or two away but the executions are coming." ∎

The Big Movement Afoot

Suddenly, everyone started running . . .

> *I have found my hero, and he is me.*
> —Dr. George Sheehan

No more could the long-distance runner claim to be lonely. In squads and lines and legions, huge numbers of Americans were running to beat, if not hell, obesity. Also, coronaries, slack muscle tone, insomnia, indigestion, emphysema, self-contempt, tensions, aggressions, depressions and flaccid sex lives. Wind-blown and bright-eyed, the heroes to themselves pumped along the crisp beaches of Florida and across the rich fields of Iowa. They toiled up Nob Hill and clacked down Beacon Hill from sunrise to sunset, and on mid-afternoon Manhattan elevators confronted the two-martini luncheon crowd with whiffs of virtue and sweat.

As many as 10 million Americans are now jogging, trotting or running,* and their numbers are waxing as fast as their waistlines may be waning. Running is the nation's fastest-growing pastime.

In jaded New York City, the grueling five-borough marathon last October attracted 4,823 starters (3,900 finished) —more than twice as many as the year before. Some 3,000 runners entered the Honolulu Marathon this year—15 times as many as the first Hawaiian marathon attracted in 1972. Such figures are only the

*There is no clear distinction between the gaits, as there is, say, between a horse's canter and gallop. However, anyone who completes a mile in eight minutes or less is said to be running.

Woman and Afghan on the run in New York
To beat, if not hell, obesity.

tip of the sneaker, because the great majority of runners prize the pursuit for the very reason that it is not competitive: a serious amateur sets and adjusts his own speed to his own satisfaction, matching his will not against anybody but against his own body. Moreover, since running —unlike golf or tennis—does not require expensive gear, or any at all, equipment sales do not reflect the extent or depth of the joggernaut's passion. Nonetheless, sales of jogging suits—which to many devotees are nothing but a status symbol —have risen exponentially in the past five years. Literally hundreds of varieties of running shoes are on the market: so many

that the October issue of the monthly magazine *Runner's World,* in its largest issue ever, devoted all 144 pages to the subject. Nike, one of the top U.S. manufacturers, reports that sales are increasing at the rate of about 75% a year (to nearly $50 million in 1977).

At least 200 major corporations now subsidize physical activities—including running—for their employees. There are enough new books on running to pave Central Park's six miles of roads. *Runner's World,* which is shoehorned full of advice from the Olympic to the podiatric, is as minutely scrutinized by its 200,000 subscribers as the label on a vitamin bottle—and has propelled its publisher, Bob Anderson of Mountain View, Calif., into other sports-news enterprises that gross $5 million a year.

Swimming and bicycling are less grueling. Squash and tennis are more companionable. The very act of running blisters the foot, strains the kneecap, jars the spine, discombobulates the intestines, overpalpitates the heart and reduces strong lungs to wheezing. Jogrunners proudly catalogue their cramps, stitches, pulled muscles, torn ligaments, heel spurs, shin splints, chondromalacia patellae and Achilles' tendinitis. So what is this addiction? Why do people run? The reasons are not simple. They have both a compelling rationality and an impenetrable mystique. Running, for most devotees, is not so much a sport as—in its literal sense—a recreation. The pain and the monotony lead—so the heavy breathers maintain —to a new euphoria, the addictive exaltation of goddammit I did it. It can become a way of life and—for some—a lifesaver.

Nearly 5,000 runners crossed the Verrazano-Narrows Bridge at start of New York City's grueling five-borough marathon last October

Larry Kirshbaum, 32, a Manhattan marketing executive who laced up his first track shoes in 1977, says blithely: "Before I started running I was very hyper, uptight and a son of a bitch. Now I'm just a son of a bitch." More specifically, Jesse Bell, 52, president of the Cleveland-based Bonne Bell cosmetics company, admits that four years ago he was "drinking too much, losing my wife and my business." He took up running and was joined by his wife; now, wherever they may be, from Oslo to Tokyo, the Bells ring up some 60 miles a week.

For good reason, doctors are among the most assiduous evangelists of jog. James King Jr., 37, a vascular surgeon now based in Portland, Ore., used to jog seven miles a day between three Atlanta hospitals (he does not make house runs). George Sheehan, (*Dr. Sheehan on Running*), an erudite New Jersey cardiologist, became a record-breaking miler when he was 50 (he is now 59), and argues that running is intellectual as well as physical therapy. He goes so far as to say: "Trust no thought arrived at sitting down." Thaddeus Kostrubala, 47, an equally engaging author (*The Joy of Running*) and a San Diego psychiatrist, believes that running can allay almost any kind of psychological disorder. He maintains: "Jogging is a whole new way of getting into contact with our unconscious selves. We are basically hunters and runners who have become urbanized. By jogging, we get back to our normal selves." The most renowned running medic of all is of course Kenneth Cooper, 46, a former Air Force medic, whose 1968 book *Aerobics* explained to millions how the body can more efficiently use oxygen through exercise.

Physicians are by no means unanimously agreed that running can confer all the physical and psychological benefits that the true believers claim. No Kinseys or Masters/Johnsons have yet emerged to track the long-distance sexual highs claimed by the Adidas set. Undeniably, however, running buffs do generally reduce or eliminate smoking and drinking. They usually eat sensibly and trim excess weight. A new study of 16,936 Harvard alumni has shown conclusively that those who engaged regularly in strenuous activities like running, swimming and squash were far less susceptible than sedentary types to heart attacks. Since 54% of all deaths in the U.S. occur through diseases of the heart and blood vessels—diseases that are associated with physical inactivity—the runner would be, even to a cold-eyed life insurance agent, a better actuarial risk than the sedentary, overweight caricature of a body that *Americanus flabiosus* lugs around.

Few authorities believe that jogrunning is a '77 fad, an instant remedy for the ills of affluence, industrialization and urbanization that will quietly expire at some unannounced finish line in '78. Whatever other reasons people may have for huffing and puffing at dawn or dusk, they will always feel good doing it. ∎

Fashion Avenue Gulps Mighty Lungfuls of Self-Assurance

The results: free-form, fluid, roomy, romantic and relaxed

American women live and dress quite differently from Europeans, and they remain faithful to their fashion. Never was this more true than in 1977, when French couturiers tried and formidably failed to create the free, frisky, practical yet romantic clothes that carry *l'américaine* from breakfast to bed. At the same time, U.S. designers from Manhattan's Fashion Avenue (a.k.a. Seventh) to Sunset Boulevard gulped mighty lungfuls of self-assurance. The fashions they produced—and those the customers snapped up—were the most distinctive expression to date of the casual-sportive American Look. Indeed, their handiwork has been called the most significant evolution in fashion since that memorable year when Christian Dior dropped hemlines almost to the parquetry.

What has emerged in the past year —what women are wearing—is a softer, more graceful and sophisticated chic. The hard-edged image has yielded to what Designer Albert Capraro, 34, calls "an easy, unconstructed, unbulky mood. Everything is softer, softer, softer." Says Halston, the Indiana-reared *doyen* (at 45) of American design: "The look is more sophisticated, the view is more utilitarian." Adds *Vogue* Editor-in-Chief Grace Mirabella: "American fashion is more polished now, not as scatty, not as bits-and-piecey. Casual by day holds, but it's a little more dressed in the evening, in fabrics that suggest richness." Some fashion observers, who have over the centuries perceived acute sociological significance in the vagaries of women's dress, attribute the new look to the victories of the feminist movement. No longer do women have to wear blazers and pants to assert themselves in the office world. As California's rising star, Harriet Selwyn, puts it, "We can afford now to look pretty."

The silhouette is larger, but not bulky; it shows off the body but does not constrict it. The clothes are more natural and more unabashedly feminine than before. The tiered, layered look has evolved, notably with shawls, ponchos and scarves, from self-consciousness to self-confidence, with ruffles and flounces, soft jerseys, big blouses, tweed and flowered skirts, simple wrap-arounds, patchwork waistcoats and chamois trousers, delectable fabrics and toothsome hues. Says Mirabella: "The layered look has become the thinnest thing over the thinnest thing." Last year's gear look has been refined, so that the wearer no longer looks like a model from the L.L. Bean catalogue but rather a cover girl from *Field & Stream*. Quilted jackets, for every good climatic reason, are still in, and boots are, as Mirabella says, "the anchor of everything."

American women are buying fewer garments but spending more and devoting greater thought to the wardrobes they assemble. That, to the celebratory eye, can be observed in any daytime elevator or all-night disco. The same eye will also record that American women are re-dressing and uninhibiting for the evening. As Halston notes, "It's considered bad taste for a woman to draw high-fashion attention during the day. At night, she can be slit to the waist, or whatever she wants. At night, anything goes." ∎

A soft, blouson silhouette

"We can afford now to look pretty."

Clockwise from upper left: ABC Programming Chief Fred Silverman and some of his network's biggest hits: The Fonz in *Happy Days;* the controversial new serial *Soap; Laverne & Shirley* (rated No. 1); and *Three's Company*

Static and Confusion

ABC has changed the ABCs

Along Manhattan's Network Row you could almost hear the Alka-Seltzer fizzing—and the heads rolling. The most prosperous year in television history was also the most troubled. Not since radio gave way to TV in the early '50s had broadcasters been so uncertain about what they were doing or where they were going. "There never has been a season so complicated. Or so confusing," complained CBS President Robert Wussler in August, just before the new shows were unveiled. By October Wussler was an ex–CBS president—one of many victims of TV's year of static and confusion.

The chief cause of turmoil was as simple as ABC—the American Broadcasting Co. For 20 years the boundaries of the TV world had been fixed and immutable. CBS—the home of such innovative hits as *I Love Lucy, The Mary Tyler Moore Show* and *All in the Family*—was first in the ratings. NBC was not far behind, and ABC, a distant third, hardly a competitor. In the early '70s, however, ABC began making changes. It designed its programming to appeal to young peo-

ple, and, under the flashy direction of Roone Arledge, it concentrated more than the other networks on sports.

At the end of the 1976-77 season last April, the network claimed the four top-rated shows in the country, and seven of the top ten. Its overall average in the Nielsen ratings was 21.5, which put it far in front of CBS (18.7) and even farther ahead of NBC (18.0). For eight consecutive nights in January, moreover, ABC did not just beat the opposition. It obliterated and humiliated it with its dramatization of *Roots,* Alex Haley's bestseller about his search for his origins in black Africa. The most popular show in history, *Roots* at its peak drew an audience of some 130 million—or almost two out of every three men, women and children in the U.S.

Heady from the unaccustomed smell of success, ABC—guided by Fred Silverman, the programming whiz it had snatched from CBS—decided to push its advantage with the new season. Instead of premiering its new shows in mid- to late September, as custom dictated, ABC

pushed the schedule ahead to Sept. 6, the day after Labor Day. Hoping for another ratings bonanza like *Roots,* it also started off with its biggest hitter: six consecutive nights of *Washington: Behind Closed Doors,* John Ehrlichman's fictionalized account of high deeds and low in the Nixon White House.

Down the street, network executives fumed that ABC had broken the rules, and denounced its upstart arrogance for trying to catch them off guard. "It's essential to knock *Washington* off on Tuesday," NBC Program Vice President Paul Klein told his network's affiliates. "And if we can injure *Washington* on Wednesday, then we will have done a job on them. When the numbers come in, they will either have a success or a huge failure —and the season will be over." Belatedly, the other networks scheduled expensive counterprogramming—movies and specials that they had planned to hold for the peak viewing nights of the fall—but their efforts were too little, if not too late: ABC took the first week's ratings with *Washington,* and it also captured every other week of the season but one.

The single exception went to NBC, which devoted four nights in November to the saga of *The Godfather,* nine hours

LeVar Burton as the hero of *Roots*
Seen by almost two-thirds of America.

of footage, some of it never before shown publicly, from Francis Ford Coppola's *The Godfather* and *The Godfather, Part II*. But even that victory was a disappointment for NBC, which hoped that *The Godfather* would dominate the airwaves as *Roots* had. In fact, though *The Godfather* did well, it did not do well enough to justify its enormous cost—a staggering $10 million to $12 million, according to most estimates.

As the year ended, ABC appeared almost certain to stay in front for the rest of the season—and possibly for the rest of the decade. The latest rating gave ABC five of the top ten regularly scheduled series, with *Laverne & Shirley* and *Happy Days* the first two. ABC has clearly found a formula the viewing public likes —broad-gauged, comic-book humor and as much sex as the tube will allow—and neither CBS nor NBC has been able to successfully duplicate that combination.

In the one area where the network was still demonstrably third-rate—news—ABC was energetically trying to catch up. Roone Arledge took over the news division, even while retaining sports, and CBS and NBC, still No. 1 and 2 in news ratings, expected and feared his usual headlining innovations. "The ABC powerhouse has clearly established itself as the General Motors of the business," says Mike Dann, a TV consultant who was CBS's programmer during the glory days of the '60s. "It might develop that we'll have one General Motors and two American Motors."

To forestall that dire possibility, both CBS and NBC brought in whole new teams to run their networks. NBC, apparently sensing doom, replaced President Robert Howard with Robert Mulholland at the start of the season. A few weeks later it announced that it would lay off more than

300 employees, including many near the top. CBS waited for disaster to be announced in the fall Nielsens before taking action. Not only did it change a few name plates, but it also totally revamped its corporate structure for what it hoped would be a more streamlined, alert operation. Its model? ABC, of course, the network it only dimly recognized as recently as three or four years ago. "CBS is not a No. 3 network," asserted Chairman William Paley, contradicting the ratings that put it there. "CBS is not a No. 2 network. CBS is a No. 1 network. I feel it. I know it." Surveying all the carnage in plush suites, Producer Norman Lear wryly observed: "They talk about violence on TV! There is more violence being done on the corporate level than anything we see on television."

Yet even as they battle, the network executives have another reason for breaking out the Alka-Seltzer. After 30 years of fascination, the public seems to be somewhat bored by TV—all TV. For the first time in memory, television viewing is down substantially. According to Nielsen, the daytime drop from November 1976 to November 1977 was 6.4%, a figure roughly equivalent to the combined populations of Detroit and San Francisco. The nighttime drop, 3.1%, is less dramatic, but it is nonetheless significant. If this trend does continue, the

ABC News Chief Roone Arledge
An emphasis on youth.

advertisers, who sometimes pay well over $200,000 for one commercial minute of prime time, will undoubtedly begin to wonder where their money is going. The title of No. 1 may no longer be the prize it once was. — *Gerald Clarke*

Rule Britannia!

In the winter, after the start of Anthony Trollope's *The Pallisers*, liquor stores reported a run on orange curaçao, the favorite drink of Trollope's crusty old Duke of Omnium. In the spring, when *Upstairs, Downstairs* ended after 3½ years, it seemed as if there was not a dry eye in the country, and many addicts were asking whether poor James Bellamy really had to kill himself. In the summer, it was time for the swashbuckling adventures of *Poldark*, a romance of the 18th century, and in the fall it was the turn of *I, Claudius*, a riveting drama of the vices and violences of the first four Roman emperors.

The four series had only two things in common: they were all splendidly done, and they all bore the stamp "Made in Britain." In 1977, as in the rest of the '70s, the British dominated quality TV in America. "What would public television be," quipped Public Broadcasting Service (PBS) President Lawrence Grossman, "if the British didn't speak English?"

One American company, Children's Television Workshop (CTW), which

Derek Jacobi as Claudius

has produced outstanding children's shows like *Sesame Street*, sent a staff member to London for a year to learn the secrets of the masters. Based on her study, CTW produced its own historical drama, *The Best of Families*. Set in New York in the late 19th century, *Families* looked at three different kinds of families—rich, poor and middle class—much as *Upstairs, Downstairs* had focused on masters and servants in Britain. The results were somewhat different, however. *The Best of Families* was the Biggest of Bores.

The secret of British quality, like the purloined letter, stares at all those who can turn on a set. It is a trust in the intelligence of the audience. Commercial TV hasn't had it for some time, and PBS isn't sure it knows what the term means. Until it finds out, the BBC will remain the best network in America. — *G.C.*

The Punks Are Coming!

They bring driving sound, a dumb look—and outrage

Once again a highly publicized quartet of British rockers is invading the U.S., but history is repeating itself with some differences. The Sex Pistols are not adorable moptops who want to hold your hand. Lead Singer Johnny Rotten informs audiences at Pistols concerts that he hates them, then spits at them to drive home his point. His contribution last summer to Elizabeth II's Silver Jubilee was a scabrous single called *God Save the Queen* (sample lyrics: "God save the Queen,/ She ain't no human being ... the fascist regime made you a moron"). To promote

any case, something old and new is happening: rock 'n' roll is stirring up outrage.

The Sex Pistols and their unpleasant shenanigans deserve much credit for this resurgence of public bile. But they are only one of a welter of noisy groups now on the verge of making the catchall term "punk rock" a household word—or a household curse. The punk phenomenon has been simmering on both sides of the Atlantic for several years. Working-class social protest fuels much British punk. England's economic woes and ossified class system have created a receptive, restive

Spiv Bators of the Dead Boys
Any kid can pick up a guitar.

Johnny Rotten of the Sex Pistols
A scabrous view of the Queen.

CHRIS LITTLE—CAMERA 5

BOB GRUEN

this tribute, the Pistols' record company distributed stickers showing a picture of the Queen with a safety pin jammed through her lip. Two of the four Sex Pistols have been physically assaulted by fellow countrymen. Their attackers may have been furious royalists; perhaps they were just old-fashioned music lovers. In

audience for the Sorrows of Young Rotten: "We're stinking poor and have nothing to do." Some punk groups in England flaunt swastikas and flirt with totalitarianism in their lyrics; the Sex Pistols' first hit single was *Anarchy in the U.K.*

U.S. punks, including such groups as the Ramones, Television, Talking Heads, Richard Hell and the Voidoids, and the Dead Boys, stage aesthetic rather than political assaults. Their target: the lush, middle-of-the-road pop rock that now dominates AM and FM airwaves, exemplified in the work of such perky millionaires as Elton John and Peter Frampton. The punk groups that have recorded have done so chiefly on small labels; their live performances have been largely confined to raucous city clubs like New York's C.B.G.B. and the Whisky in Los Angeles. U.S. punks give the impression that they would not know a Moog synthesizer if one arrested them. Not for them the ov-

erdubbing, string sections and cavernous echoes of MOR rock. The sound they want is raw, nerve flaying, an aggregate of amplified guitars in a tin garage.

Despite these differing approaches, British and American punk rockers produce much the same kind of music: hard-driving, double-clutch beats, with unintelligible lyrics hurled into a metallic din. Extended guitar riffs and solos, the mark of hard rock, rarely appear in the punk repertoire; the tempos are too fast to accommodate them, and few punk guitarists have displayed enough mastery to play them. Punk scorns slickness and professionalism in favor of lumpen proletariat amateurishness. Says the New York–based *Punk* magazine: "Any kid can pick up a guitar and become a rock 'n' roll star, despite or because of his lack of ability, talent, intelligence ..."

Similarly, punk fans have cultivated an aggressively dumb look: strategically torn T shirts; safety pins stuck through clothes, cheeks and ear lobes; fishnet hose; cropped and dyed hair. Bred in equal measure by trash-strewn city streets and soft-core S-M boutiques, punk fashion has already percolated into such class stores as Bloomingdale's in New York and Giorgio's in Beverly Hills.

To the May-fly mentality that permeates the rock world, every variation is brand new. Punk, as it happens, is old. It dates back at least as far as Elvis' sideburns, sneer and pegged pants. The young Bob Dylan posed scruffily against Greenwich Village backdrops, cigarette dangling from his lips, smoke in his eyes. Before the Beatles became cuddly, they wore black leather jackets and bawled out tough-boy protests. When the Liverpudlians were embraced by a waiting world, Mick Jagger and the Rolling Stones were ready in the wings to become the reigning hoodlums of rock. "We're the best punk band of all," says Jagger, casting a figurative look backward at a horde of hungry young rockers roughly half his age.

Thanks to their notoriety, the Sex Pistols have earned the first chance to challenge Jagger's hypothesis in the arena that matters most—the vast American music market. The November release of their first U.S. album, *Never Mind the Bollocks, Here's the Sex Pistols,* was effected almost secretly by Warner Bros. records: no advertising blitz, a green and shocking pink album cover that suggests new meanings for the term tacky. The commercial response to this album, which includes a vivid description of an aborted fetus, will be carefully watched by U.S. rock entrepreneurs. Success will almost certainly spur a switch toward primitive, minimalist rock. Should the album bomb, punk will simply be where it has always felt most comfortable: down but not out, and still threatening to come out of the water closet at any moment.
— *Paul Gray*

Theater

The Tawny, Frolicking Cubs

A new generation of playwrights surprises Broadway

For season after season, a recurring plaint has been "Where are the new young American playwrights?" That question was not asked in 1977. The fitting question now is "Where are they not?" Indeed, 1977 may prove to have been the year in which the fresh, able and agile members of a rising generation of playwrights captured and held significant theatrical ground from coast to coast.

One instructive example is to follow the trail of *The Shadow Box,* by Michael Cristofer. This drama on the difficult subject of facing up to imminent death was launched at Los Angeles' Mark Taper Forum under the venturesome leadership of that theater's artistic director, Gordon Davidson. The equally adventurous Arvin Brown, who presides over New Haven's Long Wharf Theater, brought the play East. This underscored the growing role of the regional theaters as seedbeds of new talent. It also showed the way in which they are increasingly enriching each other through cross-fertilization. The leap to Broadway followed, and there *The Shadow Box* won the Tony Award and the Pulitzer Prize.

Beyond Cristofer a whole phalanx of new talent is at work. In 1977 one or more plays by the following alphabetically listed dramatists could be seen from one end of the U.S. to the other: Ed Bullins, Christopher Durang, John Guare, Israel Horowitz, Preston Jones, Albert Innaurato, David Mamet, Ronald Ribman, Ntozake Shange, Sam Shepard, Steve Tesich, Richard Wesley, Lanford Wilson and Robert Wilson.

Perhaps the first thing to say about these dramatists, whose ages range from the mid-20s to the mid-40s, is what not to expect from them. Do not expect the eloquent elegies for the violated heart that come from a Tennessee Williams. Do not expect the staunch moral quests for justice that come from an Arthur Miller. Do not expect some savage duel of the sexes such as Edward Albee provided in *Who's Afraid of Virginia Woolf?*

By and large, these playwrights seem to be post-absurdist, post-psychoanalytical, apolitical, nondidactic and virtually immune to social outrage. Though some of them began writing in the '60s, they have shed the mentality and the causes of the '60s. Even the black playwrights, Bullins, Shange and Wesley, seem to draw their emotional force more from precise camera images of black life than from breast-beating lamentations and vituperative hostility toward "whitey."

These playwrights represent a kind of social and aesthetic diaspora. They reflect splintered ethics, fragmented ethnic identities, eroded mores, and an America that no one can truly call home because each increasingly feels like a wanderer in a strange land. Their works imply moral neutrality, and playgoers who want to distinguish the good guys from the bad guys find this unnerving. Most of the plays are infused with a marvelous abundance of humor—some zany, some ironic, and some that draws blood with the startling swiftness of a paper cut.

As a rule, the new playwrights prize the word over the primal scream, though the words are often unhousebroken. David Mamet, whose *American Buffalo* won the New York Drama Critics' Circle Award for Best American Play in 1977, may be the keenest wordsmith of the lot. He has perfect pitch and uses language like a poet of the blue-collar class, with abrasive inflections of his native Chicago. Mamet believes language is a form of action and intimidation, a tactic by which one man holds another at bay much in the manner of a lion tamer. The theme of *American Buffalo* is the betrayal of friendship through greed. Mamet means it to have wider implications—his title derives from the vanishing breed that once graced the coin of the realm.

The theme of betrayal—in sorrow rather than in anger—also possesses Sam Shepard. He seems to yearn for the untarnished majesty of wide-open spaces. Though fast cars, mechanical gadgetry, chrome and plastic festoon his works, they form a symbolic veneer under which, he

seems to be saying, older American ideals are shriveling. Shepard is also haunted by the laconic, mythical American cowboy-sheriff hero. In *The Tooth of Crime,* which is possibly the most durable single play yet written by any of the new dramatists, Shepard urbanizes the mythical setting. Hoss, a rock star, is the robber baron of the Western freeways. An upstart maverick named Crow contests his dominance. In a sacrificial stomping dance both men are entangled in electric cords and outthrust microphones as they engage in a musical cutting session and a machine-gun duel of far-out words. It is as chillingly primordial as a tribal rite in which the young warrior snatches primacy from the aging patriarch.

Sharing Shepard's fascination with myth is Christopher Durang. In *A His-*

Playwright Michael Cristofer (right) with cast of Tony Award–winning *The Shadow Box*

The new writers reflect splintered ethics and fragmented identities.

tory of the American Film, staged in Hartford, Los Angeles and Washington in 1977, he strip-mines the Hollywood mother lode, ranging from the films of D.W. Griffith to *The Exorcist,* to show how Americans create myths, cherish them and are eventually enslaved by them.

Alternating with the mythical strain in the new dramatists is a strong undercurrent of neonaturalism and domestic tragicomedy. Alberto Innaurato made impressive debuts both on and off Broadway in 1977 with *Gemini* and *The Transfiguration of Benno Blimpie.* In these two quite different plays, the family was his basic text, the family in its care, compassion and animal warmth, and in its blood-blister pain and criminal fury.

The new dramatists are the tawny, frolicking cubs of our rudely vigorous theater. The once-and-future lion may soon be roaring in their midst. — **T.E. Kalem**

Art

The Reign of Entropy

Several shows raise a question: What are museums for?

In art, the year 1977 produced no geniuses, movements or other whales on flatcars. Indeed, the very word movement now looks, in the face of what is being produced in America, quite anachronistic. It has joined its sibling, the word avant-garde, as part of the archaeology of modernist culture. How long has it been since a group of significant American artists worked together, however loosely, to achieve some serious cultural aim that was not merely part of a promotional apparatus? Ten years? Twenty?

And how long has it been since anyone of intelligence was able to utter the word avant-garde in the context of today's art without a feeling of mild embarrassment? There is, of course, no dearth of nominally avant-garde activity. X draws a scratchy line on his Sheetrock wall and so transforms his loft into an "environment." Y collects "documentation" of his trip to Tijuana in the form of a thousand blurred Polaroid shots. Z carves out lumps of turf with a bulldozer. The conceptual-process artists keep on with

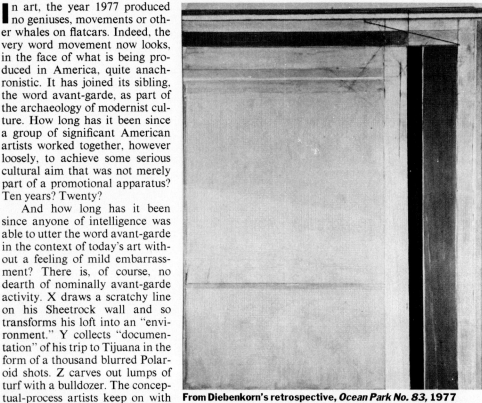

From Diebenkorn's retrospective, *Ocean Park No. 83*, 1977

their uninteresting classification and pseudo sociology. The video people scrutinize their navels. Tiny aesthetic gestures crawl like stag beetles about the landscape, pushing unwieldy masses of documentation before them.

As for the "mainstream" we used to hear so much about—the style of flat acrylic-on-duck abstraction, which, for formalist critics a decade ago, seemed to be the painted version of the categorical imperative—that, too, has run dry. Its contents look more and more like either decor or super-graphics, if one may judge from the Guggenheim Museum's retrospective of Kenneth Noland last April, or the recent show of Helen Frankenthaler's astute, peachy and vacuous canvases at Manhattan's André Emmerich Gallery.

Thus we are, to put it mildly, in a lull. Most of the art being made in America today either promises so little or delivers so tepidly, that to talk of trends or movements makes no sense. The art world is still suffering from a hangover. Its proximate cause was the binge of the '60s.

Beyond that, however, lies a deeper malaise. It is the feeling that the very language of the static visual arts is no longer of crucial importance—that painting and sculpture, thrust from

The *Bathers* (1898-1900), from the Cézanne exhibition in New York's Museum of Modern Art

their old centrality by film, TV and photography, cannot embody major meanings, and must be content either with fragmentary ruminations in a generally ironic mode, or else with decoration. A modern Rubens, or even a contemporary Delacroix, is unimaginable: most new painting, for the time being, has abandoned the ambition to create large coherent fictions. The artists who most resemble the old masters may be neither painters nor sculptors, but film makers: notably, Bunuel.

Was '77 a wasteland, then? By no means. But it is surprising, all the same, that most of the memorable exhibitions were made by men and women of 50 or more, and not by younger talent. One thinks, among other things, of those two masterly affirmations of the language of the brush, Richard Diebenkorn's 35-year retrospective and the survey of Robert Motherwell's paintings and collages produced by the Musée d'Art Moderne in Paris. Robert Rauschenberg's traveling circus of images continued to tour America, and Jasper Johns' retrospective opened at the Whitney; and in private galleries there were remarkable shows by Lee Krasner, Anthony Caro, Jim Dine, Nancy Graves, Louise Nevelson, and that very underrated sculptor Hans Hokansen, the best large-scale wood carver in America.

The reign of entropy favors backward glances, and it was no surprise that most of the best exhibitions were retrospectives and re-evaluations—the kind of work museums do best. The clear winner in this category was an encyclopedic show called "Trends of the Twenties," organized in West Berlin by the Council of Europe: several thousand works in all media, from photography to architectural models, giving the most complete picture of the European avant-garde at the time of the Weimar Republic that has ever been assembled. No historical survey mounted by an American museum equaled this one in scope, energy or appositeness, although the traveling exhibition of "Women Artists, 1550-1950," organized by the Los Angeles County Museum, opened a tract of art history long ignored by institutions here and in Europe.

But there were, in America, memorable one-artist museum shows. The Cézanne exhibition at the New York Museum of Modern Art was a curatorial masterpiece, rivaled only by the Courbet retrospective at the Grand Palais in Paris. The Brooklyn Museum had Lewis Hine's photographs, and a notable show

of the first 100 years of photography —Niepce to Atget, drawn from the Jammes collection—is still running at the Art Institute of Chicago. And then, most ravishing of all, there was the collection of Matisse's late paper cut-outs at Washington's National Gallery of Art.

From Matisse's paper cut-outs, *Beasts of the Sea*

The memorable exhibitions did not come from young talent.

But if 1977 was the year of the museums, in terms of remarkable exhibitions, it was so in another sense as well, for a long-simmering debate over the future use of museums, and their policies, was brought to full boil on both sides of the Atlantic. In America it revolved around New York's Metropolitan Museum of Art, and in Europe its subject was Paris' Centre Pompidou, which drew huge crowds to its new building but opened with an ambitious and badly bungled survey of the reciprocal traffic between two great centers of modern art over

the last 75 years, "Paris–New York."

At the Met, the issue was the relation —or lack of it—between the museum's task of conservation and connoisseurship, and its role as educator and merchant. That the two were in conflict, few could doubt. One only needed to visit the Met's big retrospective of Andrew Wyeth, the only large-scale show of a living artist the Met had in 1976-77, to realize that the overriding issue in the museum director's mind was box office. Thomas Hoving's ten years as director ended with his retirement in December, but the legacy of his work, good and bad, will continue to profoundly affect not only the Metropolitan but also every other museum in the country. It poses, in essence, the question of how far any museum can go in the direction of high-class vulgarization. In some respects, the Met's installations—the Tiffany-style spotlighting and exaggerated plushiness of the recent "Treasures of Early Irish Art" and the concurrent "Age of Spirituality"—betray an almost schizophrenic flamboyance, whereby the historical and aesthetic meaning of each object is forced to battle against its preciousness.

This yearning for Aladdin's Cave presents a real problem in seeing, and it is not rendered less awkward by the Met's obsessive souvenir selling. The merchandising of replicas, prints, Tut cuff links and the like (together with restaurant and parking receipts) generated 54% of the museum's income in 1976-77. Of course, every major museum in the world sells replicas of objects in its collection. But none do it with quite the Met's aggressiveness. Its current policy, for spectacle shows like Irish art or Wyeth, is to line the exit with souvenir counters, so that one goes straight from the real to the fake. This raises a problem: how far, for the average viewer, does it blur the distinction between original and replica?

The uniqueness of the object is, after all, the supreme reason for the existence of museums. They have one purpose, to which all others are secondary: to enable people to contemplate works of art, in conditions as close to clarity and privacy as possible, helped by the most accurate scholarly information available. No other matters —not merchandising, not grandiose visual-aids programs, not the vanity of potential donors—should interfere with that. It may be that, in the museum world, 1977 will be remembered as the year in which the lines of that issue were most clearly drawn. — *Robert Hughes*

Books

A Bit of Reassuring News

And a warning of blockbusters ahead

In the world of book publishing, 1977 was less a year of trends than of tendencies. Biographies of Ring Lardner, Simone Weil and Vladimir Nabokov aroused interest but not revivals. Except for a few major missing links, it was too late for first-person disclosures about Watergate and too early for remote historical overviews. Authors could, however, begin to perceive the Viet Nam war at some historical remove. The year began with Gloria Emerson's *Winners and Losers,* a collage of tragic memories and sharp analyses, animated by the author's fury. It ended with Michael Herr's *Dispatches,* which cast a much colder eye on the conflict to examine flaws of hawk and dove rhetoric—and the implications of battles that would not leave the American mind even after guns were stilled.

Between these parentheses came scores of volumes from the unknown, the emerging and the established. Perhaps the most reassuring news arrived within a few weeks, when three writers of grandfatherly demeanor produced books of astonishing vigor and technique. At the age of 64, John Cheever offered *Falconer,* a demonstration that hell is a place much like an American prison, where "loneliness can change anything on earth." Cheever's studies of prisoners burning in their own memories showed an aesthetic and moral relation to Walker Percy's *Lancelot.* Percy, 60, conferred upon his central character an ironic title and territory. Lancelot Andrewes Lamar is a brute cavalier

locked in an insane asylum. There he rants at a world in which flaccid tolerance is as malign as rigid bias—a world as crazy as he. Two weeks later, Robert Penn Warren, at 71, proved with *A Place To Come To* that he could still aim fiction at the gut without offending the head. The failure of promise, the annealing power of love and lust, the illusions present in time as well as space have always been War-

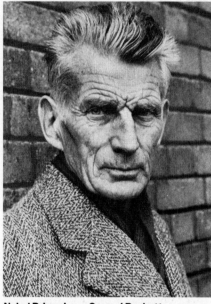
Nobel Prizewinner Samuel Beckett
Earth must have got stuck, one sunless day.

ren's turf; in *A Place To Come To* he made them the prose equivalent of his poetic statement: "In our imagination/What is love?/One name for it is knowledge." Gray power was also asserted by Nobel Prizewinner Samuel Beckett, whose two little volumes *Ends and Odds* and *Fizzles* once again presented his audience with the bones of aphorisms: "The earth must have got stuck, one sunless day, in the heart of winter ... this gag has gone on long enough for me."

Not on that level, but of substantial quality, were other works of imaginative fiction. The durable ironist Kingsley Amis wrote *The Alteration,* limning a what-if world where the Protestant Reformation has never occurred. Italo Calvino's *The Castle of Crossed Destinies* went Amis one better: his novel depended upon the random deal of tarot cards. Other novelists tried the far reach: Thomas Gavin's twinkling *Kingkill* was based upon a 19th century chess-playing automaton secretly animated by a hidden dwarf. Robert Coover wasted his considerable gifts upon the year's most wrenching rewrite of history, *The Public Burning,* in which Spies Julius and Ethel Rosenberg are executed in Times Square to the jeers of a half-dressed villain named Richard Nixon.

Traditional novels provided some of the year's greatest aesthetic rewards: Joan Didion's *A Book of Common Prayer* was a remarkable contemporary version of Henry James' *Portrait of a Lady.* In *Daniel Martin,* the polished surface of John Fowles' prose reflected the traditional philosophical question of how to live, as posed by a wandering scenarist on leave from Hollywood. In *Song of Solomon,* Toni Morrison tracked the stations of a

Novelist & Short Story Writer John Cheever
Loneliness can change anything on earth.

Novelist & Essayist Walker Percy
Lancelot is a brute locked in an asylum.

Novelist, Poet & Critic Robert Penn Warren
In our imagination, what is love?

family risen from slavery to its contemporary angst—a kind of illuminated *Roots*. And the espionage novel reached the province of art with John le Carré's highly traditional dissection of betrayal and allegiances in *The Honourable Schoolboy*.

The novel was not confined either to the aging or to the skilled, however. The year's most prodigious bestseller was an overweight (530 pages) chronicle of the Cleary family's rise from New Zealand obscurity to Australian wealth and London prominence. No Cleary ascended with greater velocity than Author Colleen McCullough: paperback rights to *The Thorn Birds* were sold for a record $1.9 million. The novel became the least-talked-about bestseller of the year; it seemed to rise without a trace.

The Thorn Birds Author Colleen McCullough
It seemed to rise without a trace.

Bestsellers, in fact, often seem impervious to criticism. The only certainty about them is they imitate each other from year to year. So although the authors of the hits of 1977 are already fading into oblivion and the star authors of 1978 are not yet known, the titles of some predictable 1978 hits seem almost inevitable:

▶ *Corruption, How to Abuse It* is an extrapolation of Michael Korda's manual, *Power*, which warned against eye contact with rivals and sex in the office. *Corruption* shows how to avoid both hazards by slipping Baggies over the heads of colleagues until quitting time. A very special guide offers tips on how to give competitors cholera, how to acquire a desk-size nuclear device, how to rise in the corporate world by the use of blackmail and extortion.

▶ *Visas.* Like Gail Sheehy's *Passages*, which examines mid-life crises, *Visas* turns to that most crucial period of life, kindergarten. In a series of case histories, the book shows why boys at the age of four begin yearning to make snakes out of clay and how girls turning 3½ frequently have tantrums when the word bedtime is uttered. The apppendix includes a useful manual about chocolate chip cookies, gerbils and other tranquilizers.

▶ *The Book of Leftovers*, like *The Book of Lists* compiled by David Wallechinsky and family (Irving Wallace, *et al.*), offers yet another series of arbitrary groupings. In this case, we learn about food-stuffs found in the iceboxes and refrigerators of Presidents from George Washington (cherries, acorn soup) to Richard Nixon (crow, humble pie).

▶ *Feathers* is in the style of Alex Haley's black saga *Roots* and Robert S. Elegant's *Dynasty*, the story of a Chinese family that rises to global prominence. A Sioux band gathers at Little Bighorn, then asserts itself in succeeding generations. At the book's close, one princess is President of the U.S., her brother is a Mafia chieftain, and their little sister is the beautiful seducer of the Los Angeles Dodgers.

▶ *It Didn't Start With Rome.* Taking a leaf, dust jacket and binding from Victor Lasky's *It Didn't Start with Watergate*, this scathing, hysterically researched book shows that the excesses of Caligula (arbitrary executions, bestiality, promoting his favorite horse, Incitatus, as consul) were, in fact, necessary to Roman foreign policy. And besides, Nero was a major loon, Claudius a minor one and Tiberius a poisoner, thereby excusing Caligula's child's play and, anyway, Incita-tus was the only official to finish in the money at the chariot races.

▶ *Margaret* extends the tradition of *Judy* and *Vivien Leigh*, which retailed the tragedies of actresses, complete with backstage gossip and innuendo. Nude parties, Hollywood orgies that might shame Petronius, sexual aberrations—none of these was remotely connected with Margaret Dumont, the queen dowager of the Marx Brothers comedies. But every possible insinuation is magnified into horsefeathers.

▶ *No Fault Living* will be the year's best-selling self-improvement book. It begins with the premise that everything unpleasant is somebody else's fault and provides charts to show how blame can be apportioned to parents, friends, wives, husbands, children, doormen, cleaning ladies and the American Constitution, which only promises the pursuit of happiness instead of its capture and imprisonment.

▶ *The Doctors' Sahara Diet* capitalizes on the new fascination with the Middle East and applies it to the old concern with overweight. Starting simply, the new reduction plan begins by cutting out carbohydrates, fatty meat, seeds, nuts—in fact, all animal and vegetable products. Finally, table salt is removed, whereupon the dieter is left with three full meals of sand.

▶ "Amanda gazed with trepidation at the long cold granite stairway leading to the castle. Was Lord William under a curse? Could she run away? Something larger than herself seemed to pull her up the steps, closer, closer ..." This traditional opening is combined with the standard prelude to aerobics (workouts are no good unless the pulse beats 120 times a minute) to create *The Gothic Exercise Manual*. This invaluable volume shows how the hero or heroine can use those stone stairs to advantage, ascending and descending them rapidly to provide the heart, lungs and goose flesh with a thorough workout.

▶ *Paperweights of the Gods.* Proof positive that the Taj Mahal, pyramids and even the Sunday New York *Times* are, when viewed from the air, status symbols of extraterrestrial beings constantly monitoring the earth. Pictures of the artifacts, plus rare holographs of such inimitable paperweights as Eric Von Daniken and Uri Geller are shown in their two dimensions.

▶ *The Family Way.* The first blockbuster to tell the story of the Carter family from the inside. Joe Bob Colt, a house painter who used to look in the windows, spins stories of the Carters in the old days, when Billy drank Royal Crown Cola and the only promise about Jimmy was the one to get a better grade in American history next year. — *Stefan Kanfer*

DRAWING BY WM. HAMILTON © 1977 THE NEW YORKER MAGAZINE, INC.

"I tell you, the book has everything—sex, history, consciousness, and cats!"

Americana

The Lone Eagle of 1927

Charles Lindbergh had been dead for three years, but many a middle-aged man could still remember from his remote childhood something of the thrill of Lindbergh's great adventure: the small, silver monoplane with its 220-h.p. engine; the gangling young flyer with his five sandwiches, his gallon and a half of water, fighting off sleep for hours, occasionally dropping the *Spirit of St. Louis* down just above the troubled surface of the North Atlantic to double-check his drift by watching which way the wind was blowing the wavetop foam; the prayers of a waiting world; and then, after 33½ hours, the mobs cheering his landing at Le Bourget. It was May 21, 1927, just a half-century ago.

Newspaper headlines hailed him as "The Lone Eagle" and "Lucky Lindy." The latter was inaccurate, as Lindbergh was swift to point out. He had a trained engineer's mind as well as a flyer's heart. He not only helped design his rugged, high-winged Ryan aircraft, but coldly calculated his chances down to the last detail. He flew without a navigator because he figured that a man's weight translated into extra fuel would give his plane three more hours in the air (an added 300 miles of range). To Lindbergh, the flight was a triumph for meticulous planning, not a stunt. "I never asked to be a hero," he once remarked, "I don't want to be a hero and, what's more, I never was a hero."

History and the public disagreed. After he returned home to ticker-tape parades, and a hard-working career as engineer, inventor, and pioneer of airline routes for Pan American, both press and public unrelentingly pursued him. Wealth and publicity, he felt, led to the kidnaping and murder of his baby son in 1932. He never forgave the U.S. press, took to wearing disguises, finally escaped to Europe for four years. On the eve of World War II, he joined America Firsters in deploring U.S. intervention. That clouded his popularity, but not his fame.

As America celebrated the Lindbergh anniversary, some people wondered why his public impact had lasted so. Partly, perhaps, because he seemed a throwback, a symbol for his nostalgic countrymen of frontier qualities that they still like to think of as typically American. A towering, skinny young man, he was taciturn, modest, inventive, courageous.

But Lindbergh was also riding a wave of the future that still rolls onward. The once lonely sky over the North Atlantic is now dense with Boeing 747s, each one more than eight times as long as the *Spirit of St. Louis*. Their pilots seem more like bus drivers than heroes. By contrast, as Lindbergh wrote of that lonely flight, "I live only in the moment in this strange, unmortal space, crowded with beauty, pierced with danger." His was indeed a rare moment, when personal confidence and skill were still in partnership with machines, not overwhelmed by them. ∎

Lindbergh and the *Spirit of St. Louis*
He didn't want to be a hero.

The Human Fly of 1977: What Price Glory?

When Toy Designer George Willig sat down to a breakfast of steak and eggs early one morning in May, he was as obscure as any other typical 27-year-old resident of Queens. But by mid-morning the nation and a good deal of the world knew his name and trim-bearded face. Though Willig's rise to celebrity was amazingly quick, few were inclined to follow in his footsteps: these had led him straight up one of the World Trade Center's twin towers—110 stories, 1,350 ft.

The amateur mountaineer's thoroughly broadcast feat riveted millions of Americans in dizzy suspense for more than three hours. At the outset it almost drove Center's security guards themselves up the wall. "Hey! Crazy man! Get down here right now!" yelled one of the guards who flocked to the plaza below soon after a young man wearing jeans, T shirt and a burnt orange backpack started scaling the South Tower.

Willig, however, proceeded up, up, up. Soon traffic in lower Manhattan was paralyzed as spectators thronged the streets to gape incredulously as Willig nimbly, almost nonchalantly, headed skyward. No one except close relatives and friends knew that Willig had spent months meticulously planning the adventure. He had devised and constructed special gear—T-shaped metal blocks that fit into the tower's vertical scaffold guides and were locked into place by his weight. During hours off from his job at the Ideal Toy Corp., Willig had gone to the tower several times late at night to test the devices. Now, on Ascension Day, he worked them expertly.

Finally, when Willig had outdistanced all shouted commands from below, the official reaction, reasonably enough, was to lower a scaffold bearing New York Police Suicide Specialist DeWitt C. Allen and a fellow policeman to intercept and rescue a putative lunatic. Yet when at the

Willig climbing the World Trade Center
Few were inclined to follow in his footsteps.

60th floor the scaffold drew alongside a climber who seemed cool, self-possessed, confident and competent, the police discarded all rescue tactics.

As Willig gained the roof after 3½ hours of climbing, a jubilant cheer roared up from the streets below. New York City officialdom was slow to hear the ovation. It arrested Willig on the roof and threatened to sue him for $250,000 for all the trouble and expense he had caused. As the hurrah-for-Willig continued, Mayor Abraham Beame finally joined the crowd, grinned and slashed the price Willig would have to pay for his glory: $1.10—a penny per floor of the tower. ∎

Current Affairs Test

After reading this *Year in Review,* why not test yourself on how well informed you are? Take the 44th annual TIME Current Affairs Test. This 100-question review of 1977, prepared by the TIME Education Program, is available (with answer sheet and key) for 50¢. Classroom/bulk quantities can be provided at a reduced cost. To order this test or to find out more about the TIME Education Program (a classroom service, which includes free teaching units) write:

Time-Life Building
Rockefeller Center
1271 Avenue of the Americas
Room 30-66
New York, N.Y. 10020